The Law of International Conflict

The Composition of the Curatorium of the Xiamen Academy of International Law

The titles published in this series are listed at *brill.com/ccxa*

The Law of International Conflict

Force, Intervention and Peaceful Dispute Settlement

VOLUME 5
2015

By

Hanspeter Neuhold

BRILL
NIJHOFF

LEIDEN | BOSTON

Library of Congress Cataloging-in-Publication Data

Neuhold, Hanspeter, author.
The law of international conflict: force, intervention and peaceful dispute settlement / Hanspeter Neuhold.
pages cm -- (Collected courses of the Xiamen Academy of International Law ; 5)
Includes bibliographical references and index.
ISBN 978-90-04-29991-7 (hardback : alk. paper) -- ISBN 978-90-04-29993-1 (e-book : alk. paper) 1. Pacific settlement of international disputes. 2. Arbitration (International law) 3. Conflict management. 4. Aggression (International law) 5. International relations. I. Title.

KZ6010.N34 2015
341.5--dc23

2015034132

This publication has been typeset in the multilingual 'Brill' typeface. With over 5,100 characters covering Latin, ipa, Greek, and Cyrillic, this typeface is especially suitable for use in the humanities.
For more information, please see brill.com/brill-typeface.

ISSN 1875-4678
ISBN 978-90-04-29991-7 (hardback)
ISBN 978-90-04-29993-1 (e-book)

This book is printed on acid-free paper.

Printed by Printforce, the Netherlands

Contents

List of Abbreviations

ABM	anti-ballistic missile
AJIL	American Journal of International Law
ASEAN	Association of South East Asian Nations
ASIL	American Society of International Law
AU	African Union
BYIL	British Yearbook of International Law
CIA	Central Intelligence Agency
CSCE	Conference on Security and Co-operation in Europe
DDOS	distributed denial of service
ECCAS	Economic Community of Central African States
ECOMOG	ECOWAS Monitoring Group
ECOSOC	Economic and Social Council
ECOWAS	Economic Community of West African States
EJIL	European Journal of International Law
EU	European Union
FRY	Federal Republic of Yugoslavia (Serbia and Montenegro)
FYROM	Former Yugoslav Republic of Macedonia
HJIL	Heidelberg Journal of International Law
ICBM	intercontinental ballistic missile
ICC	International Criminal Court
ICISS	International Commission on Intervention and State Sovereignty
ICJ	International Court of Justice
ICSID	International Centre for Settlement of Investment Disputes
ICTY	International Criminal Tribunal for the Former Yugoslavia
IDI	Institut de Droit international
IGO	intergovernmental organization
ILC	International Law Commission
INTERFET	International Force in East Timor
ISAF	International Security Assistance Force
Max Planck YBUNL	Max Planck Yearbook of United Nations Law
MPEPIL	Max Planck Encyclopedia of Public International Law
MONUSCO	Mission de l'Organisation des Nations unies pour la stabilisation en République démocratique du Congo
NATO	North Atlantic Treaty Organization
NGO	non-governmental organization
OAS	Organization of American States

OAU	Organization of African Unity
ONUC	Opération des Nations unies au Congo
OSCE	Organization for Security and Co-operation in Europe
PCA	Permanent Court of Arbitration
PCIJ	Permanent Court of International Justice
PLO	Palestine Liberation Organization
RCADI	Receuil des cours de l'Académie de droit international
RDD	radiological dispersion device
RGDIP	Revue générale de droit international public
SADC	South African Development Community
SCADA	supervisory control and data acquisition
SFRY	Socialist Federal Republic of Yugoslavia
UN	United Nations
UNAMA	United Nations Mission in Afghanistan
UNDOF	United Nations Disengagement Observer Force
UNEF	United Nations Emergency Force
UNIFIL	United Nations Interim Force in Lebanon
UNOSOM	United Nations Operation in Somalia
UNPROFOR	United Nations Protection Force
UNTAC	United Nations Transitional Authority in Cambodia
UNTAG	United Nations Transition Assistance Group
U.S.	United States
WTO	World Trade Organization
VCLT	Vienna Convention on the Law of Treaties
WEU	Western European Union
ZAÖRV	Zeitschrift für ausländisches öffentliches Recht und Völkerrecht

CHAPTER 1

Introduction

That the subjects of a legal order ought to comply with all its rules is stating the obvious. This maxim naturally also applies to international law. However, some of the rules of the international legal system are of particular importance because they reflect meta-legal values of the international community and constitute the foundations on which the other, more specific norms are based.[1] If these cornerstones of the international legal order are violated, the consequences of the breach are particularly serious and far-reaching. These principles are enshrined, first and foremost, in Article 2 of the Charter of the United Nations (UN) which some international lawyers regard as the constitutional instrument of the international community.[2] They were further defined in additional documents at the global and regional levels. The Declaration on Principles of International Law concerning Friendly Relations and Co-operation among States (henceforth referred to as Friendly Relations Declaration) adopted by the UN General Assembly in 1970, 25 years after the entry into force of the UN Charter,[3] and the Declaration on Principles Guiding Relations between Participating States in the Final Act of the Conference on Security and Co-operation in Europe (CSCE),[4] which the heads of state and government of the 35 participating states signed in Helsinki on 1 August 1975, merit special mention in this context.[5]

---

1 Zemanek, 'Basic Principles of UN Charter Law', in: Macdonald and Johnston (eds.), *Towards World Constitutionalism: Issues in the Legal Ordering of the World Community* (2005) 401.

2 Verdross and Simma, *Universelles Völkerrecht. Theorie und Praxis* (3rd ed. 1984) 59; Simma, 'From Bilateralism to Community Interest in International Law', 250 *RCADI* (1994) 229 (258); P.-M. Dupuy, 'The Constitutional Character of the United Nations Charter Revisited', 1 *Max Planck YBUNL* (1997) 1; Fassbender, 'The United Nations Charter as Constitution of the International Community', 36 *Columbia Journal of Transnational Law* (1998) 531.

3 As annex to Resolution 2625 (XXV) on 24 October 1970. No sources for treaties, court decisions and other documents will be given, since they can be accessed today more easily and rapidly in the Internet than in printed sources like the United Nations Treaty Series, International Legal Materials or other documentations. The same is true of the judgments and advisory opinions of the International Court of Justice (ICJ). IJC judgements will be quoted without the words *Case concerning*.

4 Since this Declaration comprises ten principles, it is sometimes also referred to as the 'CSCE Decalogue'.

5 The CSCE, which became an institutionalized diplomatic process in the wake of the initial Conference (1973–1975), was renamed Organization for Security and Co-operation in Europe (OSCE) at the Budapest summit meeting in December 1994; this decision took effect on 1 January 1995. However, despite its name it is not an intergovernmental organization (IGO) in the

 | DOI 10.1163/9789004299931_002

It stands to reason that the rules governing various forms of coercion, above all the resort to armed force, are included among these principles.[6] In the light of the continuously growing destructive power of weapons especially in the recent past, resort to their use ought to be regulated and restricted by law. However, more powerful states may also employ other, subtler forms of coercion like political and economic pressure in order to impose their will on weaker countries. Consequently, what is called intervention in the affairs of other states should also be outlawed. Yet, such prohibitions do not solve the conflicts which lead to the use of armed and other forms of force. Therefore, conflicting parties must be obligated to settle their controversies peacefully, and the means for the pacific solution of disputes ought to be adequately developed.

The following chapters are devoted to these three inter-related principles – the prohibition of the threat or use of force, non-intervention, and the peaceful settlement of international disputes. The author already dealt with them in some detail in the 1970s.[7] The invitation by the Xiamen Academy of International Law which he gladly accepted offered a welcome opportunity to update his discussion of these principles during the Cold War and ascertain whether his conclusions at that time were correct or not.

---

technical legal sense since it still lacks a constituent treaty and international legal personality. The OSCE at present comprises 57 participating states, including the United States and Canada from the beginning of the CSCE, and the Central Asian states after the disintegration of the Soviet Union. For the OSCE, Europe thus denotes the region from Vancouver to Vladivostok.

6 Strictly speaking, it is not force but the subject, whether an individual or the forces of a state, using weapons that is armed. The same is true of an armed attack.

7 Neuhold, *Internationale Konflikte – verbotene und erlaubte Mittel ihrer Austragung. Versuche einer transdisziplinären Betrachtung der Grundsätze des Gewalt- und Interventionsverbots sowie der friedlichen Streitbeilegung im Lichte der UN-Prinzipiendeklaration und der modernen Sozialwissenschaften* (1977); idem, 'Die Prinzipien des KSZE-Dekalogs und der Friendly-Relations-Deklaration der UNO-Generalversammlung. Ein Vergleich aus transdisziplinärer Sicht', in: Simma and Blenck-Knocke (eds.), *Zwischen Intervention und Zusammenarbeit. Interdisziplinäre Arbeitsergebnisse zu Grundfragen der KSZE* (1979) 441. On the Friendly Relations Declaration see also Rosenstock, 'The Declaration of Principles of International Law Concerning Friendly Relations: A Survey', 65 *AJIL* (1971) 713; Arangio-Ruiz, 'The Normative Role of the General Assembly of the United Nations and the Declaration of Principles of Friendly Relations', 137 *RCADI* (1972) 419; Sahović, 'Codification des principes du droit international des relations amicales et de la coopération entre Ètats', ibid. 243; Sahović (ed.), *Principles of International Law concerning Friendly Relations and Cooperation* (1972); Dohna, *Die Grundprinzipien des Völkerrechts über die freundschaftlichen Beziehungen und die Zusammenarbeit zwischen den Staaten. Die Arbeit des UN-Sonderausschusses über die völkerrechtlichen Grundsätze betreffend die freundschaftlichen Beziehungen und die Zusammenarbeit zwischen den Staaten und das geltende Völkerrecht* (1973).

CHAPTER 2

A Problem-Oriented Approach to International Law

The approach adopted by the writer does not constitute a separate theory of international law. What it may contribute is a different focus and additional perspectives. The rules of international law relevant to the topics under scrutiny will be presented against their non-legal background. It is submitted that the normative tip of the iceberg visible to a positivist lawyer's eye can be better understood if the part below the legal water surface is also looked at. This implies the inclusion of the reasons why a norm came into existence at a given point in time. In other words, the non-legal problems to be solved by law should be identified.

Depending on the issue at hand, such an approach requires at least a basic knowledge of the relevant political, military, strategic, economic, technological, ecological and other aspects.[8] Frequently, useful insights may be gained from other disciplines, above all International Relations. This discipline deals with the same reality as international law. It tries to establish causal relationships and behaviour regularities in the relations between the actors of the international system which lawyers call subjects of international law.[9]

---

8 The approach suggested by this author may also be applied to legal doctrine. Although under Article 38 of the Statute of the ICJ even 'the teachings of the most highly qualified publicists of the various nations' merely constitute subsidiary means for the determination of rules of law, the writings of scholars play an important part in the practice of international law and are quoted on an equal footing with the 'primary' sources of international law, i.e., customary international law, international treaties and general principles of law. The views of writers are widely regarded as authoritative statements on the existence or non-existence of legal rules which are based on thorough research, even if this is not always the case. The overall political backdrop against which an author develops legal theories, concepts and arguments also deserves closer attention. In order better to understand why a certain scholar argues the way he or she does, it may also be helpful to know more about their personality, including his/her biography, education, professional career, ideological/religious beliefs, etc.

9 Some of these behaviour standards have 'hardened' into legal rules with specific consequences, in particular in case of non-compliance with them. These consequences range from reprisals/countermeasures resorted to by the victim of an unlawful act under the law of state responsibility and enforcement measures adopted by the international community, in particular the UN, to proceedings before international courts or tribunals. However, unfortunately for the international legal order, the effectiveness of these consequences tends to be limited. For further details see *infra* 116, 199.

 | DOI 10.1163/9789004299931_003

Both disciplines would benefit from a more intensive dialogue. Political scientists tend to underrate the role played by lawyers in the practice of foreign policy. As a rule, the views of legal experts are taken into account by decision makers. Admittedly, important decisions are sometimes taken without consulting the legal advisers, or these lawyers may be instructed to come up with arguments to justify a legally dubious decision after it has been made. However, foreign and other ministers are well advised to involve their legal experts before they make up their minds. They may still conclude that political considerations outweigh legal objections, but lawyers may help them to reduce the negative consequences of such a decision.

For example, in the 1962 Cuban missile crisis the administration of President John F. Kennedy relied on arguments proposed by the legal advisers which limited the unwelcome precedent effect of the naval blockade of the island. It termed the use of armed force a 'defensive quarantine'[10] and did not justify it as the exercise of the right of self-defence but rather invoked a recommendation of the Organ of Consultation comprised of the Foreign Ministers of the contracting parties to the 1947 Inter-American Treaty of Reciprocal Assistance (also called the Rio Treaty).[11]

On the other hand, international lawyers should know more about the political system in which international law is just one and not the most important element.

From the problem-oriented perspective advocated by this writer two different basic scenarios have to be distinguished.[12] Legal rules are relatively easy to establish if there is general consent within a society, national or international, on which behaviour is desirable or unacceptable.[13] For example, it is hard to

---

10 'Quarantine' is primarily a medical term denoting the isolation of individuals suffering from dangerous contagious diseases in order to protect the rest of the population. It is a fine question whether this euphemism stressing the exceptional character of the recourse to force by the United States ought to be applauded, or whether it is a case of (bad) old wine in a bottle with a new label that should not be allowed to deceive public opinion. Neuhold, 'Legal Crisis Management: Lawfulness and Legitimacy of the Use of Force', in: Fastenrath et al. (eds.), *From Bilateralism to Community Interest: Essays in Honour of Judge Bruno Simma* (2012) 278 (282).

11 Although this legal basis is problematic it is more difficult to obtain the support of one of the few existing regional organizations than unilaterally to claim to act in self-defence.

12 This approach is reminiscent of the German legal concept of *Interessenjurisprudenz*. Heck, *Begriffsbildung und Interessenjurisprudenz* (1932); Müller-Erzbach, *Wohin führt die Interessenjurisprudenz? Die rechtspolitische Bewegung im Dienste der Rechtssicherheit und des Ausbaus der Rechtswissenschaft* (1932).

13 Yet, differences of opinion may still arise if and when details, including possible exceptions or the distribution of costs, are formulated.

imagine a lack of consensus within the overwhelming majority of the citizens in a state on the prohibition of murder.[14]

Striking a normative balance between contradictory values and/or interests is more difficult if opinions are more or less equally divided over which of the two ought to be given priority. Such a situation is known, in the terminology of game theory, as a zero-sum game. What one party wins the other loses, so that the sum of gains and losses is zero. For the problem at hand, it means that one value or interest can only be safeguarded and promoted by legal rules at the expense of the other.

This dilemma is particularly acute if matters of principle are at stake and sound arguments can be advanced by both sides. For instance, in the area of international law such a conflict may arise between two pillars of the modern legal order, the sovereignty and territorial integrity of states on the one hand and self-determination of peoples on the other. If it is accepted that the latter principle includes a people's right to have its own state,[15] it will have to be exercised on the territory of an existing state.[16] This dilemma is exacerbated by the lack of a rule on primacy between conflicting principles of international law. The relevant codifications offer no solution. According to both the Friendly Relations Declaration and the Declaration on Principles of the CSCE Helsinki Final Act, each of the principles they contain, including self-determination of peoples and sovereignty and territorial integrity, ought to be interpreted taking into account all the others.[17] A choice will therefore have to be made on the basis of values and political preferences.[18]

A closer look at legal rules striking a normative balance between such conflicting values and interests leads to several, mostly sobering general observations, in particular it the area of international law. Although they are truisms, it might be appropriate to recall them occasionally.

---

14 However, in some countries, and not the least important ones, there is strong support for capital punishment as a sanction for particularly heinous crimes, in other words an exception to the principle of the sanctity of human life.

15 However, this 'external' right of self-determination of peoples is controversial.

16 For a concrete example provided by the Kosovo issue see *infra* 89.

17 The CSCE Declaration adds that all the principles it contains are of primary significance.

18 Another example is provided by the important issue of the lawfulness of reservations to international treaties. On the one hand, the principle of the integrity of the treaty text leads to a restrictive solution. On the other, according to the principle of universality, as many parties as possible should be bound by the treaty concerned; therefore, reservations should be admitted rather generously. The rules laid down in the 1969 and 1986 Vienna Conventions on the Law of Treaties (VCLT) lean toward this second solution, since their Article 19 permits reservations in principle, subject to certain exceptions.

(1) A given rule aimed at a balance between contradictory values and interests, both of which have their merits, can at best only provide the relatively optimal solution. Furthermore, if the background conditions – the political or economic situation, the development of technology or the state of the environment, etc. – change, the hitherto relatively best option should be replaced with a new rule. A new normative balance ought then to be sought.

(2) One important basis for the establishment of legal norms is provided by the values shared by the subjects of a legal system. The more solid their common value platform, the easier the creation of law will be.[19] Unfortunately, the common value fundament is thinner at the international than the domestic level. During the Cold War, for example, given their diametrically opposed ideologies, capitalist and communist states found it particularly difficult to agree on common legal rules. While the end of the East–West conflict apparently enlarged this platform in favour of the West, Western values have increasingly been challenged in recent years in the context of a trend towards multipolarity in the global system, in particular by the propagation of Eurasianism by Russia under President Vladimir Putin and Islamic fundamentalism. [20]

(3) The normative balance between conflicting interests is indeed also determined by power. As a result, the weaker parties must make more concessions than the more powerful subjects when legal norms are established. International law reflects the power (im)balance more crudely than its domestic counterpart.[21]

The existing power relationship is reflected in both major sources of international law. In spite of the principle of sovereign equality of states, the practice of great powers is more relevant to the development of customary international law than that of small and medium-sized countries. In negotiations leading to the conclusion of an international treaty, the weaker parties are likely to have to make more concessions than the more powerful ones.[22]

---

19 For instance, it is easier to solve political or economic conflicts if all parties accept the principles of multi-party democracy and the rule of law or market economy, respectively, than if they disagree on these systemic principles.

20 Lukin, 'What the Kremlin is Thinking: Putin's Vision for Eurasia', 93 *Foreign Affairs* No. 4 (July/August 2014) 85; idem, 'Eurasian Integration and the Clash of Values', 56 *Survival* No. 3 (June–July 2014) 43.

21 Within democratic states, the struggle for power is usually not fought with bullets but with the ballot box. However, economic power plays an ever increasing role in determining the outcome of elections. Parties and candidates with more financial resources can conduct more expensive campaigns that influence voters.

22 Theoretically, the weaker party could invoke coercion as a ground for the invalidity of a treaty in extreme cases in accordance with Article 52 of the 1969 VCLT. However, in practice it is likely to refrain from taking this step for fear of further negative, also unlawful,

Not surprisingly, developing countries that gained their independence in the process of decolonization after World War II objected to international legal rules which had been created without their participation in the past and failed to take their interests into account.

(4) The adaptation of international law to changing circumstances is more difficult than that of domestic law. The 'horizontal' international system, which – to the surprise of some observers – is still dominated by sovereign states that remain the main subjects of international law – lacks central organs, including norm-creating institutions like national parliaments. In principle, the modification of existing rules therefore needs the consent of all parties bound by them. However, a change of the political, economic, technological and other background circumstances may upset the normative balance to the detriment of some and to the advantage of other parties. The latter, which now benefit from the rule more than before, are unlikely to agree to changing it. Especially if powerful states refuse to adjust legal rules to new challenges, 'bad' law that offers increasingly inadequate solutions to the problem at hand, remains in force.[23] Changes often require insights into the long-term negative consequences of the legal status quo.[24] Unfortunately, apparent short-term advantages tend to prevail, as can be seen in the area of international environmental law.

Another aspect of legal analysis which will be encountered on more than one occasion below is also worth mentioning at the outset. It may be called the 'grey-area phenomenon'. Complex issues may be seen as a spectrum between

---

responses by the more powerful party. Otherwise the less powerful side would not have agreed to the unequal treaty in the first place.

23 The law of international treaties – Article 62 of the VCLT – allows contracting parties to invoke a fundamental change of circumstances in order to suspend or even terminate/withdraw from a treaty. However, the conditions posed by the Convention are not easily met, their fulfilment is more often than not likely to be controversial, and an important category of treaties, those establishing a boundary, is excluded by Article 62(2)(a). Moreover, even if the prerequisites for invoking a fundamental change of circumstances clearly exist, weaker parties may again hesitate to exercise this right against the objections of more powerful parties.

24 The failure of initiatives to reform the UN Security Council may be mentioned as an example. Although the Council is widely regarded as not representing the power realities in today's world, demands for increasing the number of its members, including the exclusive circle of those with a permanent seat, haven fallen on the deaf ears of those five privileged member states whose consent is needed for any amendment to or revision of the UN Charter. They appear more jealous than ever of their privileges which give them a decisive advantage over the so-called newly emerging powers in the Security Council. This seems particularly true of France and the United Kingdom whose power has considerably declined over the years. As a result of the opposition of the permanent members to reform the Security Council is facing a growing legitimacy crisis. See *infra* 116.

two points or clusters, between behaviour which is obviously lawful and which is definitely illegal. Instead of a clearly identifiable dividing line or threshold separating right from wrong, there is a more or less broad 'grey area' of acts or omissions the legality of which is controversial and assessed differently by governments and scholars.

This problem is not unknown in domestic law but exacerbated for its international counterpart by the 'primitive' structure of the legal system. In domestic legal systems, such issues can be clarified relatively quickly and effectively by courts with compulsory jurisdiction and appropriate additional legislation which are lacking at the international level. By contrast, the jurisdiction of international courts and tribunals is still based on its recognition by the parties which they are in general hesitant to give. Only relatively few international organizations have the power to request an advisory opinion from the International Court of Justice (ICJ), and the majority necessary for such a request may be difficult to obtain.[25] As pointed out above, the same is true of the consent of all states involved to reducing ambiguities by entering into treaties, and the conclusion of a treaty is often a time-consuming process so that urgent problems cannot be solved quickly. The development of customary law usually takes even more time.

Finally, another introductory remark is in order. 'Classical' international law, which governed international relations from the 1648 Westphalian Peace Treaties to the end of World War I in 1918 and still provides the foundation of the contemporary international legal order, was essentially shaped by Western, above all European, states in order to defend and promote their values and interests.[26] They enjoyed a decisive superiority in relevant technological areas, above all weapons and navigation, as well as in the fields of administration and organization. Their governments also had the political will to use these advantages in order to conquer territories and enforce their interests and impose their values on the inhabitants of other continents.

These interests and values also found their expression in international law. The resulting legal system was challenged after the October Revolution in Russia by the Soviet Union, and after World War II by other 'socialist' states and the countries of the so-called Third World, which gained their independence in the process of decolonization after 1945. Both groups of states accepted rules of 'classical' international law if they perceived them also to take their values and interests into account. Otherwise they called for new norms but as a rule only succeeded if their demands were backed by sufficient power.

---

25 See *infra* 196.

26 And beginning in the 19th century also the United States.

CHAPTER 3

The Prohibition of the Threat or Use of Force

3.1 Legal Strategies to Limit the Use and the Effects of Force in International Relations

Especially in the 'horizontal', decentralized system of international law, the use of force by individual subjects beyond self-defence may, at least at first sight, not only be viewed as a negative social phenomenon. It could, theoretically, also serve positive purposes. States as the main subjects of international law may have recourse to force as a means of last resort to bring about compliance with legal rules; or they may be employ it in order to establish new norms if they regard existing law as dysfunctional and unjust, in other words if they do not perceive law as legitimate.[28]

However, on closer analysis these two functions are highly problematic in the international legal system. Due to the absence of centralized effective law enforcement mechanisms individual subjects of international law may indeed have to 'take the law into their own hands', resorting to armed violence at least if other means fail. Yet in practice, the resulting state of affairs will be highly unsatisfactory from the legal point of view. The powerful actors with the necessary military and non-military resources to enforce the law usually do not

---

27 Wehberg, 'L'interdiction du recours à la force : Le principe et les problèmes qui se posent', 78 *RCADI* (1951) 7; Waldock, 'The Regulation of the Use of Force by Individual States in International Law', 81 *RCADI* (1952) 451; McDougal and Feliciano, *Law and Minimum World Public Order: The Legal Regulation of International Coercion* (1961); Brownlie, *International Law and the Use of Force by States* (1963); Wengler, *Das völkerrechtliche Gewaltverbot: Probleme und Tendenzen* (1967); Žourek, *L'interdiction de l'emploi de la force en droit international* (1974); Neuhold, *supra* (fn. 7) 55; Cassese (ed.), *The Current Legal Regulation of the Law of Force* (1986); Weisburd, *Use of Force* (1997); Cannizzaro (ed.), *Customary International Law on the Use of Force* (2005); Corten, *Le droit contre la guerre. L'interdiction du recours à la force en droit international contemporain* (2008); Gray, *International Law and the Use of Force* (3rd ed. 2008); Zemanek, 'The Prohibition of the Use of Force after Sixty Years of Abuse', in: Buffard et alii (eds.), *International Law between Universalism and Fragmentation: Festschrift in Honour of Gerhard Hafner* (2008) 287; Corten, *The Law Against War: The Prohibition of the Use of Force in Contemporary International Law* (2010); Moir, *Reappraising the Resort to Force* (2010); Dinstein, *War, Aggression and Self-Defence* (5th ed. 2012); Arend and Beck, *International Law and the Use of Force* (2nd ed. 2013).

28 Neuhold, 'Legitimacy: A Problem in International Law and for International Lawyers?', in: Wolfrum and Röben (eds.), *Legitimacy in International Law* (2008) 335.

 | DOI 10.1163/9789004299931_004

need to actually use them. For weaker states are unlikely to violate their obligations in their relations with more powerful ones for fear of harmful consequences inflicted by the latter. Conversely, as a rule, the less powerful victims of violations of their rights dare not employ force. For they have to expect defeat in a forcible confrontation with their stronger adversaries. In the end, they would be left worse off than if they reluctantly resigned themselves to their fate as the losers in the international self-help system.

The international legal order also lacks norm-creating institutions similar to national parliaments whose members share a broad platform of common values and take majority decisions. If force is used to change existing or create new law, might is likely to make right, again favouring the more powerful parties even more than in the negotiations leading to the adoption of the text of a treaty.

But even if force is also viewed in a positive light and war as 'the father of all things'[29] leading to ultimately desirable change, progress in weapons technology in particular resulted in early attempts to limit the resort to physical violence in international relations by legal means. As ethological research has shown, human beings, although physically relatively weak since they lack fangs or claws, nevertheless succeeded in surviving in an initially hostile environment.[30] They did so thanks to two assets: superior intelligence and high aggressiveness. Later on, thanks to his ingenuity, *homo sapiens* came, for better or worse, to dominate the world, without reducing his now less necessary aggressiveness. One by-product of his creativity was the development of more and more destructive arms, including those of mass destruction, which today enable him to annihilate humankind as a whole.

As a result, there seemed to be an increasingly urgent need, not only for humanitarian reasons, to limit the human suffering and material damage and destruction caused by the resort to armed force. However, the powerful international actors were reluctant to renounce the exploitation of their military superiority for their political purposes, above all the extension of their power in terms of conquered territory and its human and material resources.

Given this conflict of interests and values, attempts to submit the use of force in international relations, first and foremost armed violence, to legal restrictions took a long time. Efforts to this effect were undertaken in three directions.

1) Firstly, these efforts were aimed at limiting the situations in which such force may be employed lawfully and establishing prerequisites for its use,

29 According to the Greek philospher Heraclitus.

30 Lorenz, *Das sogenannte Böse. Zur Naturgeschichte der Aggression* (1963) 317; Storr, *Human Aggression* (1970).

called in Latin *jus ad bellum*, i.e., the right of states to go to war. The focus of this chapter will be placed on this aspect, the evolution and current issues of the prohibition of the threat or use of force in international relations as enshrined, above all, in the UN Charter.

2) Secondly, attempts were made to limit the negative consequences also of the legal resort to force by prohibiting attacks on certain targets and the use of certain means and methods in international armed conflicts. This part of international law is traditionally called *jus in bello*, the law of war, which was subsequently extended to the concept of international humanitarian law. For instance, attacks on civilians and non-military targets were prohibited under the law of war. Certain weapons, for example those causing unnecessary suffering, were outlawed. Some tactical 'tricks', such as wearing the enemy's uniform, were banned as perfidious. Reciprocity ensured at least minimal compliance with these rules, which, however, tended to take a back seat to the overarching principle governing war, that of military necessity: in principle, everything that helps to achieve the goal of war, namely the defeat of the enemy, is allowed.

3) Thirdly, states tried to reduce the numbers of or completely eliminate certain weapons. This is the most effective way to reduce the harm inflicted by the use of armed force. The main difficulty complicating international disarmament and arms control is the fact that they cannot be imposed on sovereign states – except by the victors on the defeated belligerent(s) at the end of an armed conflict or, more recently, by a decision of the UN Security Council under Chapter VII of the Charter.[31] Otherwise, states tend to consent to measures in this area that may be called military 'window-dressing'. They abandon arms races in sectors which, for whatever reason, are no longer attractive; or they may formally renounce weapons or weapon systems which are out of their reach for technological or financial reasons. The 1963 Partial Test Ban Treaty which still allowed for underground nuclear tests is an example of the former, the 1972 Anti-Ballistic Missile (ABM) Treaty[32] of the latter variant of 'window-dressing'. Substantial reductions of the parties' arsenals are likely to be accepted only if the relations of the contracting states are free of major tensions, in which case they will probably not consider using those weapons against each other anyway.

---

31 See *infra* 47.

32 Both parties, the Soviet Union and the United States, realized that they could not achieve an effective missile-defence system.

The three main above-mentioned efforts do not necessarily run parallel. Restrictions on the *jus ad bellum* may not go hand in hand with more respect for the *jus in bello*. On the contrary, if the use of force for a just cause is recognized as lawful, warring parties could feel that the just end justifies all possible means, including those that are normally prohibited. Limits to the resort to armed force and the development of the *jus in bello* are not automatically accompanied by arms control and disarmament. Banned weapons must not be used but remain available.

3.2 From the *Justa Causa* Requirement to the *Jus ad Bellum* as an Element of State Sovereignty

Early concepts to limit the lawful use of force were set forth not only in Europe but, for instance, in ancient India and China as well. However, since, as pointed out above, the focus of this chapter will be on developments in the West because of their decisive impact on the evolution of 'classical' international law which remains the foundation of the contemporary international legal order.[33]

For a long time war, i.e., the use of armed force between independent entities,[34] was not absolutely prohibited but considered lawful only if it was 'just'. The just nature of recourse to such force was defined according to two different criteria in the course of history. On the one hand, the fulfilment of certain formal requirements was regarded as decisive. On the other, a 'just' war depended, above all, on the objective, the cause for which it was waged.

In ancient Rome, the gods were supposed to be on the side of the Romans if, after a final appeal to comply with Rome's demands, war was properly initiated.[35] This was the task of a college of priests, the *fetiales*. Its spokesman, the *pater patratus*, opened war by a declaration of war, which was formalized by throwing a spear, with a fire-hardened tip, the so-called *hasta praeusta*, into enemy territory, and recited traditional legal formulas.

After centuries of persecution, Emperor Constantine the Great finally allowed Christians to practice their religion under the Edict of Milan in 313 AD. The year before, he is supposed to have had a vision predicting victory if he chose a Christian symbol as his emblem. Constantine followed this advice and

---

33 For a recent historic survey see Kleinschmidt, *Geschichte des Völkerrrechts in Krieg und Frieden* (2013).

34 On the problems caused by more sophisticated definitions of war see *infra* 14.

35 Nussbaum, *A Concise History of the Law of Nations* (2nd ed. 1954) 16; Kotzsch, *The Concept of War in Contemporary History and International Law* (1956) 28.

defeated his rival Maxentius at the Battle of the Milvian Bridge over the river Tiber. Less than a century later, in 380, Christianity became the state religion of the Roman Empire under Emperor Theodosius.

Subsequently, famous Christian theologians developed a different concept of just war. According to Augustine, wars '*quae ulciscuntur injurias*', which avenged wrongs, in other words redressed a wrong which the party concerned had suffered at the hands of another, were just.[36] Thomas Aquinas further refined this doctrine by posing two additional conditions. Belligerents had to be guided by a just intention ('*intentio recta*'), promoting the good and avoiding the evil. Moreover, Thomas required a just authority ('*justa auctoritas*'): only princes but not private individuals had the right to wage war.[37]

Later debates revolved around the issues of whether the crusades and the *conquista*, the conquest of overseas colonies by Spain, were 'just'. Not surprisingly, leading scholars advanced arguments which justified the use of force for these purposes in accordance with the general prevalent doctrine. Islam equally developed a theory of just, of 'holy' war, the *djihad*, which was also interpreted more or less extensively in the course of history, in particular to support Arab expansionism.

With the advent of the Reformation, the Pope ceased to be the generally recognized supreme authority to decide, in the event of conflicting claims, which side fought for the just cause.[38] A decisive step was taken by Balthazar Ayala, born in Antwerp of noble Spanish parentage, in the 16th century.[39] He served as Auditor General with the troops of King Philip II of Spain which were sent to the Netherlands to crush an uprising against the Spanish rule.[40] Once again, law was adapted so as to serve the political interests of great powers and their ruling elites. Ayala insisted that only princes, who derived their authority from God, but not rebels had the right to wage war, thus providing a legal foundation for the political goals of the Spanish King. According to this new theory, the *justa causa* was only of moral and political significance.

The right to go to war at will, irrespective of the cause for which it was fought, became an important element of the sovereignty of states in the international system that emerged in the wake of the Westphalian Peace Treaties. This approach was epitomized in the famous dictum by Carl von Clausewitz

36 Von Elbe, 'The Evolution of the Concept of Just War in International Law', 33 *AJIL* (1939) 665 (668).

37 Nussbaum, *supra* (fn. 35) 42; Kotzsch, *supra* (fn. 35) 32.

38 McDougal and Feliciano, *supra* (fn. 27) 133.

39 Von Elbe, *supra* (fn. 36) 676; Nussbaum, *supra* (fn. 35) 74.

40 Wehberg, *supra* (fn. 27) 23; Nussbaum, *supra* (fn. 35) 74.

who defined war as the 'mere continuation of politics/policy by other means'.[41] The paradoxical result of this development was a legal system which was based on the sovereignty of its subjects but at the same time allowed a state to violate or even terminate the sovereignty of another state by defeating it in a war.

However, although states, especially great powers, were reluctant to restrict, let alone renounce, their unrestricted *jus ad bellum*, they continued to invoke the justice of their cause when they launched an armed attack against another state. They did so in order to motivate their population, in particular their soldiers who risked their lives on the battlefield. Moreover, with the subsequent advent of democracy, absolute monarchs lost their exclusive power to shape foreign policy as they deemed fit. Parliaments and public opinion, which was increasingly influenced by newspapers as the principal mass medium, had to be taken into account. Governments therefore asserted the enforcement of legal rights in order to justify recourse to armed force. These rights were often rather general and ill-defined, such as self-preservation and self-defence, the defence of national honour or the protection of national interests. In order to avoid parliamentary approval, the use of force was not referred to as war but as reprisal, intervention or pacific blockade.

Moreover, the definition of war under international law has given rise to difficulties.[42] Not only one but two different definitions were put forward, and both also entail major problems.[43] According to what may be called the common sense view, war means large-scale military hostilities between states with a view to defeating the enemy and imposing the victor's will on him. Armed force may be used for limited purposes, like the cession of a piece of the other state's territory, or be aimed at unconditional surrender in a 'total war' like World War II. When war was finally outlawed, this material definition, which also focuses on the scope of armed force, raised the question of measures below the threshold of war which were not covered by the prohibition and therefore remained legal.

This problem exemplifies the above-mentioned 'grey-area phenomenon'.[44] At one end of the normative spectrum, the use of armed force indisputably

---

41 *'Die bloße Forstsetzung der Politik mit anderen Mitteln'.* Von Clausewitz, *Vom Kriege. Hinterlassenes Werk* (1832), Book 1, Chapter 1, sub-chapter 24.

42 Apart from the rather loose use of the term in everyday non-legal parlance in order to underline the gravity of a challenge and the seriousness of efforts to cope with it, like 'war on terror', 'war on poverty', 'war on drugs', 'Cold War' or 'class war'. Megret, 'War? Legal Semantics and the Move to Violence', 13 *EJIL* (2002) 361 (362); Dinstein, *supra* (fn. 27) 3.

43 For a critical discussion of these two definitions see Greenwood, 'The Concept of War in Modern International Law', 36 *ICLQ* (1987) 283 (286).

44 See *supra* 7.

constitutes war, for instance an all-out invasion of the territory of another state; at the other, it equally clearly does not, as for example a small border skirmish or the shooting down of a single plane. In between lies a 'grey area' where opinions may be divided on whether war is waged or not. Criteria for drawing the line include the number of human casualties, the extent of material damage and the size of territory occupied.

According to another definition, a subjective criterion, the *animus belligerendi*, which could be formally expressed by a declaration of war, leading to the formal state of war,[45] is decisive:[46] a state decides to break off all peaceful relations with another state and apply the *jus ad bellum* instead of the international law of peace. This concept of war entails two rather strange consequences. A state can be at war with another state without firing a single shot. It is nevertheless allowed to take measures that would be illegal under the international law of peace. For example, it has the right to arrest and intern nationals of the enemy state and confiscate their property, as Guatemala did after declaring war on the German *Reich* in World War II in the case of Friedrich Nottebohm whom it regarded as a German citizen.[47] Conversely, a state may resort to massive armed force against another state without being at war with the latter if it denies its *animus belligerendi*.

During the centuries of the unrestricted *jus ad bellum*, European history was nevertheless not characterized by permanent war and large-scale bloodshed. This was due to the remarkable homogeneity of the balance-of-power system which existed until World War I.[48] European states shared similar political, military, economic and cultural systems. The members of the ruling dynasties and aristocratic families were related to each other. The foreign policy professionals, the diplomats, formed an international 'caste'. They spoke the same language and were often hired by foreign governments.[49] The absence of nationalism as a divisive ideology also led to moderation in armed conflicts. Moreover, the complete elimination of a major actor was ruled out for another reason: today's

45 This concept of war as a legal status was developed by Hugo Grotius against the backdrop of the Thirty Years' War which was characterized by periods during which actual fighting did not take place at all. Kotzsch (fn. 35) 38.

46 Greenwood, 'War, Terrorism and International Law', 56 *Current Legal Problems* (2003) 505 (513). Among the critics of this concept see Dinstein, *supra* (fn. 27) 14.

47 The resulting dispute with Liechtenstein, whose nationality Nottebohm had obtained, was decided by the ICJ in 1955. *Nottebohm Case* (*Liechtenstein v. Guatemala*), Second Phase.

48 Gulick, *Europe's Classical Balance of Power* (1955); Rosecrance, *Action and Reaction in World Politics: International Systems in Perspective* (1963). Schroeder, *The Transformation of European Politics 1763–1848* (1996).

49 For instance, the most outstanding diplomat and the most successful military leader in Austrian history, Prince Metternich and Prince Eugene of Savoy, were foreigners.

enemy could be needed in the future as an important ally in a new coalition in order to preserve the balance of power against another member of the system who aimed at hegemony. Although not too rosy a picture of that past European system ought to be painted, it already had some features which are considered major achievements in the process of European integration that was launched in the 20th century after two world wars which all nations on the continent lost.

From the legal viewpoint, the situation resulting from the unfettered *jus ad bellum* as an element of sovereignty was highly unsatisfactory. For if a state resorted to war in order to defend and enforce its rights, the application of the *jus in bello* instead of the international law of peace placed the two belligerents on an equal legal footing, irrespective of the previous lawfulness or illegality of their positions. The situation was similar to that of two men fighting a duel.[50] If the state fighting for its rights was defeated it even had to reckon with further losses under an eventual peace treaty, in particular the cession of territory to the victor.[51]

Moreover, in the second half of the 19th century, weapons became increasingly 'effective' as a result of technological progress, causing more and more casualties and destruction. This led to efforts to humanize warfare by developing the law of war. In this context, the First Red Cross Convention signed in Geneva in 1964 may be mentioned; it was designed to improve the lot of wounded and sick soldiers.[52] The 1868 St. Petersburg Declaration banned explosive ammunition weighing less than 400 grammes.[53] This process culminated in the Hague Conventions of 1899 and 1907 which codified and further developed the law of war. The First Hague Peace Conference was initially convened by Russia in order to achieve progress in the third above-mentioned dimension of limiting the effects of international armed conflict, i.e., disarmament and arms control, but no agreement could be reached on the Russian

50 The Latin word for war, *bellum,* is derived from the older word *duellum,* as Grotius already noted. Wright, 'The Outlawry of War and the Law of War', 47 *AJIL* (1953) 365 (369); Dinstein, *supra* (fn. 27) 163.

51 Neuhold, *supra* (fn. 7) 59.

52 The initiative for the Convention for the Amelioration of the Conditions of the Wounded in Armies in the Field was taken by Henri Dunant, a citizen of Geneva, who witnessed the deaths of thousands of Austrian and French-Piedmontese wounded soldiers on the battlefield of Solferino in 1859. Many of them could have been saved if they had received proper medical treatment in time.

53 Declaration Renouncing the Use, in Time of War, of Explosive Projectiles Under 400 Grammes Weight. The purpose of the treaty, hardly recognizable at first sight, was to avoid unnecessary suffering: the objective of war could be accomplished by the employment of highly destructive weapons, whereas less deadly explosives would merely injure soldiers and thereby prolong their suffering. See *supra* 11.

proposals to this end. These issues already receded into the background during the preparations for the Second Conference.

With regard to the *jus ad bellum*, two of the 1907 Hague Conventions are important in the present context.[54] Convention III Relative to the Opening of Hostilities again emphasized the formal aspect. According to its Article 1, hostilities between the contracting parties had to be preceded by previous and explicit warning, in the form either of a reasoned declaration of war or of an ultimatum with conditional declaration of war.[55] However, if a party disregarded these formalities it could nevertheless bring about the state of war in its relations with the victim of its attack. It merely committed a breach of international law which was by far outweighed, however, by not losing the surprise factor that could decide the outcome of an armed conflict. This Convention was therefore of minor practical relevance.

In contrast, Convention II Respecting the Limitation of the Employment of Force for the Recovery of Contract Debts was based on a substantive approach. It outlawed recourse to armed force (and not war) for the recovery of contract debts claimed from the government of one by the government of another country as being due to its nationals. However, this prohibition did not apply when the debtor state refused or did not reply to an offer of arbitration, or after accepting the offer, prevented any compromise from being agreed on, or, after the arbitration, failed to submit to the award. To put it more simply, the contracting parties renounced the forcible collection of debts owed to their nationals by another party, unless the latter failed to accept arbitral proceedings.[56]

---

54 Mention may also be made of the watered-down commitments under Article 2 of the 1899 and 1907 Conventions I for the Pacific Settlement of International Disputes. The parties agreed that in case of serious disagreement or conflict, before an appeal to arms, they would have recourse, *as far as circumstances allow* (italics added), to the good offices or mediation of one or more friendly Powers.

55 This treaty was mainly concluded because of widespread disapproval of the attacks without a declaration of war on Russian warships by Japanese torpedo boats at the beginning of the 1904/1905 war between these two major powers.

56 This treaty is also known as the Drago-Porter Convention. It was named after the Argentinian foreign minister Luis Maria Drago who put forward the underlying principle, the application of which was made conditional on arbitration by the US representative to the 1907 Hague Conference, Horace Porter. Drago developed his doctrine, in particular, under the impression of the blockade of Venezuela by Germany, Italy and the United Kingdom in order to force the payment of private debts in 1902/1903. Hershey, 'The Calvo and Drago Doctrines', 1 *AJIL* (1907) 26. Other (in)famous cases of 'gunboat diplomacy' by European colonial powers and the United States include the two 'Opium Wars' (1839–1842 and 1856–1860) which forced China not only to permit opium imports but also to open ports and make territorial concessions, as well as the 'opening' of Japan by the 'Black Ships' of Commodore Matthew C. Perry (1853–1854).

Another step in this direction prior to World War I was taken by U.S. Secretary of State William Jennings Bryan. On his initiative, the United States concluded, in 1913/1914, a number of bilateral Treaties for the Advancement of Peace excluding or at least postponing the use of force between them.[57] Under these Bryan Treaties, the contracting parties engaged to submit for investigation and report to a five-member commission all differences between them which could not be composed by diplomatic methods or a tribunal of arbitration. They committed themselves not to declare war nor open hostilities before the commission presented its report. These treaties thus first called for a diplomatic settlement or arbitration. If a dispute could not be solved by these methods, a conciliation procedure was provided for which would lead to a clarification of controversial facts and non-binding proposals for a settlement by the commission. Since both war and hostilities were prohibited while the conciliation commission performed its task which had to be completed within one year, a cooling-off period was introduced. Hopefully, the time thus gained would reduce animosities and tensions between the parties so that they would not resort to force even after the commission had presented its report.[58]

Despite the carnage and destruction caused by World War I, the 'war to end war',[59] states were not yet ready to really renounce their *jus ad bellum*. This reluctance was, in particular, reflected in the Covenant of the League of Nations[60] which did not abolish this right but solely introduced limitations on its exercise.[61] The rather tortuous provisions of the League's constituent treaty[62] obligated member states to respect and preserve against external aggression the territorial integrity and existing political independence of all League members.[63]

---

57 Finch, 'The Bryan Peace Treaties', 10 *AJIL* (1916) 882.

58 An expectation which is not always borne out by reality, as labour disputes show where such cooling-off periods are practiced, for example under the 1947 Taft-Hartley Act in the United States.

59 The phrase was coined by the British author H.G. Wells.

60 The driving force behind the establishment of the League of Nations was U.S. President Woodrow Wilson. In his address to the U.S. Congress on 8 January 1918 in which he formulated in 14 points the principles for a peace settlement after World War I, he urged that 'XIV. A general association of nations must be formed under specific covenants for the purpose of affording mutual guarantees of political independence and territorial integrity of great and small states alike'. Ironically, the United States did not become a member of the League because of the refusal of the isolationist Senate to approve the Covenant.

61 Wehberg, *supra* (fn. 27) 31; Waldock, *supra* (fn. 27) 469; Brownlie, *supra* (fn. 27) 55.

62 See Articles 12, 13 and 15 of the Covenant of the League of Nations.

63 Article 10.

Member states also agreed to submit disputes likely to lead to a rupture to arbitration, to adjudication by the Permanent Court of International Justice (PCIJ)[64] or to enquiry by the League Council.[65] Furthermore, they undertook not to resort to war against a member that complied with the arbitral award, the judgment of the PCIJ or the recommendations in a report which the Council adopted unanimously (excluding the votes of the conflicting parties).[66] Otherwise they had to wait for three months before going to war, meaning they had to respect a rather short cooling-off period.[67]

The gaps in this fairly complex system consisted in the choice of conciliation by the Council, where the party that wanted to go to war could expect at least one member of this body supporting its position to prevent the unanimous adoption of a report, or in resorting to armed hostilities 'short of war'.[68] If a League member used these 'back doors', the sanctions under the system of collective security of the League would not be applied against it.[69]

It was only in 1928 that the change from the *jus ad bellum* to the *jus contra bellum*, the principled prohibition of war, was achieved by the Briand-Kellogg Pact.[70]

---

64 The Court whose creation was envisaged in Article 14 of the Covenant was established by its 1920 Statute and first sat in 1922. See *infra* 192.

65 Under Article 12, the arbitral award or judicial decision had to be made 'within a reasonable time', the report of the Council within six months after the submission of the dispute.

66 Articles 13 and 15(6). On the enforcement measures within the system of collective security of the League see *infra* fn. 181.

67 Article 12.

68 See *supra* 15. Moreover, if the time limits in Article 12 were exceeded, member states were also no longer bound by the prohibitions of the Covenant.

69 However, the resort to force still conflicted with the obligation under Article 10 to respect the territorial integrity and independence of member states. For attempts to solve the problem by attributing primacy to either Article 10 or Article 15(6) see W. Komarnicki, 'La définition de l'agresseur dans le droit international moderne', 75 *RCADI* (1949), 5 (22), and Brownlie, *supra* (fn. 27) 62. Attempts to strengthen the League of Nations system by the 1924 Geneva Protocol outlawing wars of aggression and the 1928 Geneva General Act on the Peaceful Settlement of Disputes, as well as the 1925 Locarno Treaties between Belgium, Germany, France and the United Kingdom, failed to produce the desired effect. Fassbender, 'Die Gegenwartskrise des völkerrechtlichen Gewaltverbotes vor dem Hintergrund der geschichtlichen Entwicklung', 31 *Europäische Grundrechte Zeitschrift* (2004) 241 (245).

70 The treaty owes its name to the two driving forces behind it, the then French Foreign Minister Aristide Briand and his U.S. opposite number, Secretary of State Frank Billings Kellogg. It was signed in the French capital and is therefore also referred to as the Pact of Paris. Kellogg, 'The War Prevention Policy of the United States', 22 *AJIL* (1928) 253; Wehberg, 'Le problème de la mise de la guerre hors de la loi', 24 *RCADI* (1928) 151; Wright, 'The Meaning of the Pact of Paris', 27 *AJIL* (1933) 39. On the political background of the

Under Article I, the contracting parties renounced war as an instrument of national policy in their relations with one another. They also agreed, pursuant to Article II, to seek to settle disputes among them by pacific means only. Although this treaty marked a turning point in the history of international law, it still suffered from several major shortcomings.

1) Firstly, it only banned war but not force, so that according to the above-mentioned subjective and objective or factual definitions of war a party was still allowed to resort to armed hostilities if it claimed to act without *animus belligerendi* or employed force 'short of war'.[71] The two above-mentioned 'back doors' in the two definitions of war thus remained open.[72]
2) Secondly, no genuine sanctions against breaches of the Pact were provided for. The denial of the benefits of the treaty to the party violating it in the preamble merely reiterated an existing principle of international law[73] which did not have a genuine deterrent effect on a powerful party considering an attack on a weaker one, although this provision applied not only to the victim of the breach but all the other parties as well. Yet, these parties had the right but not the obligation to go war with the state that violated the Pact of Paris. Whether they would do so in order to

---

treaty see Lesaffer, *Kellogg-Briand Pact*, MPEPIL. References will be made to paragraphs in the electronic version of the Encyclopedia which is more easily accessible and has the advantage of updates and the addition of new articles.

71 The authors of the Pact should have been aware of the problem in the light of the so-called Corfu incident of 1923. The members of a commission appointed to delineate the border between Albania and Greece headed by the Italian General Enrico Tellini were ambushed and killed near the town of Ioannina. Italy held Greece responsible for the assassination and made far-reaching demands, some of which were not accepted by the Greek government. Thereupon Italian forces occupied the island of Corfu. Italy defined this measure as temporary pacific occupation. A commission of five experts chaired by the Japanese lawyer Mineitciro Adatci was established by the League of Nations Council and gave a delphic answer to the issue: it was for the Council to decide on the merits of each case whether the use of force constituted unlawful war or a measure 'short of war'. Strupp, 'L'incident de Janina entre la Grèce et l'Italie', 31 *RGDIP* (1924) 255.

72 The renunciation of war as 'an instrument of national policy' was also problematic since it seemed to permit the interpretation that war was still lawful as 'an instrument of international policy' for such purposes as the enforcement of arbitral awards and court judgments or even in response to any breach of international law by the victim. However, this conclusion ran counter to the principle in Article II to seek to settle disputes peacefully.

73 The rule that a party violating a treaty is not entitled to compliance with the treaty by the party or parties victims of the breach (*inadimplendi not est adimplendum*).

defend the victim of an attack in violation of the Pact would depend on the expected costs in terms of casualties and material damage and the degree of solidarity with the attacked party.

The United States tried to fill this legal gap in the Briand-Kellogg Pact with its response to the invasion of Manchuria in 1931 by Japan, which subsequently established the puppet state of Manchukuo there. This reaction was similarly unlikely to impress an aggressor. The following year, Secretary of State Henry Lewis Stimson sent a note to China and Japan in which the American government declared that it would not recognize any situation, treaty, or agreement brought about by means contrary to the Pact of Paris.[74] This 'Stimson Doctrine' was endorsed by the League of Nations Assembly. Unfortunately, however, time often works in favour of breaches of international law. Non-recognition is difficult to uphold in the face of a lasting unlawful but effective factual situation.[75]

3) Thirdly, the prohibition of war was not accompanied by an effective mechanism for the peaceful solution of disputes between the parties as an alternative to their settlement by force of arms. The obligation in Article II merely to seek a solution by pacific means was not sufficient.[76]
4) Fourthly, the Pact was eroded by reservations and restrictive interpretative declarations of some of the contracting parties.[77] In particular, the United Kingdom declared that it would not tolerate interference by other states in regions of special and vital interest to it. Furthermore, the United States, the United Kingdom, Japan, France, Germany and other parties excluded war in self-defence.[78]

---

74 Wright, 'The Stimson Note of January 7, 1932', 26 *AJIL* (1932) 342; McNair, 'The Stimson Doctrine of Non-Recognition – A Note on its Legal Aspects', 14 *BYIL* (1933) 65; Grant, 'Doctrines (Monroe, Hallstein, Brezhnev, Stimson)', MPEPIL.

75 The principle *ex injuria jus not oritur* is overruled, sooner or later, by *ex factis jus oritur* – 'law does not originate from illegality' by 'law originates from facts'. The latter principle is known in German as the *'normative Kraft des Faktischen'* ('the normative power of the factual') according to Georg Jellinek.

76 Strictly interpreted, the duty to 'seek' would not be violated if efforts resulted in failure.

77 These declarations were not reservations in the technical sense. For they were made in the course of the diplomatic correspondence preceding the signing of the Pact of Paris but were not repeated on the occasion of the signature of the treaty or the deposit of the instruments of ratification. Wright, *supra* (fn. 74) 43.

78 The Foreign Relations Committee of the U.S. Senate also wanted to add the Monroe Doctrine which, however, was not included in the official declaration of the American government. Brownlie, *supra* (fn. 27) 245.

Therefore, although the Briand-Kellogg Pact did enter into force after all 15 signatory states had ratified it in accordance with its Article III and almost all states – 63 altogether – were bound by the treaty in 1939,[79] it could not prevent World War II. The treaty thus became an example of the fallacy of the so-called idealist school in the theory of International Relations.[80]

3.3 The Prohibition of the Threat or Use of Force under the UN Charter

Under the influence of the horrors of World War II which caused millions of deaths throughout the world, the authors of the UN Charter closed some of the main gaps in the rules governing the resort to force in international relations. The new key principle was laid down in Article 2(4) of the constituent treaty of the UN which reads as follows:

> All Members shall refrain in their international relations from the threat or use of force against the territorial integrity or political independence of any state, or in any other matter inconsistent with the Purposes of the United Nations.[81]

This provision marks progress over previous international law in several respects.[82]

---

79 Among the members of the League of Nations, four Latin American States (Argentina, Bolivia, El Salvador and Uruguay) did not ratify the Pact of Paris but became parties to its American equivalent, the Saavedra Lamas Pact signed in Rio de Janeiro in 1933. It is named after its main author, the then Foreign Minister of Argentina, Carlos Saavedra Lamas.

80 The adherents to this school, such as Alfred Zimmern, Philip Noel-Baker and Norman Angell, believed in the effectiveness of international law and institutions as the foundations of world peace.

81 In addition, according to paragraph 7 of the Preamble to the Charter, the peoples of the United Nations are determined to ensure, by the acceptance of principles and the institution of methods, that armed force shall not be used, save in the common interest, …' U.S. President Franklin D. Roosevelt and British Prime Minister Winston Churchill had already, in the eighth principle of the Atlantic Charter of 14 August 1941, expressed their belief 'that all of the nations of the world, for realistic as well as spiritual reasons, must come to the abandonment of the use of force'.

82 Schrijver, 'Article 2, Paragraphe 4', in: Cot, Pellet and Forteau (eds.), *La Charte des Nations Unies* (3rd ed. 2005) 437; Randelzhofer and Dörr, 'Article 2(4)', in: Simma et alii (eds.), The Charter of the United Nations: A Commentary (3rd ed. 2012) 200 (208).

1) Firstly, Article 2(4) outlaws force and not war. It thereby closes the legal loopholes left open under the Briand-Kellogg Pact to states that either use armed force below the threshold of war or claim to act without *animus belligerendi.*
2) Secondly, the Charter also prohibits the threat of force which can be as effective as the actual recourse to armed violence in the relations between a powerful and a weak state.[83] For the threat of force to be illegal actual resort to force must be prohibited. Consequently, if a state that feels threatened by another declares its intention to exercise its right of self-defence if attacked, this warning would not be contrary to Article 2(4).[84] While an explicit menace to use unlawful force undoubtedly constitutes a threat, the situation is less clear with regard to potentially hostile acts, such as military exercises close to the borders of a neighbouring state without a verbal message to the latter.[85] The question, in particular the seriousness and credibility of the threat, will have to be decided on the merits of a given case.
3) Thirdly, the new interdiction also applies to non-members of the UN. On the one hand, Article 2(4) extends its protection to 'any state'. On the other, it ought to be read together with Article 2(6), according to which the Organization shall ensure that states which are not Members of the UN act in accordance with the Principles of the Charter, which include the prohibition of the threat or use of force, so far as may be necessary for the maintenance of international peace and security. It may be objected that this provision is legally problematic since its runs counter to the rule that treaty obligations must not be imposed on non-parties without their consent.[86] Yet, the prohibition in Article 2(4) has in the meantime

---

83 Article 10 of the League of Nations Covenant already provided for advisory action by the Council not only in the case of aggression but also in the event of any threat or danger of external aggression. Article 11 declared any war or threat of war, whether immediately affecting any of the Members of the League or not, a matter of concern to the whole League. See also Sadurska, 'Threats of Force', 82 *AJIL* (1988) 239; Wood, 'Use of Force, Prohibition of Threat', MPEPIL.

84 This aspect was emphasized by the ICJ in its 1996 advisory opinion on the *Legality of the Threat or Use of Nuclear Weapons*, paragraph 47.

85 The ICJ also clarified that the mere possession of arms, including nuclear weapons, is not unlawful as proof of a state's aggressive intent and a threat according to Article 2(4) in its 1986 judgment on *Military and Paramilitary Activities in and against Nicaragua (Nicaragua v. United States of America)*, Merits, paragraph 269, and its 1996 advisory opinion on the *Legality of the Threat or Use of Nuclear Weapons*, paragraph 48.

86 In accordance with Article 35 of the 1969 VCLT which even requires express acceptance of a treaty obligation in writing by a third state. Article 2(6) was occasionally

become part of universal customary law which is also binding on non-member states of the UN. Moreover, since practically all states of the world are today members of the World Organization, its actual relevance is minimal anyway.[87]

4) This positive assessment is further reinforced by the establishment of a system of collective security by the UN Charter which, at least on paper, is much more effective than that of the League of Nations.

As a result, 'primitive', decentralized international law has caught up with its more developed domestic counterpart with regard to the use of force. As under internal criminal law, physical violence is either an unlawful act, legal self-defence, or the application of force by those institutions and their organs endowed by the law with the power to do so – the police and the armed forces under domestic law on the one hand and action by the Security Council of the UN under Chapter VII of the Charter on the other.

3.4 Enhancing the Prohibition of the Threat or Use of Force in International Relations

After the entry into force of the UN Charter, several developments strengthened and extended the principle laid down in Article 2(4).

1) As mentioned above, the prohibition of the threat or use of force became a rule of universal customary law and thus not binding just on member

---

referred to in UN practice, for example in Security Council (SC) Resolutions 338 (1976) and 409 (1977) on Southern Rhodesia. Moreover, many resolutions of the General Assembly and the Security Council, including binding decisions by the latter, have been addressed to all states (and not just members of the UN). SC Resolution 757 (1992) on comprehensive sanctions against the Federal Republic of Yugoslavia (Serbia and Montenegro – FRY) may be quoted as an example. See *infra* fn. 261. This practice posed particular problems for permanently neutral Switzerland which was admitted to the World Organization as late as 2002. Mahiou, 'Article 2, Paragraphe 6', in: Cot, Pellet et Forteau (eds.) *supra* (fn. 82) 475; Talmon, 'Article 2(6)', in: Simma et alii (eds.), *supra* (fn. 82) 253. See also Falk, *The Authority of the United Nations over Non-Members* (1965).

87 Furthermore, it could be argued that the enforcement of the principle in Article 2(4) of the Charter against a non-member state that resorts to the illegal use of force constitutes the lawful exercise of the right of collective self-defence as it existed in 1945.

> states of the UN.[88] However, since almost all states – 193 at this writing – have been admitted to the World Organization this does not constitute a major breakthrough.

Moreover, the principle was also included among the few rules that are generally recognized, in particular also by the International Law Commission (ILC), as part of *jus cogens* which reflects the fundamental values of the international community.[89] Treaties conflicting with such peremptory norms are void.[90]

In addition, acts affecting *jus cogens* are excluded from countermeasures which used to be called reprisals.[91] These measures are taken by the victim of a breach of international law against the perpetrator and are designed to make the latter comply with its legal obligations. They also consist in violations of the rights of the perpetrator but are legal because of the previous unlawful act committed by the perpetrator state.[92]

Furthermore, like all *jus cogens* rules,[93] the principle in Article 2(4) of the Charter belongs to the obligations with *erga omnes* effects. This means, in the words of the ILC, for obligations of a universal character that they are owed to the international community as a whole.[94] As a result, not only the direct victim

---

88 As stated, for instance, by the ICJ in 1986 in the *Nicaragua* case. *Military and Paramilitary Activities in and against Nicaragua (Nicaragua v. United States of America)*, Merits, paragraphs 183–192.

89 Article 50 of the Articles on the Responsibility of States for internationally wrongful acts elaborated by the ILC which the UN General Assembly welcomed and commended to the attention of governments in Resolution 56/83 of 28 January 2002. The ILC had already mentioned the interdiction in Article 2 (4) of the Charter as an example of a peremptory rule in the commentary to Article 50 of its Draft Articles on the Law of Treaties which provided the basis for the 1969 VCLT. Yearbook of the International Law Commission 1966 II 247. In its judgment in the *Nicaragua case*, the ICJ referred to this statement of the ILC. *Military and Paramilitary Activities in and against Nicaragua (Nicaragua v. United States of America)*, Merits, paragraph 190. Schrijver, *supra* (fn. 82) 459.

90 Articles 53 and 64 of the 1969 VCLT.

91 The duty of states to refrain from acts of reprisals involving the use of force was already stated in paragraph 6 of the first principle of the 1970 Friendly Relations Declaration, the duty of states to refrain from the threat or use of force in international relations.

92 However, the practical relevance of this innovation is limited, since the use of force as countermeasure would usually violate the principle of proportionality between the initial unlawful act and the response to it, another requirement that must be met when countermeasures are taken.

93 Zemanek, 'New Trends in the Enforcement of erga omnes Obligations', 4 *Max Planck YBUNL* (2000) 1 (6).

94 Article 48 of the Articles on the Responsibility of States for internationally wrongful acts. See *supra* fn. 89.

of a breach of the prohibition but any state may claim from the perpetrator the cessation of the wrongful act, assurances and guarantees of non-repetition, as well as performance of the obligation of reparation, in the interest of the injured state or of the beneficiaries of the obligation breached.

Finally, according to Articles 40 and 41 on the Responsibility of States for internationally wrongful acts,[95] a serious, i.e., a gross or systematic, breach of a peremptory norm of general international law entails specific consequences: the obligation of states to cooperate to bring such a breach to an end through lawful means; and the prohibition on recognizing as lawful a situation created by a serious breach of a *jus cogens* norm, as well as rendering aid or assistance in maintaining that situation, in other words the 'Stimson Doctrine' which was already included in the Friendly Relations Declaration.[96]

2) In addition, Article 2(4) is deemed applicable, together with other rules of international law including those on responsibility, not only to states but also to *de facto* regimes,[97] i.e., entities that possess the attributes of statehood, including an effective government, but are not recognized by existing states. In particular, their opponents are numerous enough to prevent the admission of these regimes to international organizations, above the UN as well as specialized agencies. During the Cold War, the 'socialist' parts of the divided states of Germany, Korea and Vietnam were cases in point. Such regimes also have to comply with and are protected by the prohibition of the threat or use of force.
3) Similarly, demarcation and armistice lines, such as those agreed on in Germany, Korea, the Middle East and Vietnam after World War II, are regarded as covered by the prohibition in Article 2(4). This view was confirmed by the Friendly Relations Declaration in 1975.[98]
4) The definition of force prohibited under the UN Charter gave rise to three major issues: the 'indirect' use of force; the inclusion of non-military coercion, political and economic pressure; and, more recently, 'cyber force'. Article 2(4) undoubtedly outlaws the employment by a state of its regular armed forces which wear uniforms and use conventional weapons.[99]

95 See *supra* fn. 89.

96 See *supra* 21.

97 Frowein, *Das de facto-Regime im Völkerrecht* (1968).

98 Principle 1 on refraining from the threat or use of force, paragraph 5.

99 With regard to nuclear weapons, the ICJ, by a vote of seven votes to seven, by President Bedjaoui's casting vote, stated in its 1996 advisory opinion on this issue that the threat or use of these weapons would generally be contrary to the rules of international law

Complications arose because those other forms of force came to play an increasingly important role soon after the entry into force of the UN Charter as a result of political, technological and strategic developments.

a) A direct military confrontation between East and West, in particular between the two superpowers, the United States and the Soviet Union, in the pursuit of their goals could have spelt disaster for both of them and the rest of mankind if the conflict had escalated across the threshold of the use of nuclear weapons. This risk, albeit less seriously, also existed if one of these powers used armed force outside the territory of the other bloc, since the other power could have entered or have been drawn into the conflict.

This did not mean that the superpowers and their allies renounced the extension of their zones of influence. However, they considered direct control over additional territories less important than in the colonial period and shifted their priorities to establishing or maintaining governments in other countries which shared their ideological and political orientations. These aims could also be achieved by using or supporting irregular, paramilitary forces and armed bands that operated abroad by providing them with weapons, as well as by training and sheltering them, by hostile propaganda or destabilizing another state by other means. Such use and assistance could remain covert and be denied officially, at least for some time.[100] It also avoided or reduced criticism by public opinion which would, at least in Western democracies, often vehemently protest against the open use of direct armed force. 'Indirect force' also had the advantage of making self-defence and countermeasures by the governments of states against which it was directed legally and politically more difficult. Moreover, the government under attack could be blamed for the political and economic problems in the country, which led to violent opposition. This strategy thus helped the superpowers and their blocs, which usually found

---

applicable in armed conflict, and in particular the principles and rules of humanitarian law. However, the Court could not conclude definitely that it would be lawful or unlawful in an extreme circumstance of self-defence, in which the very survival of a state would be at stake. *Legality of the Threat or Use of Nuclear Weapons,* paragraphs 97, 105. This assessment may be extended to other weapons of mass destruction, i.e., biological, chemical and also radiological weapons. See *infra* 121.

100 All these activities have recently received growing attention in the context of 'hybrid warfare' of which the West is accusing the Russian Federation in Ukraine.

themselves in opposite camps in the pursuit of those 'milieu goals',[101] to achieve these objectives at lower costs than if they employed their regular armed forces.

These forms of force were soon widely condemned in principle, in particular by the UN General Assembly, for example in its Resolutions 110 (II), 290 (IV – 'Essentials of peace'), 380 (V) and 381 (V). However, opinions were usually divided on which side had actually or first used 'indirect force' in a specific conflict.

The plenary organ of the World Organization reiterated its position in 1974 when it adopted its definition of aggression.[102] The list of acts of aggression in Article 3 includes lit. (g), which reads as follows: '[t]he sending by or on behalf of a State of armed bands, groups, irregulars or mercenaries, which carry out acts of armed force against another State of such gravity as to amount to the acts listed above, or its substantial involvement therein'. The ICJ ruled in the *Nicaragua* case in 1986 that these acts were banned under customary international law.[103]

In accordance with Principle II, entitled 'Refraining from the threat or use of force', in the Declaration on Principles in the CSCE Final Act of 1975, participating states will refrain from the direct, as well as indirect, use of force against another participating state.

The UN General Assembly confirmed its broad understanding of unlawful armed force in 1970 in paragraph 8 of the first principle in the Friendly Relations Declaration, the prohibition of the threat or use of force: 'Every State has the duty to refrain from organizing or encouraging the organization of irregular forces or armed bands, including mercenaries, for incursion into the territory of another State'.

Seventeen years later, the Assembly included a similar obligation in the Declaration on the Enhancement of the Effectiveness of the Principle of Refraining from the Threat of Use of Force in International Relations.[104]

---

101 In the terminology of Wolfers who distinguishes these goals from the traditional territorial 'possession goals'. Wolfers, *Discord and Collaboration* (1965) 274.

102 Annex to Resolution 3314 (XXIX) of 14 December 1974. See *infra* 63.

103 *Military and Paramilitary Activities in and against Nicaragua* (*Nicaragua v. United States of America*), Merits, paragraph 195.

104 Annex to Resolution 42/22 of 18 November 1987. According to Article 6, 'States shall fulfil their obligation under international law to refrain from organizing, instigating, or assisting or participating in paramilitary, terrorist or subversive acts, including acts of mercenaries, in other States, or acquiescing in organized activities within their territory directed towards the commission of such acts.' See also Treves, 'La Déclaration des Nations Unies sur le renforcement de l'efficacité du principe du non-recours à la force', 33 *AFDI* (1987) 379.

These broad formulations raise the question whether any support constitutes the use of force or whether a line should be drawn below which assistance 'merely' violates the prohibition of intervention in the internal affairs of states. The ICJ held the latter view with regard to the supply of funds to rebels in the *Nicaragua* case.[105]

b) Another controversy revolved around the extension of the prohibition in Article 2(4) of the Charter beyond armed force to political and economic pressure.

The debate on this issue took place in various forums, in particular in the context of the codification of the law of treaties and the definition of aggression.[106] It led to a major debate at the Vienna Conference on the Law of Treaties in 1968/1969 where it was agreed that a treaty was void if its conclusion had been procured by the threat or use of force in violation of the principles of international law embodied in the Charter of the United Nations.[107] The problem was also discussed within the Special Committee charged by the UN General Assembly with formulating the principles of the Friendly Relations Declaration.[108]

The principal political argument on which the advocates of the inclusion of non-military coercion in the prohibition relied was the contention that, although its visible effects were less dramatic than the human fatalities and the destruction caused by armed force, it could also result in substantial concessions, which the victim would otherwise not make, to the state exerting such pressure. The legal debate focused on the UN Charter, the preparatory work of this treaty, and legal developments after its entry into force.

(1) Those in favour of an extensive interpretation of force argued that whenever the authors of the UN Charter understood force narrowly they expressly referred to armed force, as in the preamble and Articles 41 and 46. The opponents pointed out that in Article 44 force was mentioned

105 *Military and Paramilitary Activities in and against Nicaragua* (*Nicaragua v. United States of America*), Merits, paragraph 228.

106 See *infra* 63.

107 Article 52 of the 1969 VCLT. Neuhold, 'The 1968 Session of the United Nations Conference on the Law of Treaties', 19 *Österreichische Zeitschrift für öffentliches Recht* (1969) 59 (80); idem, 'Die Wiener Vertragsrechtskonvention 1969', 15 *Archiv des Völkerrechts* (1971) 1 (38).

108 In Resolution 1966 (XVIII). For details see Neuhold, *supra* (fn. 7) 179.

without any qualification; however, it was clear from the context that military force was meant. For Article 44 had to be read together with Article 42 which dealt with action taken by the Security Council using air, sea or land forces.

(2) Moreover, the *travaux préparatoires* of the 1945 San Francisco Conference where the text of the Charter was adopted were quoted in order to prove that force was to be interpreted restrictively. At that conference, Brazil submitted an amendment including economic coercion in Article 2(4). However, this proposal was rejected by an overwhelming majority of 26:2. This result could only mean that the authors of the Charter wanted to limit unlawful coercion to armed force. The counterarguments against this conclusion were not convincing: that the Brazilian amendment was rejected as redundant, since force was generally understood to include non-military pressure as well; or because a specification of illegal force could open dangerous gaps for other forms of coercion not covered by the prohibition but producing the same unacceptable result. The more honest response would be to admit that the effectiveness of non-military force was not fully realized at a time when most of the weak states of the Third World were still colonies.

(3) In addition, the supporters of a broad definition invoked legal developments after 1945, such as provisions of the Charter of the Organization of American States (OAS), several UN General Assembly resolutions[109] and declarations adopted by the Non-Aligned Movement. The opponents objected that the constituent treaty of the OAS only obligated the contracting parties; that resolutions of the plenary organ of the UN were not legally binding; and that documents of the non-aligned states were not relevant to non-members of their movement and 'soft law' anyway. Since Western states consistently opposed an extensive interpretation of force, it could not have become general customary law.

A broad definition is particularly problematic in the context of the law of treaties and is a further illustration of conflicting interests and contradictory legal principles as described in the introduction.[110] On the one hand, the effectiveness of non-military pressure on small and weak states, especially developing countries, resulting in unequal treaties, cannot be denied. On the other, the conclusion of each treaty inevitably involves a 'give-and-take' process. The line between unlawful coercion and the exchange of acceptable concessions may

109 For instance, Resolutions 2131 (XX) and 2160 (XXI). See *infra* 166.

110 See *supra* 5.

often be difficult to draw. An extensive definition of unlawful pressure rendering a treaty void would undermine the *pacta sunt servanda* principle and result in undesirable uncertainty about the validity of a treaty after its conclusion.

The negotiators at the Vienna Conference on the Law of Treaties eventually settled for a compromise. The invalidity of treaties concluded under economic and political pressure was not included in the text of the Convention. In exchange, the Conference adopted a declaration solemnly condemning the threat or use of pressure in any form, military, political, or economic, which was included as an Annex in the Final Act of the Conference.[111]

The UN General Assembly took a position on the issue in 1987 in the above-mentioned Declaration on the Enhancement of the Effectiveness of the Principle of Refraining from the Threat of Use of Force in International Relations.[112] Article 8 of this declaration on the prohibition in Article 2(4) of the Charter echoes the Declaration in the Final Act of the Vienna Conference: 'No State may use or encourage the use of economic, political or any other type of measures to coerce another State in order to obtain from it the subordination of the exercise of its sovereign rights and to secure from it advantages of any kind'.

Beyond the debate on the inclusion of non-military coercion as outlawed force, its illegality can more easily be asserted under the principle of non-intervention in internal affairs.[113] This principle would be meaningless if non-military coercion were also covered by the prohibition of the threat or use of force.

c) More recently, the use of a new type of weapon in a broad sense has attracted growing attention and is emphasized as one of the most alarming threats in contemporary strategic doctrines, in particular those of the European Union (EU), the United States and the North Atlantic Treaty Organization (NATO): 'cyber force'.[114] The Internet has been called the battlefield of the 21st century and the fifth dimension of war after land, sea, air and outer space. To make matters worse, it can be used not only by states but also by terrorists and 'ordinary' criminals.

111 Neuhold, *supra* (fn. 107: 'The 1968 Session…') 83; text in: 14 *Archiv des Völkerrechts* (1968–1970) 380.

112 See *supra* 28.

113 See *infra* 159.

114 Lynn III, 'Defending a New Domain: The Pentagon's Cyberstrategy', 89 *Foreign Affairs*, No. 5 (September/October 2010) 97; see also Betz and Stevens, *Cyberspace and the State: Toward a Strategy for Cyber-Power* (2011).

Computer software and hardware have become equally vulnerable. Attacks on hardware, causing design deficiencies or tampering with computer chips, are even more difficult to detect and defend against than interference with software, such as stealing secret military or civilian industrial information, destroying or changing computer systems and data.[115] Distributed-denial-of-service (DDoS) attacks may disturb or paralyze vital communication systems for protracted periods of time.[116] Nightmare scenarios envisage attacks on vital military and civilian infrastructure. They would be aimed at supervisory control and data acquisition (SCADA) systems, such as air-traffic-control systems, power grids and health and financial systems. Such attacks could not only cause heavy material damage but also thousands of human casualties.

Major incidents in recent years include a DDoS attack against Estonia in 2007 dubbed by some 'Web War I'. Numerous government, corporate and media sites were bombarded by computers with requests for data, and some of them stopped working for three weeks. Damage caused was estimated at €28 million.

Another spectacular attack was directed simultaneously against the United States and South Korea over the 4th of July weekend in 2009. The targets included websites of the White House, the Department of State and the New York Stock Exchange in the United States, and the Blue House, i.e., the office of the South Korean President, as well as the Defence Ministry and the National Assembly in Seoul.

In 2010, The Stuxnet Trojan Worm attack on Iranian nuclear installations received worldwide coverage.[117] In 2011, groups of unidentified hackers known as LulzSec and Anonymous launched real barrages of attacks on the computer systems of prominent targets, such as the International Monetary Fund and NATO, the FBI and the CIA, Lockheed Martin, Google and Sony. In 2012, the 'Flame' virus, according to some reports more sophisticated than Stuxnet and already used for years in the Middle East and again, in particular, against Iran, made headlines. The embarrassment caused by the revelations of confidential military and diplomatic reports by the whistle-blower Wikileaks should also be mentioned in this context.

---

115 A distinction can be made between cyber exploitations and disruptive cyber-attacks. The former monitor computer systems as well as copy data; the latter alter, disrupt, deny, degrade or destroy computer systems and the information in or transiting through these systems. Woltag, 'Cyber Warfare', MPEPIL; Goldsmith, 'How Cyber Changes the Laws of War', 24 *EJIL* (2013) 129 (130).

116 Clark and Levi, 'Securing the Information Highway: How to Enhance the United States' Electronic Defenses', 88 *Foreign Affairs*, No. 6 (November/December 2009) 2 (4).

117 Farwill and Rohozinski, 'Stuxnet and the Future of Cyber War', 53 *Survival* No. 1 (February–March 2011) 23.

To make matters worse for the victims, cyber warfare, crime and terrorism are often asymmetrical and favour the attackers.[118] The latter are hard to identify because they are able to operate from remote locations and may benefit from a time lag between the initiation and the actual occurrence of their attacks. In addition to the low risk of being caught, their costs are low. Consequently, a strategy of deterrence against digital attacks is much less effective than against armed attacks that can be clearly attributed to a state or non-state actors.

The use of the 'cyber weapon' also raises a number of thorny legal questions. One concerns the extension of the prohibition in Article 2(4) of the UN Charter to cyber warfare.[119] The definition of force should focus on the results of a given activity. Not all cyber-attacks cause human casualties or substantial material damage; but if they do, they ought to be considered force and outlawed by the interdiction in the Charter. It should be borne in mind that a single digital attack may have more disastrous consequences than the use of heavy conventional weapons. The definition of arms covered by the prohibition in Article 2(4) ought therefore to be based on their effects.[120]

The same considerations apply to the exercise of the right of self-defence against cyber-attacks.[121] If the – indirect – physical effects of a digital attack amount to those required for an armed attack under Article 51 of the UN Charter, resort to force should be considered lawful.[122]

---

118 Asymmetrical warfare is practiced, above all, by a technologically and/or numerically weaker opponent who attacks the weak spots of a 'physically' stronger adversary while evading the latter's strengths. See *infra* fn. 118.

119 Other issues arise in the areas of the laws of war and neutrality. Joyner and Lotrionte, 'Information Warfare as International Coercion: Elements of a Legal Framework', 12 *EJIL* (2001) 825; Schmitt and O'Donnell (eds.), *Computer Network Attack and International Law* (2002).; Woltag, *supra* (fn. 115); Goldsmith, *supra* (fn. 115).

120 According to the U.S. Air Force, weapons are 'devices designed to kill, injure, or disable people or to damage or destroy property'. Farwell and Rohozinski, *supra* (fn. 117) 30.

121 '...the United States reserves the right, under the laws of armed conflict, to respond to serious cyber attacks with a proportional and justified military response at the time and place of its choosing'. Deputy Secretary of Defense William J. Lynn announcing the new U.S. cyber defence strategy on 14 July 2011. http://www.rferl.org/articleprintreview/24266548.html. See also *infra* 122.

122 Computer attacks do not cause direct physical damage or harm to persons, but their effects may well do, for example a plane crash or collision after a cyber-attack on an air control system. In any event, in paragraph 72 of their declaration at the end of their Newport summit meeting of 4–5 September 2014, NATO member states affirmed that cyber defence was part of NATO's core task of collective defence. A decision as to when a cyber-attack would lead to the invocation of Article 5 would be taken by the North Atlantic Council on a case-by-case basis. Similarly, the UN Security Council could determine that a major

Moreover, could the use of the 'cyber weapon' also constitute aggression? According to Article 3(b) of the definition adopted by the UN General Assembly in 1974, aggression also consists in the 'bombardment by the armed forces of a State against the territory of another State or *the use of any weapons by a State against the territory of another State*'.[123]

Further complications are caused by the above-mentioned difficulties, first to identify the authors of a cyber-attack and, if they are known, to attribute the responsibility for their activity to a state. Governments may 'outsource' cyber warfare to hackers who are not their organs but more or less closely associated with them.[124]

3.5 A Major Gap in the Charter System Prohibiting Force in International Relations: Non-International Armed Conflict

Article 2(4) of the UN Charter prohibits the threat or use of force in international relations but remains silent on internal relations within states. The founders of the World Organization obviously paid little attention to domestic conflicts in 1945. The horrors of World War II overshadowed those of the Spanish Civil War (1936–1939), although the bloody confrontation between the leftist Republicans and the right-wing Nationalists on the Iberian Peninsula was a kind of rehearsal for the former.

However, after 1945 internal strife escalating to what used to be called civil war and more recently tends to be referred to, at least in legal terminology, as non-international armed conflict soon became and still remains the dominant type of the resort to armed force.[125] The violent struggle for independence by the indigenous inhabitants of many dependent territories in the decolonization process, one of the major developments of global significance after World War II, fell into this category. In addition, the armed conflicts in Greece between the pro-Western government and its communist opponents (1946–1949),[126] in China between the Kuomintang Nationalists and the communists (1946–1950), or

cyber-attack constitutes a threat to, if not a breach of the peace, under Article 39 of the UN Charter and take enforcement measures in the context of the system of collective security under Chapter VII. See *infra* 45. On self-defence see *infra* 122.

123 Italics added. For further details of the definition of aggression see *infra* 63.

124 Klimburg, 'Mobilising Cyber Power', 53 *Survival*, No. 1 (February–March 2011) 41.

125 Since non-lawyers continue to speak of 'civil war', this term will also be used here.

126 Both sides were supported by states sympathizing with their respective positions.

in Nigeria (1967–1970), which was caused by the secession of Biafra, may also be mentioned in this context.

Moreover, this type of conflict has not receded into the background with the completion of decolonization in the Third World. The causes and goals of intra-state armed force have been manifold and often mutually reinforcing: secession of part of the population of a state fighting for independence; the imposition of a religion and the law based on it in a country; ethnic enmity; control over natural resources, in particular precious minerals; ousting a repressive authoritarian regime and introducing multi-party democracy and basic human rights. Many of these internal conflicts have been fought with egregious brutality, with civilians massacred and other atrocities like mass rape and torture committed at random, sometimes by drugged child soldiers.

The disintegration of the former Yugoslavia and the conflicts in Afghanistan, Sierra Leone, Liberia, Sudan and, more recently Libya, Mali, the Central African Republic and South Sudan, as well as Syria and Iraq, may be mentioned as examples.

As in the case of force 'short of war' in international armed conflict, not every use of armed force within states constitutes a non-international armed conflict. A distinction ought to be made between riots, sporadic terrorist attacks and other forms of domestic unrest and violence on the one hand and a non-international armed conflict on the other.

Governments confronting even large-scale violent domestic opposition are usually reluctant to recognize the conflict as civil war for legal and political reasons. For at least according to the non-intervention principle that, as will be shown below, has been gaining some ground, they are thereby precluded from receiving outside military assistance, which is lawful in domestic conflicts 'short of civil war'. Moreover, by admitting the existence of civil war in their countries they indicate that resistance has reached a scope beyond the level of domestic unrest and constitutes a serious challenge to their legitimacy, if not their very existence.

As for the definition of war and an armed attack required for the exercise of the right of self-defence under Article 51 of the UN Charter,[127] preferably quantifiable criteria for crossing the threshold from lesser violence to a non-international armed conflict should be sought.[128] On the basis of an analysis of relevant practice, the Committee of the International Law Association on the Meaning of Armed Conflict in International Law concluded, in its 2010 report,

---

127 See *supra* 15 and *infra* 121.

128 The distinction is important, since the existence of an armed conflict triggers the application of international humanitarian law. This means that some human rights need not to be respected; for instance, persons may be killed without warning or detained without trial.

that two characteristics were relevant:[129] on the one hand, the existence of organized armed groups, including their command structure, training and recruiting ability, communications, procurement and logistical capacities; on the other hand, engagement in fighting of some intensity, which could be measured by the number of fighters and the types of weapons used, the numbers of casualties, the amount of material destruction, territorial extension and protraction. None of these factors were necessarily decisive; rather, the low level of one could offset the high degree of another. It may be added that what is important is not just the respective figures as such but also their share of the size of the population, the territory and the economy of the country.[130]

If permanent control by the rebels over a sizeable part of the territory of the state in which they operate is required for civil war/non-international armed conflict, problems arise if, as is frequently the case, guerrilla warfare is waged against the government. Opposition fighters practicing this strategy who do not wear uniforms and cannot be distinguished from the rest of the population at least initially launch most of their attacks at night. As a result, government forces seem to be able to maintain order and security in most of their state's territory during the day, but lose control over large areas once night sets in. Similarly, the exact size of insurgent forces and the number of their supporters are hard to establish.

At the other end of the spectrum the extent of outside support to the insurgents which transforms a domestic into an international armed conflict may be discussed. If this assistance amounts to an armed attack under Article 51 of the UN Charter, the government may in turn request military help from other states in the exercise of the right of collective self-defence, even if non-intervention is accepted as the principle governing foreign involvement in civil war.[131] The parties involved tend to define a conflict differently according to their political interests. For example, while the Bosniaks regarded the 1991–1995 conflict in Bosnia and Herzegovina as international as a result of aggression by the Federal Republic of Yugoslavia (Serbia and Montenegro – FRY), the latter party considered it a civil war.[132]

---

129 www.ila-hq.org/download.cfm/docid/2176DC83-D-268-413.

130 See *infra* 123.

131 See *infra* 38.

132 Gray, 'Bosnia and Herzegovina: Civil War or Inter-State Conflict? Characterization and Consequences', 67 *BYIL* (1996) 155; Meron, 'Classification of Armed Conflict in the former Yugoslavia: Nicaragua's Fallout', 92 *AJIL* (1998) 236; for other examples see Gray (fn. 27) 83.

The key legal issue in a civil war/non-international armed conflict was and is the legality of support by other states to the conflicting parties.[133] The question concerns, above all, military assistance in various forms, from sending troops to supplying military equipment and training, as well as the provision of funds for these purposes. As pointed out above, this issue became particularly urgent with the shift by great powers to 'milieu' instead of 'possession goals' and to 'indirect force'[134] and numerous 'civil wars by proxy', and has remained topical. Significantly, no simple answer can be given to this question on the basis of treaties and other relevant documents and an unambiguous state practice.[135]

1) The 'classical' solution favouring the status quo limits outside support to assistance to the 'legitimate' government according to the traditional definition, i.e., the government against which part of the population, which may also have formed a government or other representative body of its own, has taken up arms. On the legal level, it is argued that only that government represents the state concerned in its international relations. From the political point of view, this rule is said to have the advantage of shortening the conflict and reducing its negative effects, bloodshed as well as material damage.

---

133 The ICJ ruled in the *Nicaragua* case that the arming and training of the insurgents, the *contras,* by the United States against the Nicaraguan government could certainly be said to involve the threat or use of force against Nicaragua whereas the mere supply of funds to them, while undoubtedly an act of intervention in the internal affairs of this state, did not in itself amount to a use of force. *Military and Paramilitary Activities in and against Nicaragua* (*Nicaragua v. United States of America*), Merits, paragraph 228.

134 See *supra* 27.

135 In addition to works on recent specific non-international armed conflicts see Potter, 'L'intervention en droit international moderne', 32 *RCADI* (1930) 611; Siotis, *Le droit de la guerre et les conflits armés d'un caractère non-international* (1958); Pinto, 'Les règles du droit international concernant la guerre civile', 114 *RCADI* (1965) 455; Castren, *Civil War* (1966); Falk (ed.), *The International Law of Civil War* (1971); Farer, 'The Regulation of Foreign Intervention in Civil Armed Conflict', 142 *RCADI* (1974) 297; Moore (ed.), *Law and Civil War in the Modern World* (1974); Neuhold, *supra* (fn. 7) 88; Cassese, 'La guerre civile et le droit international', 90 *RGDIP* (1986) 553; Tanca, *Foreign Armed Intervention in Internal Conflict* (1993); Nolte, *Eingreifen auf Einladung. Zur völkerrechtlichen Zulässigkeit des Einsatzes fremder Truppen im internen Konflikt auf Einladung der Regierung* (1999); Corten, *supra* (fn. 27) 174; Nolte, 'Intervention by Invitation', MPEPIL; on other aspects see Hurwitz (ed.), *Civil War and the Rule of Law: Security, Development, Human Rights* (2008).

These arguments can easily be refuted. The very occurrence of a civil war proves that the government can no longer speak on behalf of the entire people. Moreover, despite the existence of numerous authoritarian governments, it may be argued today that legitimacy also requires that a government be democratically elected so that its simple prior existence is not sufficient. As a result, undemocratic and repressive regimes would not be legitimate. In addition, 'intervention by invitation' runs counter not only to the prohibition of the threat or use of force but also to another cornerstone of modern international law, the right of self-determination of peoples. This principle would come into play if opposition to the incumbent government were widespread and protracted.

As regards the practical consequences of assistance, keeping a weak and widely unpopular regime in power by providing military support to it may prolong the conflict and on the contrary entail losses that could otherwise be avoided.

However, the principle of 'Metternich legitimacy' as practiced by the Holy Alliance in the 19th century, is backed, *inter alia*, by the Havana Convention on Duties and Rights of States in the Event of Civil Strife of 1928[136] and more recently by the 1975 Helsinki Final Act[137] of the CSCE, as well as by the ICJ in its 1986 judgment in the *Nicaragua* case.[138]

2) According to another rule demanding strict non-intervention in internal affairs, other states must not provide military aid to either party to a civil war.[139] A major legal argument in favour of this solution is the exercise of the above-mentioned right of self-determination which entitles a people

136 For instance, under Article 1(3) of the Convention, the parties are obligated, 'to forbid the traffic in arms and war material, except when intended for the Government, ...'.

137 Paragraph 4 of the Principle VI of the Declaration on Principles Guiding Relations between Participating States, Non-intervention in internal affairs, reads as follows: '[] Accordingly, they (the participating States – the author) will, inter alia, refrain from direct or indirect assistance to terrorist activities, or to subversive *or other activities directed towards the violent overthrow of the regime of another participating State*.' (Italics added).

138 'Indeed, it is difficult to see what would remain of the principle of non-intervention in international law if *intervention, which is already allowable at the request of the government of a State*, were also to be allowed at the request of the opposition'. (Italics added). *Military and Paramilitary Activities in and against Nicaragua* (*Nicaragua v. United States of America*), Merits, paragraph 209. However, it is worth noting that even if the lawfulness of support to the (older) government is accepted, governments practicing apartheid or genocide are deemed precluded from requesting foreign military assistance. Nolte, *supra* (fn. 135 – MPEPIL) paragraph 22.

139 This principle must clearly be observed by a state that recognizes the insurgents as belligerents, since as a result, the recognizing state becomes neutral in the civil war and must

to choose its political, economic and social system.[140] If this choice cannot be made peacefully, force may have to be used as a means of last resort. Another reason is derived from the general objective of the non-intervention principle, the protection of a state's sovereignty and independence from foreign interference. Moreover, the interdiction of outside involvement contains the conflict and limits its negative consequences.

Support for this solution can be found, for instance, already in a treaty concluded by the five Central American States in 1907,[141] as well as several UN General Assembly resolutions, notably the Draft Declaration on Rights and Duties of States in Resolution 375 (IV),[142] the 'Non-Intervention Declaration' in Resolution 2131 (XX)[143] and the Friendly Relations Declaration,[144] by the Institut de Droit international (IDI) at its Wiesbaden Session in 1975, as well as the 1977 Protocol Additional to the 1949 Geneva Conventions relating to the Victims of Non-International Armed Conflicts.[145]

---

comply with the law of neutrality, which includes the obligation of abstention from providing military support to any belligerent party.

140 On the problem of a possible exception in favour of a people in the exercise of its right to self-determination see Corten, *supra* (fn. 27) 186. On the basis of his analysis of the divergent positions taken by states which show the lack of consensus within the international community on this question, he concludes that other states may provide humanitarian, political or economic assistance to national liberation movements. On the issue of whether peoples fighting for their independence may receive military aid from abroad on the basis of the right of collective self-defence against colonialism as a form of armed attack see *infra* 155.

141 Article II of the Additional Convention to the General Treaty of Peace and Amity signed in Washington on 20 December 1907: 'No Government of Central America shall in case of civil war intervene in favor of or against the Government of the country where the struggle takes place'.

142 Article 4: 'Every State has the duty to refrain from fomenting civil strife in the territory of another State, and to prevent the organization within its territory of activities calculated to foment such civil strife'.

143 Declaration on the Inadmissibility of Intervention in the Domestic Affairs of States and the Protection of Their Independence and Sovereignty. Paragraph 2 reads as follows: '...no state shall organize, assist, foment, finance, incite or tolerate subversive, terrorist, or armed activities directed towards the violent overthrow of the regime of another State, *or interfere in civil strife in another State*'. (Italics added). See *infra* 166.

144 This second Declaration contains the same text.

145 Article 3(2): 'Nothing in this Protocol shall be invoked as justification for intervening, directly or indirectly, for any reason whatsoever, in the armed conflict or in the internal or external affairs of the High Contracting Party in the territory of which that conflict occurs'.

More recently, at its Rhodes Session in 2011, the IDI adopted another resolution on the issue. It permits military assistance, i.e., the sending of armed forces by a state, to a requesting state. However, the resolution only applies to situations of international disturbances and tensions, such as riots, isolated and sporadic acts of violence and other acts of a similar nature, including acts of terrorism. These situations remain below the threshold of non-international armed conflict in the sense of Article 1 of Protocol II Additional to the Geneva Conventions relating to the Protection of Victims of Non-International Armed Conflicts of 1977. In these conflicts, however, the principle of non-intervention has to be observed.[146] The same rule was also included in the 2010 Kampala definition of aggression in the context of the Statute of the International Criminal Court (ICC).[147]

3) The problem with this principle, however (relatively) attractive it may be, is the lack of support by relevant international practice. The same is true of the first above-mentioned, the 'classical' solution to the problem. States have tended to assist the party with which they shared ideological preferences, political priorities and economic interests, irrespective of whether this party was the government or the so-called rebels.[148]

The picture was further complicated by the claim that only the side fighting for the 'just cause' may be assisted. During the Cold War, this meant backing 'anti-capitalist' and 'anti-colonialist' parties[149] for the East and many young states but 'anti-communist' parties for the West. Today, in addition to political and economic interests, ethnic or religious ties often replace ideological solidarity.

146 The Institute quoted the Friendly Relations Declaration and its own Resolution on The Principle of Non-Intervention in Civil War adopted at its Wiesbaden Session in 1975.

147 See *infra* 65.

148 If only the (older) government receives military assistance from other states, the conflict remains of an intra-state nature. External support to the rebels transforms it into an international armed conflict. Once again the question of the scope of foreign military help required to bring about this result arises. For a discussion of the cases of Afghanistan and the disintegration of the Socialist Federal Republic of Yugoslavia (SFRY) as examples of the transformation of an initially intra-state into an international armed conflict see Dinstein, *supra* (fn. 27) 6.

149 On the doctrine of the legality of supporting peoples fighting 'wars of national liberation' against colonial powers see *infra* 155. According to this view, only the insurgents may be assisted and not the governments against which they take up arms – the opposite of the traditional solution.

Legal analysis of foreign involvement in domestic conflicts is further complicated by the fact that the states concerned have often relied on more than one argument which they claimed provided a lawful basis for military support: in addition to the invitation by a 'legitimate' party, military action is justified as response to prior interference by another state or other states in favour of the other party, which transforms an initially internal into an international conflict and gives rise to the right of collective self-defence in favour of the incumbent government; as support for a people in the exercise of its right of self-determination; stopping large-scale human rights abuses; as resort to force in order to protect their own threatened nationals or free hostages;[150] and in order to fight terrorism. Moreover, interference by other states is often covert, difficult to prove and officially denied by the government offering assistance.

4) Political and legal developments after the Cold War have introduced a new scenario. The end of the East–West conflict, which had paralyzed the Security Council, enabled the central organ of the UN system of collective security to play a more active role in the maintenance and restoration of international peace and security.[151] The Council may prohibit military assistance, especially by imposing an arms embargo, to all or only some parties to a civil war.[152] Since the Security Council still does not have armed forces at its disposal it is unable to take military action itself. It may, however, authorize able and willing states, as well as international organizations, to use armed force for specific purposes. If the Council adopts an authorization to provide military assistance to a party involved in this type of conflict, such support is obviously lawful.[153]

A recent innovation worth mentioning in this context is the emergence of the concept of the responsibility to protect.[154] According to this new understanding

150 For instance, the United States in the Dominican Republic (1965) and Grenada (1983). See *infra* 130. For further examples see Gray, *supra* (fn. 27) 88.

151 See *infra* 66.

152 However, its practice regarding arms embargoes has not been consistent. In some internal armed conflicts, as in the former Yugoslavia in 1991 and Libya in 2011, it imposed an arms ban on all parties. See *infra* 47, 111. In the Darfur conflict in Sudan the Security Council limited the embargo to non-governmental parties. See *infra* 47. In the ongoing crisis in Syria, the members of the Council have so far failed to agree on a prohibition to provide military equipment.

153 See *infra* 67.

154 See *infra* 104.

of state sovereignty, the international community has a secondary responsibility to protect the population of a state from major human rights violations if the latter is unable or unwilling to do so itself. As pointed out above, such abuses tend to be particularly frequent in non-international armed conflicts. This secondary responsibility is to be exercised by the UN Security Council.

In practice, the problem is that the members of the Council frequently find it difficult to agree to allow military assistance to warring parties within a state and to live up to the responsibility to protect.

The unsatisfactory conclusion to be drawn at this point in time is the lack of a clear-cut rule on the important issue of foreign involvement in civil war/non-international armed conflict, even if the principle of strict non-intervention appears most desirable politically, except when the UN system of collective security is activated.

The best practical solution would of course be efforts by non-military means – bi- and multilateral diplomacy, including within and by the UN, as well as political and economic incentives – to prevent the resort to armed force in internal conflicts, but this is more of a moral appeal than a well-defined rule of 'hard law'.

3.6 The Lawful Use of Force within the UN System of Collective Security

In order to achieve the first goal mentioned in the Preamble to the UN Charter, the saving of succeeding generations from the scourge of war, and the first Purpose of the World Organization listed in Article 1, the maintenance of international peace and security by taking effective collective measures,[155] member states established a system of collective security in the framework of Chapter VII, without mentioning the term in the constituent treaty of the World Organization.[156]

While collective self-defence is directed against an external – potential or actual – attacker, collective security provides for joint enforcement action

155 For the prevention and removal of threats to the peace and for the suppression of acts of aggression or other breaches of the peace, according to Article 1(1). The same three situations calling for action, albeit in a different order, are reiterated in Article 39. See *infra* 45.

156 However, UN organs have subsequently used the term. Collective security was referred to, for example, in the title of Chapter III and paragraph 72 of the 'World Summit Outcome', the concluding document of the high-level meeting of the UN General Assembly in 2005. See *infra* 107, and de Wet and Wood, 'Collective Security', MPEPIL.

against members of the system who resort to illegal force or commit serious violations of other major principles.[157] Successful collective security, as well as successful institutionalized collective self-defence through the creation of a military alliance, is based on effective deterrence. A potential attacker ought to refrain from carrying out planned aggressive acts because the costs to be reckoned with would outweigh the expected gains. Several requirements in four different areas must be met for a system of collective security to achieve its purpose.[158]

1) In order to produce the above-mentioned deterrence effect, sufficient resources for enforcement measures, above all armed forces and weapons, as well non-military, especially economic, sanctions have to be available. This in turn necessitates the participation of as many states as possible, above all the great powers in a global collective security system. In the case of the UN with its 193 members, this condition is, to all intents and purposes, met,[159] whereas the League of Nations suffered from the absence of some great powers throughout its history.[160]

In addition, a rough power equilibrium ought to exist among the major members; otherwise the dominant great power, no matter how benign its self-image, will be tempted to use the system for its hegemonic aspirations. This prerequisite was also fulfilled during most of the UN's history, although the West led by the only remaining superpower, the United States, enjoyed a temporary superiority after the Cold War.

---

157 However, despite the difference between the underlying concepts, the two terms are sometimes used interchangeably in practice. Neuhold, 'Terminological Ambiguity in the Field of International Security: Legal and Political Aspects', in: Dicke et alii (eds.), *Weltinnenrecht: Liber amicorum Jost Delbrück* (2005) 473 (473).

158 Claude, Jr., *Swords Into Plowshares: The Problems and Progress of International Organization* (3rd ed. 1964); Neuhold, 'Collective Security After "Operation Allied Force"', 4 *Max Planck YBUNL* (2000) 73 (74).

159 The absence of some tiny island states, the special cases of Taiwan, Palestine and Kosovo, and the Holy See does not invalidate this assessment.

160 It was one of the ironies of history that the United States, whose President at the time, Woodrow Wilson, was the main driving force behind the Covenant, never became a member of the League after its switch to isolationism. See *supra* fn.60. The Soviet Union was admitted as late as 1934 and expelled in 1939 after invading Finland. The main Axis Powers, Japan, Germany and Italy, withdrew from the organization.

2) On the legal level, a clear-cut interdiction of the threat or use of force, as well as an equally unambiguous obligation to take part in enforcement action, ought to be established. Otherwise members may use gaps in the prohibition in order to justify their recourse to force. Moreover, since enforcement measures usually entail costs not only for the target state(s) but also for those taking them, many members of the system will probably prefer to remain on the sidelines if they are given a choice. Their readiness to accept these negative consequences, from human casualties in the case of military action to the loss of market shares if trade sanctions are imposed, may increase if they have particularly close relations with the fellow member state that has been attacked, or if they must expect to be the next victims themselves. In the case of the UN, this second set of conditions is also met, by Article 2(4), on the one hand, and Articles 2(5) and 25 of the Charter on the other.
3) As regards the organizational structure of a system of collective security, the founding members have a choice between a decentralized or a centralized system. The former alternative allows each member state to decide whether enforcement action is required and what kind of action is to be taken. In a centralized system, the key decisions for the activation of collective security are entrusted to a central organ. Ideally, this body would be independent of the member states, have the power to make decisions that are binding on all members of the system, and have effective enforcement resources, including military means, at its disposal. However, in a world of states jealous of their sovereignty, especially in the crucial area of security, this option is still out of reach, above all on the global level. A realistic variant of centralized collective security provides for a small organ on which only some member states are represented. The delegates forming the central body remain bound by the instructions of their national governments. Yet this construction is still deemed to be more effective than a decentralized model of collective security, since in principle a smaller organ may be expected to act more expeditiously and resolutely.

As mentioned above, the UN Charter marked progress over the collective security system created by the League of Nations Covenant in this respect.[161] The Security Council, which still comprises only 15 members, acts as the central enforcement organ.[162] Member states gave the Council what looks like a blank

161 See *supra* 24.

162 De Wet, *The Chapter VII Powers of the United Nations Security Council* (2004).

cheque with regard to five decisions: (1) whether (2) against whom (3) which kind of action (4) is to be taken by whom, and (5) when.

a) The first question to be addressed concerns the need to activate the system of collective security. Does a given conflictual situation require action by the World Organization? Article 39 of the UN Charter contains a threefold answer to this question and charges the Security Council with the task of determining the existence of any threat to the peace, breach of the peace, or act of aggression, before making recommendations or deciding what measures shall be taken.

The broadest, by far most frequently invoked of these three scenarios is a threat to the peace. The practice of the Council shows that such a threat does not necessarily include the use of armed force and does not have to be an international conflict. It may consist in an apartheid regime or a humanitarian disaster within the borders of a single state, for which the cases of Southern Rhodesia after 1965[163] and South Africa in 1977[164] – thus already during the Cold War – on the one hand and of Somalia in 1992[165] and Rwanda in 1994[166] on the other provide examples.[167]

A state committing a breach of the peace typically launches large-scale military attacks against another state and therefore triggers a more serious situation than a threat to the peace. Among the few examples in UN history, the invasion of South Korea by North Korea in 1950[168] and the invasion of Kuwait by Iraq in 1990[169] may be mentioned.

The Security Council has never formally determined the occurrence of an act of aggression in the sense of Article 39.[170] However, it referred to 'aggression', 'armed aggression' or 'acts of aggression' descriptively on several occasions, for

---

163 See *infra* 54.

164 Ibid.

165 SC Resolution 794 (1992).

166 SC Resolution 929 (1994).

167 In 2014, the Security Council determined that the unprecedented extent of the Ebola outbreak in Africa constituted a threat to international peace and security in Resolution 2177 (2014).

168 SC Resolution 82 (1950).

169 SC Resolution 660 (1990).

170 Nor has it ever expressly quoted the definition of aggression which the General Assembly adopted as guidance for determining the existence of aggression. See *infra* 63, and Dinstein, *supra* (fn. 27) 137 and 318.

example, in the context of the Israeli raid on Palestine Liberation Organization (PLO) targets in Tunisia[171] and the attacks by South Africa on neighbouring Angola[172] in the 1970s and 1980s. It may also be noted that, contrary to what one would expect from the order in which the three situations are listed in Article 39, those acts of aggression were less serious than, for example, the 'mere' breaches of the peace committed by North Korea in 1950 and Iraq in 1990.

Moreover, the Security Council also condemned acts of aggression perpetrated by non-state actors, i.e., mercenaries, against Benin, and also condemned, without naming them, states permitting or tolerating the recruitment of mercenaries and providing facilities to them.[173] Yet, the Security Council is free to choose the measures it deems appropriate in a crisis regardless of the qualification of the situation pursuant to Article 39.[174]

UN member states cannot escape action by the Security Council in an Article 39 situation by invoking the principle of non-intervention in their internal affairs. For, although Article 2(7) of the Charter does prohibit the UN from intervening in matters which are essentially within the domestic jurisdiction of any state, this principle shall not prejudice the application of enforcement measures under Chapter VII.[175]

b) Secondly, the Security Council has to decide against whom – only some or all parties involved – enforcement action should be taken. This question does not, at first sight, pose a difficult problem. The target of the measures adopted ought to be the party responsible for the threat to the peace, breach of the peace or act of aggression. However, the side which seems to have fired the first shot is not necessarily the aggressor.[176] The beginning of World War II was a case in point. During the night from 31 August to 1 September 1939, Nazi

171 SC Resolutions 573 (1985) and 611 (1988).

172 SC Resolutions 387 (1976), 454 (1979), 475 (1980), 546 (1984), 567 (1985), 571 (1985), 574 (1985), 577 (1985), 602 (1987). In the last two resolutions, the Security Council strangely qualified the pursuance of the acts of aggression as a serious threat to international peace and security.

173 SC Resolutions 405 (1977) and 419 (1977).

174 Dinstein, 'Aggression', MPEPIL.

175 Preuss, 'Article 2, Paragraph 7 of the Charter of the United Nations and Matters of Domestic Jurisdiction', 74 *RCADI* (1949) 553; Watson, 'Auto-Interpretation, Competence and Continuing Validity of Article 2 (7) of the UN Charter', 71 *AJIL* (1977) 60; Guillaume, 'Article 2, Paragraphe 7', in: Cot, Pellet and Forteau (eds.), *supra* (fn. 82) 485; Nolte, 'Article 2(7)', in: Simma et alii (eds.), *supra* (fn. 82) 280.

176 See *infra* 64.

Germany staged an attack by SS agents dressed in Polish uniforms on the radio station in the German border town of Gleiwitz, and Hitler announced that Germany was firing back.

Another problem in this context arises from the extension of sanctions to all conflicting parties irrespective of which of them bears the main responsibility for a given conflict. The arms embargo which the Security Council imposed on Yugoslavia in 1991, which affected all new states on the territory of the former Socialist Federal Republic of Yugoslavia (SFRY), provides an example.[177] The wisdom of this decision was indeed debatable. On the one hand, it could be argued that the fewer weapons which the parties to the conflicts in the wake the disintegration of the SFRY obtained, the better. But, on the other, the embargo played into the hands of the FRY which was widely regarded as the aggressor. Since it controlled the former Yugoslav National Army it enjoyed decisive military superiority over the other parties.[178] The same considerations apply to the general arms embargo decided by the Security Council in the Libyan civil war in 2011.[179] Conversely, in the Darfur crisis in 2004, the Security Council limited an arms ban to the non-governmental parties and thus exempted the government in Khartoum, although most of the blame for the atrocities in that Sudanese province was generally placed on the latter.[180]

c) Thirdly, with regard to enforcement action taken, the Security Council can choose between measures not involving the use of armed force and military action in order to give effect to its decisions.[181] Article 41 contains a non-exhaustive list of the former; they

177 SC Resolution 713 (1991).

178 Bosnia-Herzegovina sought to be exempted from the embargo, arguing that this was necessary for the effective exercise of its right of self-defence against the FRY, which had priority over the embargo. However, the Security Council did not comply with this request, although the General Assembly repeatedly urged it to do so. In contrast, the arms embargo imposed on Rwanda under SC Resolution 918 (1994) was lifted in favour of the Rwandan government by SC Resolution 1011 (1995). Gray, *supra* (fn. 27) 126, 268.

179 See *infra* 111.

180 SC Resolution 1556 (2004). Neuhold, 'The International Community and "Rogue States"', in: Fischer-Lescano et alii (eds.), *Frieden in Freiheit: Festschrift für Michael Bothe zum 70. Geburtstag* (2008) 215 (232).

181 Under Article 16(1) of the League of Nations Covenant all other member states undertook immediately to take non-military measures against a member that resorted to war in disregard of the treaty: they were obligated immediately to sever all trade or financial relations

> may include complete or partial interruption of economic relations and of rail, sea, air, postal, telegraphic, radio, and other means of communication, and the severance of diplomatic relations. Should the Council consider that such non-military measures would be inadequate or have proved to be inadequate, it may, pursuant to Article 42, take such action by air, sea, or land forces as may be necessary to maintain or restore international peace and security. Such action may include demonstrations, blockade and other operations by the armed forces of member states.[182]

The problem raised by military action which the Security Council is supposed to take under Article 42 is the lack of forces of its own. Proposals for a permanent UN army were rejected at the Dumbarton Oaks conference on the Charter of the new World Organization. However, Article 43 offers a remedy to this deficiency.[183] All UN members undertake to make available to the Council, on its call and in accordance with a special agreement or agreements, the necessary armed forces, assistance and facilities, including rights of passage. Such agreement(s) shall govern the numbers and types of forces, their degree of readiness and general location, and the nature of the facilities and assistance to be provided. They shall be negotiated as soon as possible on the initiative of the Security Council.

According to the concept underlying Article 43, these agreements enable the Council to know in advance exactly on which military resources it can count from each contracting party. The latter is aware of the kind and scope of its contributions and can be sure that it does not have to comply with unexpected demands by the Security Council. Forces placed at the disposal of the

---

with the Covenant-breaking state, to prohibit all intercourse between their nationals and the nationals of that state, and to prevent all financial, commercial or personal intercourse between the nationals of the latter and the nationals of any other state, whether a member of the League or not. In contrast, in the framework of the UN system of collective security, member states are not obligated to impose non-military sanctions automatically but only on the basis of a specific Security Council decision.

182 The system of collective security established by the League of Nations Covenant was also different in this respect from that of the UN Charter. Pursuant to Article 16(2) of the Covenant, the League Council could only recommend to members to contribute armed forces to military enforcement action. The only obligation member states had with regard to military measures, in accordance with Article 16(3), was to afford passage through their territory to the forces of those members which followed a recommendation of the Council. On balance, the UN system is more effective than that of its predecessor, at least on paper.

183 Krisch, 'Article 43', in: Simma et alii (eds.), *supra* (fn. 82) 1351.

Council ought to be rapidly deployable so that necessary military action can swiftly be taken in a crisis.[184]

Under Article 43, the initiative for the conclusion of these agreements rests with the Security Council. If the Council takes this first step, then the member state concerned must, in accordance with a *pactum de negotiando et de contrahendo*[185] according to the wording of the provision, conclude the agreement.[186] However, because of disagreements among its permanent members on the modalities of the contributions to be made, the Security Council has so far not called on any member with a view to concluding an Article 43 agreement, so that this provision of the Charter has remained a dead letter.[187] As a result, the effectiveness of the UN system of collective security, which would require the option of military action by the organization itself as a means of last resort, has been severely eroded from the beginning.

d) Fourthly, pursuant to Article 48, it is for the Security Council to determine whether its decisions for the maintenance of international peace

184 Article 45 of the Charter imposes on member states an obligation to this effect with regard to air-force contingents for combined international enforcement action. This obligation is subject, however, to the conclusion of an Article 43 agreement determining the strength and readiness of these contingents.

185 While, for instance, the obligation of the parties under Article VI of the 1968 Non-Proliferation Treaty concerning effective measures relating to cessation of the nuclear arms race and nuclear disarmament and a treaty on general and complete disarmament under strict and effective international control is limited to the pursuit of negotiations in good faith.

186 However, no state is obligated to accept specific contributions in such an agreement. Therefore, the basic obligation under Article 43 cannot be implemented as long as differences of opinion exist on the contents of the agreement.

187 In 1947 the Military Staff Committee provided for under Articles 46 and 47 of the UN Charter submitted a report on the matter. However, the five permanent members of the Security Council could only agree on 27 of the 41 articles of the report. Differences of opinion concerned, *inter alia*, the numbers and the location of the troops to be made available by the permanent members themselves. In his 1992 Agenda for Peace presented after the end of the Cold War, Secretary-General Boutros Boutros-Ghali recommended that the Security Council initiate negotiations under Article 43, but his proposal fell on deaf ears. See paragraph 43 of the Agenda for Peace, Preventive Diplomacy, Peacemaking and Peace-keeping of 17 June 1992. UN Document A/47/277-S/24111. This recommendation was not reiterated in the Supplement to an Agenda for Peace issued by the Secretary-General on 3 January 1995. UN Document A/50/60-S/1995/1. Martinez, 'Article 46', in: Cot, Pellet and Forteau (eds.), *supra* (fn. 82) 1277; Martinez, 'Article 47', ibid. 1283; Neuhold, 'Agenda for Peace', MPEPIL; Reinisch and Novak, 'Article 46', in: Simma et alii (eds.), *supra*, (fn. 82) 1362; Reinisch and Novak, 'Article 47', ibid. 1364.

and security shall be taken by all or only some member states. This flexibility makes sense, because minor conflicts may adequately be dealt with by only some members, for example interested great powers and/or neighbouring states and other states situated in the crisis region.[188]

e) Fifthly, the Security Council has to decide when the actual resort to enforcement action shall commence. Its members may agree in principle on the measures to be taken, but some of them might wish to postpone their application in order give the target state a last chance to comply with the Council's demands of its own free will and thus avoid the negative consequences of sanctions.

4) The fourth crucial condition to be fulfilled by an effective system of collective security is its psychological/political foundation, the solidarity of its member states. Solidarity can be defined as the readiness of actors, be they individuals or states, to provide assistance to others and accept the resulting costs, as well as the actual granting of assistance.[189] In the realm of international security, solidarity means the willingness to help other states to cope with threats to and actual attacks on their essential values, above the physical integrity of their population, territorial inviolability and political independence.

Solidarity is in turn built on three main pillars:

(1) common interests based on shared threat perceptions, in particular concerning the threatened values, the gravity of a threat and the imminence and probability that it will actually materialize;
(2) common values shared by the partners; and
(3) positive feelings of sympathy and friendship, between both peoples and governments.

---

188 Article 48 was invoked in order to square the circle between the permanent neutrality of Austria and its membership of the UN system of collective security. After declaring its permanent neutrality on 26 October 1955, Austria requested the states with which it entertained diplomatic relations, including the permanent members of the Security Council, to recognize its new international status. This request was complied with before Austria was admitted to the UN on 14 December 1955. According to the Austrian view, the Council was therefore obligated to exercise its discretion under Article 48 and precluded from calling on Austria to take part in enforcement action which was contrary to its neutrality. Verdross, *The Permanent Neutrality of Austria* (1978) 52.

189 Neuhold, 'Common Security: The Litmus Test of International Security', in: Wolfrum and Kojima (eds.), *Solidarity: A Structural Principle of International Law* (2009) 193.

Solidarity may also be translated into the principles of the indivisibility of peace and anonymity. The former implies that all members of the system must feel directly concerned, no matter where an Article 39 situation occurs and which parties are involved in it. The second principle means that in a system of collective security member states must have neither permanent friends nor permanent foes. They must also be willing to take enforcement action against states with which they have good and close relations and assist other members with whom their relations are otherwise strained and hostile.

This fourth requirement is obviously not met within the UN. As a result, the voting rules governing decision making in the Security Council have weakened and even paralyzed the system of collective security from the beginning. Under Article 27(3) of the Charter, decisions on all non-procedural matters require the affirmative vote of nine members including the concurring votes of the five permanent members (China, France, Soviet Union/Russia, the United Kingdom and the United States – the 'P 5'). However, contrary to the clear wording of this provision, in practice the Security Council may also adopt a decision if a permanent member is absent or abstains, provided the necessary majority of at least nine votes in favour is reached.[190] Still, each of the 'P 5' can single-handedly prevent a decision that is not to its liking by its negative vote. This so-called veto power even exceeds the normal meaning of this term. A veto usually refers to the blocking of an existing legal act, for instance by the head of state objecting to a law enacted by the legislature, as in the United States. Moreover, the 'P 5' benefit from another prerogative, since their veto power already applies to the vote on whether a given issue is of a procedural or substantive nature.[191]

---

190 The ICJ endorsed this practice in its 1971 advisory opinion on the *Legal Consequences for States of the Continued Presence of South Africa in Namibia (South West Africa) notwithstanding Security Council Resolution 276 (1970)*, paragraph 22. Various explanations for this modification, for which the abstention of the Soviet Union on the Spanish question in 1946 set the stage, have been offered, including derogation by subsequent customary law; a teleological interpretation of the difference between the words 'affirmative' and 'concurrent', leading to the understanding of abstention as a 'concurring' vote; and an amendment by 'spontaneous consent', based on the object and purpose of Article 108 of the Charter, which would allow a two-thirds majority required for formal amendments of the treaty also to amend the treaty by spontaneous agreement. Resolutions of the UN General Assembly may be quoted to support this theory. Moreover, absence of a permanent member may be construed as abstention. Simma, Brunner and Kaul, 'Article 27', in: Simma (ed.) The Charter of the United Nations: A Commentary (2nd ed. 2002) 476 (493).

191 This right is referred to as the 'double veto'. The 'P 5' also agreed that any matter that could eventually lead to action by the Security Council was non-procedural and therefore subject to the veto.

It is tempting to criticize the veto of five privileged member states in the Charter and blame the founders of the UN for including it. However, the realistic choice in 1945 was not between the UN as we know it and a more perfect system of collective security, but rather between an admittedly imperfect and no global system at all. For the Soviet Union was determined to prevent a repetition of its negative experience with the League of Nations, from which it was excluded after its attack on Finland in 1939. Joseph Stalin therefore insisted on the inclusion of the veto in the Charter.

A solution to the problem that appears evident at first sight would be an amendment to or a comprehensive revision of the Charter. However, a closer look at the relevant provisions, Articles 108 and 109, shows that this proposal is equally unrealistic. Both modifications of the constituent treaty of the UN not only require adoption/recommendation and ratification by two thirds of the members of the organization. The latter majority must also comprise all permanent members of the Security Council. However, it is highly unlikely that these five states will renounce their prerogatives of their own free will.

Moreover, the veto makes sense to the extent that conflicts directly opposing the main victorious powers at the end of World War II to each other should not be subject to enforcement action under Chapter VII. What is objectionable is the fact that especially during the Cold War, the 'P 5' prevented the Security Council from dealing with other conflicts in which their respective 'clients', states that belonged to their ideological and political camps, were involved.

Furthermore, the power balance has substantially changed since 1945, especially in recent years. France and the United Kingdom can hardly be called great powers any longer, while the claims of countries like Brazil, Germany, India and Japan to a permanent seat on the Council are understandable. However, the calls for a reform of the Security Council have so far fallen on the deaf ears of the 'P 5', whose consent would be necessary for an enlargement of the Council, the extension of their privileges to newcomers or the abolition of the veto.

That the UN has not lived up to its role as guarantor of international peace and security envisaged in its Charter may be regretted but should come as no surprise in the light of insights of conflict theory. The effectiveness of its system of collective security under Chapter VII hinges on the continued close cooperation of the principal anti-Axis powers in World War II. However, the only tie that held this coalition together was the need to join forces against an otherwise too powerful common enemy. Once this single objective had been achieved with the defeat of Nazi Germany, Fascist Italy, Japan and their allies, the conflicts between the Western powers and the Soviet Union, which had been shelved temporarily, erupted again, leading to what became known as the Cold War.

It may also be pointed out that the veto power is a symptom but not the cause of the recurrent deadlock of the Security Council. The real root of the evil that prevents collective security from functioning is the differences of opinion between the 'P 5'. If these conflicts could be settled, then Article 27(3) would not have to be amended. It could remain unchanged, since the veto power would simply not be exercised, at least not as frequently as in the past.

3.7 The Record of the UN System of Collective Security during the Cold War

3.7.1 *The Paralysis of Collective Security Caused by the East–West Conflict*

The Cold War blocked the UN system of collective security from its inception. Even if Article 43 agreements had been concluded, a decision by the necessary majority within the Security Council on military action by the Council in accordance with Article 42 would have been unlikely. An apparent exception that is sometimes mentioned was the Council's response to the invasion of South Korea by North Korea in 1950. However, after qualifying the armed attack by North Korean forces as a breach of the peace,[192] all the Security Council did was to recommend that the members of the UN furnish such assistance to the Republic of Korea as may be necessary to repel the armed attack and to restore international peace and security in the area.[193] Ten days later, the Council recommended that the military forces and assistance provided by member states be made available to a unified command under the United States. It also requested the United States to designate the commander of such forces.[194] Moreover, it authorized the unified command at its discretion to use the UN flag concurrently with the flags of the various nations participating.[195]

192 See *supra* 45. During the East–West conflict, the Security Council also determined the existence of a breach of the peace in the Falkland/Malvinas crisis in 1982 (Resolution 502) and at a late stage in the 1980–1988 First Persian Gulf War between Iraq and Iran in 1987 (Resolution 598). All its members could agree on, however, was to demand an immediate cessation of hostilities and an immediate withdrawal of all Argentine forces from the islands in the first and an immediate cease-fire and the withdrawal of the forces of the two parties to the internationally recognized boundaries without delay in the second conflict.

193 SC Resolution 83 (1950).

194 The United States appointed General Douglas MacArthur.

195 SC Resolution 84 (1950). These resolutions were adopted despite the boycott of the Security Council by the Soviet Union in protest against the representation of China by the government in Taipei and not that in Beijing, and thus without the concurring vote of a permanent member. They set the stage for the modification of the voting requirements in the Security Council. See *supra* 51.

The Security Council did authorize the use of armed force in the course of the Cold War against the secessionist British colony of Southern Rhodesia. This may at first sight be surprising, since the majority of the UN members supported the process of decolonization in the Third World. However, the secession of Southern Rhodesia from the United Kingdom in 1965 was flawed in the eyes of the international community. For, the white minority led by Ian Smith who unilaterally declared the independence of the colony established an apartheid regime. The Security Council responded by condemning the declaration of independence and called upon all states (and not just member states) not to recognize the illegal racist minority régime in Southern Rhodesia and not render it any assistance.[196] Determining that the continuance of the situation resulting from the proclamation of independence by the illegal authorities constituted a threat to international peace and security, the Council then called on all states to impose an arms embargo on and to do their utmost to break all economic relations with Southern Rhodesia and on the United Kingdom to enforce these and the measures the British government had announced.[197] These sanctions were extended and tightened in several subsequent resolutions leading to the isolation of Southern Rhodesia.[198] In particular, the Security Council called on the government of the United Kingdom to prevent, by the use of force if necessary, the arrival at Beira[199] of vessels reasonably believed to be carrying oil destined for Southern Rhodesia, and empowered the United Kingdom to arrest and detain the tanker known as the *Joanna V* upon her departure from Beira in the event her oil cargo was discharged there.[200] Moreover, the Security Council authorized the use of force in the context of the UN peacekeeping operation in the Congo crisis 1960–1964.[201]

The Security Council also adopted an arms embargo against South Africa, the first sanction against a UN member state. Expressing its conviction that the situation in South Africa seriously disturbed international peace and security, it solemnly called, in 1963, upon all states to cease the sale and shipment of arms, ammunition and military vehicles to that country.[202] In 1977 the Council not only condemned the apartheid regime and other human rights violations in and the

196 SC Resolution 216 (1965).

197 SC Resolution 217 (1965).

198 See SC Resolutions 232 (1966), 253 (1966), 277 (1970), 388 (1976) and 409 (1977).

199 A port in neighbouring Mozambique, a Portuguese colony at the time.

200 SC Resolution 221 (1966). Southern Rhodesia was named Zimbabwe after the eventual collapse of the apartheid regime and its accession to internationally recognized independence following the Lancaster House Conference under the auspices of the British government in 1979/1980.

201 See *infra* fn. 212.

202 SC Resolution 181 (1963).

attacks by South Africa against neighbouring states.[203] It was also gravely concerned that South Africa was at the threshold of producing nuclear weapons. Acting under Chapter VII of the UN Charter and determining that the South African military build-up constituted a threat to the maintenance of international peace and security, the Security Council imposed on all states a mandatory prohibition on providing arms and related *materiél* of all types to and cooperating with South Africa in the manufacture and development of nuclear weapons.

Thus the Security Council did exceptionally resort to non-military enforcement measures. What Southern Rhodesia and South Africa had in common was the practice of racial discrimination which the rest of the world considered unacceptable, irrespective of how deep-seated the antagonism between the two Cold War blocs and the Third World was on other issues. In the case of South Africa, the international community was equally united in opposing the threat of the proliferation of nuclear weapons. At the same time, the West was evidently unwilling to take further measures against South Africa, which was both an important economic partner and a valued bulwark against the spread of communism and Soviet influence in the southern part of the African continent.

3.7.2 *Peacekeeping Operations*

Some modest efforts were undertaken during the Cold War to strengthen the UN as a security organization. An innovation[204] was the development of peacekeeping operations under the auspices of the UN which were not provided for in the Charter.[205] Peacekeepers were sent, for instance, to the Sinai Peninsula,[206]

---

203 SC Resolution 418 (1977).

204 Although operations within the framework of the League of Nations, for example the multilateral force established in order to maintain order during the 1935 plebiscite in the Saar territory, until then administered by the League, may be seen as precursors of UN operations. Bothe, 'Peacekeeping Forces', MPEPIL, paragraph 7.

205 Bowett, *United Nations Forces* (1964); Seyersted, *United Nations Forces in the Law of Peace and War* (1966); Cassese (ed.), *United Nations Peace-Keeping: Legal Essays* (1978); Durch (ed.), *The Evolution of UN Peacekeeping: Case Studies and Comparative Analysis* (1993); Hillen, *Blue Helmets: The Strategy of UN Military Operations* (2nd ed., 2000); Sucharipa-Behrmann, 'Peace-Keeping Operations of the United Nations', in: Cede and Sucharipa-Behrmann (eds.), *The United Nations: Law and Practice* (2001) 89; Khan, 'United Nations Peacekeeping in Internal Conflicts', 4 *Max Planck YBUNL* (2004) 543; Fernández Sánchez, *Operaciones de Paz: Operaciones de Naciones Unidas y de la Unión Europea* (2006); United Nations Department of Peacekeeping Operations, *United Nations Peacekeeping Operations: Principles and Guidelines* (2008); Bothe, *supra* (fn. 204).

206 United Nations Emergency Force (UNEF) I (1956–1967) and II (1973–1979).

the Congo,[207] Cyprus,[208] the Golan Heights[209] and southern Lebanon.[210] Forces of the three last-mentioned missions are still deployed today.

Although these so-called first-generation peacekeeping operations[211] certainly were and are useful, their military significance is limited in several respects. Their main task consists in stabilizing ceasefire agreements by monitoring compliance with them or the inter-positioning of military units between the conflicting parties. Peacekeeping is thus designed to help all parties and not to assist one of them against the other. Peacekeepers have to observe impartiality. Peacekeeping forces may use force only in self-defence.[212] However, this right came to be interpreted broadly to include the use of force in order to resist forcible attempts to prevent peacekeepers from fulfilling their duties under their mandates.[213] Moreover, since they are usually weaker, both numerically and with respect to their weapons, than the troops of the local parties, they ought to avoid armed showdowns with the latter. As a rule, the 'P 5' were not supposed to take part in these missions in order to keep the conflict concerned out of great power rivalries.[214] In addition, for obvious reasons, troops from states with particular interests in the host state were also not accepted.

As cooperative security activities, UN peacekeeping missions require the consent of all parties involved in them:

1) a mandate from the Security Council;[215]
2) the agreement of the conflicting parties, above all the host state on whose territory the peacekeepers are to be stationed;[216] and

---

207 Opération des Nations unies au Congo (ONUC) (1960–1964).

208 United Nations Peacekeeping Force in Cyprus (UNFICYP) (1964-).

209 United Nations Disengagement Observer Force (UNDOF) (1974-).

210 United Nations Interim Force in Lebanon (UNIFIL) (1978-).

211 Or 'traditional' peacekeeping operations, according to the terminology of the UN 'Capstone Doctrine'. United Nations Department of Peacekeeping Operations, *supra* (fn. 205) 20.

212 The mandate of ONUC constituted an exception to this rule. The Security Council authorized the UN and the Secretary-General to use force in order to prevent civil war and against foreign military and paramilitary personnel and political advisers not under UN command, as well as mercenaries, in SC Resolutions 161 (1961) and 169 (1961), respectively.

213 This was expressly stated in SC Resolution 467 (1980) on UNIFIL.

214 However, the United Kingdom, one of the guarantors under the 1960 Nicosia Treaty, is participating in UNFICYP. On the Nicosia Treaty of Guarantee see *infra* 153. Moreover, when the operation was launched, British troops were already stationed in Cyprus and thus quickly available. Similarly, France is one of the troop contributors to UNIFIL.

215 UNEF I was established by the General Assembly.

216 In practice, the parties to the conflict also have a say in the states participating in the operation, although the final decision on the composition of the force is made by the Security Council. Gray, *supra* (fn. 27) 301.

3) the assent of the contributing states; consequently, participation in peacekeeping operations is optional and may therefore be refused by a state requested to provide troops or other assistance.[217]

It should also be borne in mind that peacekeeping forces solely help to stabilize the cessation of armed hostilities.[218] Their functions do not include peacemaking, i.e., a settlement of the underlying dispute, and peacebuilding, i.e., measures with a view to laying the foundations for political stability and reforms, as well as economic recovery and development.[219] These tasks have to be performed by diplomats, politicians and other civilian experts.

Although the UN Charter remains silent on peacekeeping operations this does not necessarily mean that these missions under the auspices of the World Organization are unlawful. Their legality may in fact be based on more than one foundation.

1) It may be sought in the implied powers of the organization, i.e., the powers necessary fully to exercise the explicitly conferred competences and the functions of the UN.[220]
2) In addition, a basis in customary law can be established with the development of sufficient practice and the necessary *opinio juris*.
3) Moreover, the *argumentum a maiore ad minus* may be invoked: if the UN has the right to take obligatory non-defensive military enforcement action against a state without the consent of the latter under Article

217 The requirement of the consent of all actors concerned distinguishes cooperative security activities on the one hand from collective security and collective defence on the other. Collective security and collective defence measures do not need the consent of those against whom they are directed.

218 Peacekeeping operations may therefore be seen as the opposite of mandatory enforcement measures by the Security Council under Article 42, which however, as pointed out above, has remained a dead letter up to now because of the lack of Article 43 agreements. Military action by the Council would go beyond self-defence of the participating states. They would assist the victim against the aggressor and therefore be decidedly partial. Participation would be compulsory for the UN members required by the Security Council to take part. The consent of the state against which armed force is used would not be necessary. The forces of the 'P 5' would usually have to be involved in order to ensure the effectiveness of the military operation through military superiority over the target state(s).

219 See *infra* 86.

220 See the 1948 advisory opinion of the ICJ on *Reparation for Injuries Suffered in the Service of the United Nations*: 'Under international law, the Organization must be deemed to have those powers which, though not expressly provided in the Charter, are conferred upon it by necessary implication as being essential to the performance of its duties'. ICJ Reports 1949, 182.

> 42 of its Charter, operations to which the conflicting parties agree, in which armed force may only be used in self-defence and participation is optional, should also be considered lawful.

These arguments appear preferable to 'squeezing' peacekeeping operations into specific Charter provisions or, as the 'Capstone Doctrine' does, to basing them on Chapters VI, VII and VIII.[221]

Two other, albeit minor, efforts to increase the effectiveness of the UN with regard to its main purpose, the maintenance of international peace and security,[222] may also be discussed in the present context.

3.7.3 *'Uniting for Peace': Strengthening the Role of the General Assembly in the Area of International Security*

In 1950, at a time when Western member states held a comfortable majority in the General Assembly, they tried to enhance the role of the plenary organ of the organization if the Security Council was blocked by the veto of the Soviet Union. That permanent member had returned to the Council after boycotting it temporarily in June and July 1950 to protest against the representation of China by the government in Taipei.[223] The initiative was taken by the United States, presenting the 'Acheson plan' named for the then Secretary of State Dean Acheson. It led to the adoption by the General Assembly of Resolution 377 (V) 'Uniting for peace' by 52 votes in favour, five against (the five 'socialist' member states), and two abstentions (Argentina and India).[224]

The key paragraph of Resolution A read as follows:

> The General Assembly
>
> ...
>
> 1. *Resolves* that if the Security Council, because of lack of unanimity of the permanent members, fails to exercise its primary responsibility for the maintenance of international peace and security in any case where there appears to be a threat to the peace, breach of the peace, or act of aggression,

---

221 See *supra* fn. 211.

222 See *supra* 42.

223 See *supra* fn. 195.

224 Actually, the General Assembly adopted three resolutions, but only Resolution A was of practical relevance. Resolution B recommended that the Security Council should take the necessary action to live up to its responsibilities with regard to the situations in Article 39 of the Charter and apply the military provisions in Articles 43 and 45–47; Resolution C that the permanent members of the Council resolve their fundamental differences.

> the General Assembly shall consider the matter immediately with a view to making appropriate recommendations to Members for collective measures, including in the case of a breach of the peace or act of aggression the use of armed force when necessary, to maintain or restore international peace and security. If not in session at the time, the General Assembly may meet in emergency special session within twenty-four hours of the request therefor. Such emergency special session shall be called if requested by the Security Council on the vote of any seven members, or by a majority of the Members of the United Nations;

The resolution also established a Peace Observation Commission of 14 member states as an early warning institution with regard to international tension endangering international peace and security. Moreover, the General Assembly recommended that member states maintain military units that could promptly be made available to the UN. A panel of military experts appointed by the Secretary-General was to provide to members on their request technical advice on the organization, training and equipment of these units. Another subsidiary organ, a Collective Measures Committee equally composed of 14 members, was tasked with elaborating methods for maintaining and strengthening international peace and security.

The legality of Resolution 377 (V) was controversial.[225] The critics of the 'Uniting for Peace' initiative regarded it as contrary to the letter and the spirit of the UN Charter. They invoked Article 11(2), which provides that any question relating to the maintenance of international peace and security on which action is necessary shall be referred to the Security Council by the General Assembly either before or after discussion. Moreover, they relied on Article 12(1) which prohibits the General Assembly from making recommendations while the Security Council is exercising in respect of any dispute or situation the functions assigned to it by the Charter. The Security Council was said to perform these functions even if it was deadlocked by the veto of a permanent

---

225 In favour of the lawfulness of the 'Uniting for Peace' Resolution Woolsey, 'The Uniting for Peace Resolution of the United Nations', 45 *AJIL* (1951) 129; Vallat, 'The General Assembly and the Security Council of the United Nations', 29 *BYIL* (1952) 63 (96); Andrassy, 'Uniting for Peace', 50 *AJIL* (1956) 563; Jiménez de Aréchaga, *Derecho Constitucional de las Naciones Unidas* (*Comentario teórico-práctico de la Carta*) (1958) 197; against Kelsen, *Recent Trends in the Law of Nations* (1951) 953; Tunkin, 'The Legal Nature of the United Nations', 119 *RCADI* (1966) 7 (48); see also Neuhold, *supra* (fn. 7) 117; Tomuschat, 'Uniting for Peace – ein Rückblick nach 50 Jahren', 76 *Die Friedenswarte* (2001) 293; Franck, *Recourse to Force: State Action Against Threats and Armed Attacks* (2002) 31; Binder, 'Uniting for Peace Resolution (1950)', MPEPIL.

member or its discussions went on for a long time without the taking of any decision. The opponents also claimed that Article 24 conferred upon the Security Council an exclusive competence with regard to the maintenance of international peace and security.

The advocates of the lawfulness of Resolution 377 (V) interpreted the term 'action' in Article 11(2) narrowly, restricting it to binding decisions of the Security Council under Chapter VII, so that recommendations by the General Assembly were not excluded. According to them, a stalemate caused by a 'P 5' veto or protracted inaction by the Council meant that it did not exercise its functions under Article 12(1). They also focused on the wording of Article 24(1); under this provision members *confer* on the Council *primary responsibility* for the maintenance of international peace and security, and agree that it *acts on their behalf*.[226] The conclusion drawn was that (all) member states represented in the General Assembly possessed the original powers and authorized the Security Council to exercise these powers for them, and that therefore the Assembly retained a secondary responsibility for maintaining international peace and security.

Furthermore, those in favour of the legality of 'Uniting for Peace' invoked the general competence of the plenary organ of the UN to discuss and make recommendations. They also relied on the implied powers of the World Organization,[227] as well as the teleological interpretation of the UN Charter, which prioritized the maintenance of international peace and security. An enhanced role of the General Assembly would contribute to this objective. Moreover, they pointed out that the essence of Resolution 377 (V) boiled down to recommendations to coordinate the exercise of the right of collective self-defence guaranteed by Article 51 of the Charter. In addition, member states that initially opposed the resolution were said to be estopped from contesting its illegality, since they had approved its application by voting for emergency special sessions, for instance as early as in the 1956 Suez crisis. The 1967 emergency special session on the Middle East was even convened at the request of Soviet Union.

At least according to a progressive view, the General Assembly may recommend collective countermeasures, i.e., action or inaction that is unlawful in principle but exceptionally justified by a previous breach of international law by the target state(s).[228] However, a recommendation by the General Assembly does not provide a legal basis for the use of armed force unless it is used in the exercise of the right of self-defence under Article 51 of the UN Charter.

226 Italics added.

227 See *supra* 57.

228 Binder, *supra* (fn. 225) paragraph 29.

In any event, the importance of the 'Uniting for Peace' project has remained limited. The only element of practical importance was the convening of ten emergency special sessions of the General Assembly. The measures recommended in resolutions adopted by the Assembly on these occasions ranged from humanitarian assistance and the cessation of hostilities to the establishment of a peacekeeping force in the 1956 Suez crisis[229] and the isolation of member states.[230] The General Assembly also referred a matter to the ICJ for an advisory opinion.[231]

After the Western member states of the UN, the driving force behind the adoption of Resolution 377 (V), had lost their 'automatic majority' in the General Assembly they also lost interest in the 'Uniting for Peace' mechanism. The centre of gravity in the area of maintaining international peace and security therefore returned to the Security Council, where the great powers dominate politically and legally thanks to their veto. Moreover, the increased activity of the Security Council after the Cold War reduced the relevance of the General Assembly in the area of international security. However, continued dissatisfaction with the composition of the Security Council may lead the majority of member states in the Assembly to activate 'Uniting for Peace' in the future.

3.7.4 *The Definition of Aggression*

The efforts aimed at a definition of aggression are also relevant in the present context, since acts of aggression constitute the most severe violation of the prohibition of the use of force under Article 39 of the Charter, which ought to lead to action by the Security Council under Chapter VII. A more precise circumscription of that general term could be expected to help activate the UN's system of collective security, however modest this contribution may be.

The definition of external aggression which was mentioned in the League of Nations Covenant without further specification[232] already appeared on the international agenda in the inter-war period.[233] Attempts within the framework

229 General Assembly Resolution 1000 (ES-I) of 5 November 1956.

230 South Africa in General Assembly Resolution ES-8-2 of 14 September 1981 and Israel in Resolution ES-9/1 of 5 February 1982.

231 On the legal consequences of the construction of a wall in the occupied Palestinian territory. Resolution ES/14 of 8 December 2003.

232 Article 10. See *supra* 18.

233 On the history of the attempts to define aggression see W. Komarnicki, *supra* (fn. 69) 8; Žourek, 'La définition de l'agression et le droit international. Développements récents de la question', 92 *RCADI* (1957) 759 (765); Stone, *Aggression and World Order : A Critique of United Nations Theories on Aggression* (1958) 27; Brownlie, *supra* (fn. 27) 351; Chacko, 'International Law and the Concept of Aggression', 3 *IJIL* (1963) 396 (400); Giraud, 'L'interdiction du recours à la force. La théorie et la pratique des Nations Unies', 67 *RGDIP*

of the League, in the context of the draft Treaty on Mutual Assistance and the so-called Geneva Protocol, failed in 1923 and 1924, respectively.[234]

Some progress was achieved at the Geneva Disarmament Conference (1932–1935) under the auspices of the League of Nations, with the Soviet Union as the initiator.[235] The 18 members of the Committee on Security Questions of the Conference agreed on the so-called Litvinov-Politis definition, named after the Soviet Foreign Minister who proposed the definition and the Greek chairman of the Committee. The definition adopted by the Committee in 1933 largely followed the Soviet draft. It consisted of an exhaustive list of aggressive acts[236] which was combined with the priority principle. The side that committed one of these acts first was deemed the aggressor. Yet, the plenary Disarmament Conference did not accept this definition, due to the opposition of many states, including Germany, Italy, the United Kingdom and the United States.[237] It was included, however, in a number of non-aggression[238] and other treaties subsequently concluded by Soviet Union.

The term '(act of) aggression' appeared several times in the UN Charter where it equally remained undefined.[239] Amendments introducing definitions

---

(1963) 501 (506); Wittig, 'Der Aggressionsbegriff im internationalen Sprachgebrauch', in: Schaumann (ed.), *Völkerrechtliches Gewaltverbot und Friedenssicherung* (1971) 33; Neuhold, *supra* (fn. 7) 122.

234 Both were futile initiatives to extend the limited prohibition of war and to improve the system of collective security under the Covenant. See *supra* fn. 69.

235 Given its isolated position in the international community at the time, the Soviet Union had an understandable interest in the at least formal protection such a definition would offer it. W. Komarnicki, *supra* (fn. 69) 44.

236 (1) Declaration of war upon of another state; (2) invasion by the armed forces of the territory of another state; (3) attack by the land, naval or air forces, on the territory, ships and aircraft of another state; (4) naval blockade of the coasts or ports of another state; (5) support to armed bands formed on the territory of the aggressor state, which have invaded the territory of another state, or refusal to take, in its own territory, notwithstanding the request of the invaded state, all measures in its power to deprive those bands of all assistance or protection.

237 In a frequently quoted statement British Foreign Secretary Sir Austen Chamberlain rejected a definition of aggression as a 'trap for the innocent and a signpost for the guilty'. Stone, *supra* (fn. 233) 36.

238 With Afghanistan, Czechoslovakia, Estonia, Finland, Latvia, Lithuania, Persia, Poland, Romania, Turkey and Yugoslavia. These treaties did not protect several of these contracting states from eventual armed attacks by the Soviet Union.

239 In Articles 1(1) and 39 as well as in the title of Chapter VII. Moreover, Article 53(1) refers to regional arrangements directed against renewal of aggressive policy on the part of WW II enemy states, but this provision has become obsolete. Under Article 51, an armed attack

tabled by the Philippines and Bolivia at the San Francisco Conference in 1945[240] were not adopted. Similarly, the Charter of the Nuremberg International Military Tribunal declared aggression a crime without defining it.

The Soviet Union resumed its campaign for a definition of aggression in the UN. In 1950 the Soviet delegate Zarubin submitted to the 6th Committee of the General Assembly a draft definition which essentially reiterated the Litvinov-Politis definition of 1933. The Assembly first passed the issue on to the ILC, which eventually agreed with its rapporteur Jean (Ioannis) Spiropoulus and declared itself against a definition; instead, each concrete conflict should be judged on its merits. Three special committees subsequently appointed by the General Assembly to deal with the problem failed to reach an agreement. However, Soviet diplomacy, which was characterized by remarkable perseverance, was not discouraged by these setbacks and once again brought the matter before the General Assembly in 1967. A fourth special committee of 35 members was established and achieved a breakthrough in 1973/1974 in a period of East–West détente. The text drafted by the committee was adopted by the General Assembly as Annex to Resolution 3314 (XXIX) without debate by consensus.[241]

It may be recalled that two principal methods can be used for definitions, the general or synthetic and the enumerative or analytical method. A general formula has the advantage of being comprehensive and leaving no loopholes. Its disadvantage is due to the fact that it may make the qualification of a concrete case rather difficult. For instance, if aggression is defined as the use of force which cannot be justified as self-defence, the problem is merely shifted to the definition of another complex notion, that of self-defence.[242] In contrast, a list of relevant acts is much easier to apply. Yet, if such a 'check list' is exhaustive, it equally suffers from a major deficiency. Acts which produce the same objectionable result but are not included in the list remain lawful.

('*ataque armado*' in the Spanish text) – and not a breach of the peace or act of aggression – is required for the exercise of the right of self-defence. But to add to the terminological confusion, in the French text of Article 51 the term '*agression armée*' is used. See *infra* fn. 531.

240 UNICIO Documents, vol. 4, 760–791 and 828.

241 Žourek, 'Enfin une définition de l'agression', 20 *AFDI* (1974) 9; Bothe, 'Die Erklärung der Generalversammlung der Vereinten Nationen über die Definition der Aggression', 18 *GYBIL* (1975) 127; Ferencz, *Defining International Aggression : The Search for World Peace : A Documentary History and Analysis* (1975); Rambaud, 'La définition de l'agression par l'Organisation des Nations Unies', 80 *RGDIP* (1976) 835; Broms, 'The Definition of Aggression', 154 *RCADI* (1977) 299; Neuhold, *supra* (fn. 7) 124; Stone, 'Hopes and Loopholes in the 1974 Definition of Aggression', 71 *AJIL* (1977) 224; Dinstein, *supra* (fn. 174).

242 See *infra* 117.

The special committee and the General Assembly opted for the obviously best solution in 1974 by combining the two approaches, a general formula with a non-exhaustive list of acts of aggression. Thus on the one hand, Article 1 restricts aggression to armed force,[243] the first use[244] of which (merely) constitutes *prima facie* evidence of an act of aggression[245] according to Article 2.[246] On the other hand, Article 3 adds a list of seven acts of aggression. They include the invasion or attack of and the bombardment against the territory of a state and the blockade of the ports or coasts, as well as the attack on the land, sea or air forces, or marine or air fleets of a state by the armed forces of another state. The list also comprises the use of the armed forces of a state in the territory of another state in contravention of the conditions agreed on with the host state or the extension of their presence beyond the termination of the agreement; the action of a state in allowing its territory placed at the disposal of another state to be used by that state for perpetrating an act of aggression against a third state; and, last but not least, the sending by or on behalf of a state of armed bands, groups, irregulars or mercenaries, which carry out acts of armed force against another state of such gravity as to amount to the previously listed acts, or its substantial involvement therein: in other words 'indirect aggression', which became a type of force that was increasingly used after World War II.[247]

The definition adopted by the UN General Assembly remained open at both ends. Article 4 states that the listed acts are not exhaustive and the Security Council may determine that other acts also constitute aggression. Pursuant to Article 2, the Council may decide that relevant circumstances, including the fact that the acts concerned or their consequences are not of sufficient gravity,[248] justify the conclusion that no act of aggression has been committed.[249]

243 This was a concession made by the Soviet Union and Third World states which had called for the inclusion of massive economic pressure and hostile propaganda as economic and ideological aggression. Neuhold, *supra* (fn. 7) 130.

244 Contrary to the prohibition in Article 2(4) of the UN Charter, the threat to use armed force does not constitute aggression.

245 An aggressive intent of the decision makers responsible for the use of force is not required.

246 As a result of another concession by the 'socialist' and Third World countries. According to their initial position, the state perpetrating one of the acts mentioned in the definition first would automatically have been the aggressor.

247 Support for armed bands was already included in the 1933 Litvinov-Politis definition. See *supra* 62.

248 For example, a border incident in which a few shots are fired but neither human beings injured nor major material damage caused.

249 For instance, if a state on whose territory foreign troops remain beyond the time limit agreed upon uses force to compel them to leave, it would not be guilty of aggression, which would rather be committed by the other state that failed to withdraw its forces on time in accordance with Article 2(e) of the General Assembly's definition. Dinstein, *supra* (fn. 174) paragraph 21.

The practical value of this definition has remained negligible. Two expectations placed on it have not been borne out by political reality. Some supporters of the exercise assumed that the Security Council would live up to its primary responsibility for the maintenance of international peace and security once it had a better understanding of the most serious breach of international law under Article 39.[250] However, the main problem of the Council is not intellectual: its ignorance of acts that constitute aggression. It is rather political, namely the deep-seated conflicts that oppose its members, especially the 'P 5', to each other, and have led to the exercise of the veto or inadequate action by the Council. Moreover, the definition of aggression on which the General Assembly eventually agreed is not binding on the Security Council in any case.

The second hope focused on the involvement of public opinion. If the public and the media had a more precise idea about aggression, then they would identify and launch massive campaigns against aggressors, who would be impressed by the mobilization of shame and cease their unlawful behaviour. However, the author knows of no demonstrations that have taken place, for example, in front of the embassies of states accused of aggression, with the protesters brandishing copies of Resolution 3314 (XXIX) which is known only to a small circle of insiders and experts whose discussions hardly attract public attention.

It is also worth mentioning in the present context that the list of acts aggression in the definition adopted by the General Assembly in 1974 served as the basis of the definition of the crime of aggression for which individuals are responsible under the 1998 Rome Statute of the ICC.[251] In Article 8bis(2),

---

The above-mentioned problem with a synthetic definition is raised by Article 7, according to which the right of peoples deprived of their right of self-determination to seek and receive support in their struggle is not prejudiced by the Definition, in particular Article 3. Some important aspects of the self-determination principle still remain controversial, above all the definition of the people entitled to it, as well as external self-determination, i.e., the choice by a people of its international status, including the right to have a state of its own. See *supra* 5. Moreover, whether the support mentioned in the General Assembly's definition of aggression also means military assistance was and is contested. See *infra* 155.

250 In paragraph 4 of Resolution 3314 (XXIX), the General Assembly recommended that the Security Council should take account of the definition as guidance in determining the existence of an act of aggression.

251 Article 5 of the ICC Statute included aggression among the crimes with respect to which the Court has jurisdiction. However, it also provided that the exercise of jurisdiction required a definition of this crime and the setting out of the conditions under which the Court was to exercise jurisdiction with respect to it. Politi and Nesi (eds.), *The International Criminal Court and the Crime of Aggression* (2004); Ambos, 'The Crime of Aggression after Kampala', 53 *GYBIL* (2010) 463; Schmalenbach, 'The Crime of Aggression before the International Criminal Court', in: Hestermeyer et alii (eds.), *Coexistence, Cooperation and Solidarity: Liber Amicorum Rüdiger Wolfrum* (vol. II, 2012) 1259. On the ICC see *infra* 94.

adopted by consensus at the Kampala Review Conference in 2010, the acts listed in Article 3 of the Annex to Resolution 3314 (XXIX) were reiterated verbatim.[252]

3.8 The Record of the UN after the Cold War

3.8.1 *Testing Old and New Crisis Management and Peaceful Settlement Tools*

The fundamental antagonism between capitalist and 'socialist' members, which had paralyzed the Security Council time and again after 1945, came to an unexpectedly rapid and peaceful end, epitomized by the fall of the Berlin Wall in November 1989. Western values, above all individual-oriented human rights, multi-party democracy, the rule of law and liberal market economy, were also embraced by the former ideological and political foes. There were no losers raising revisionist claims. The universality of human rights was recognized on the global level by the participating states in the concluding documents of the 1993 UN World Conference on Human Rights in Vienna. The United States emerged as the only remaining superpower but appeared to act as a 'benign' hegemon in a unipolar world, combining its national interests with those of the international community. A particularly optimistic view declared the 'end of history' and predicted the emergence of a new global system in which conflicts between states would still occur but would not be settled by the resort to armed force.[253] In any event, expectations that the UN system of collective security would at long last function effectively seemed to be justified.

---

252 However, contrary to the 1974 state-centred definition of aggression in the sense of Article 39 of the UN Charter, the Kampala definition, which serves the purposes of individual criminal responsibility, is not 'open-ended'. According to the principles of criminal law, criminal responsibility must not be established *ex post facto* and the definitions of crimes have to be construed strictly. The first-strike rule was not retained either, since it is only one possible criterion for identifying an aggressor state. Ambos, *supra* (fn. 251) 487. On various aspects of individual criminal accountability for the crime of aggression see Dinstein *supra* (fn. 27) 124.

253 Fukuyama, *The End of History and the Last Man* (1992). His optimistic vision was not borne out by reality, as was the pessimistic forecast of dangerous instability in a multipolar system by the neo-realist scholar Mearsheimer. He recommended a nuclear-armed Germany to fill the security vacuum in Europe after the Cold War. Mearsheimer, 'Back to the Future: Instability in Europe After the Cold War', 15 *International Security* No. 1 (Summer 1990) 5.

The World Organization did become more active in its efforts to achieve its main purpose, the maintenance of international peace and security.[254] However, widespread hopes that the end of the Cold War would usher in a new age of peace and cooperation were soon dashed by the bloody conflicts between the peoples of the disintegrating SFRY. In the 1990s, they provided a 'laboratory' where the international community, first and foremost the UN, but also other international organizations and individual states, used old and also for the first time tested several new methods and tools of crisis management and the pacific solution of international disputes.[255] Therefore, special reference will be made below to 'experiments' at this 'Balkan testing site', and not only because the author is more familiar with developments in Europe than on other continents. The positive and negative lessons that can be learned from those efforts could also be applied elsewhere. However, some important examples from other regions will also be discussed.

3.8.2 *Authorization by the Security Council to Use Force*

Yet, despite the advent of an 'era of good feelings'[256] in international relations in the early 1990s, the Security Council did not live up to its role envisaged under Article 42 of the UN Charter. It still could not take obligatory military action against states committing one of the acts listed in Article 39. For, due to the continued lack of Article 43 agreements under which member states would have made military resources available, it did not have the necessary troops, weapons and facilities at its disposal. Therefore all the Council could do was merely to authorize member states to resort to force. There obviously is a major difference between a binding decision, which member states have to carry out, and an authorization, which the addressees are free to use or not to use.

There are two types of operations which may be based on a Security Council authorization. On the one hand, non-defensive armed force may be used without the consent of the target state(s). On the other, military enforcement

254 During the 15 years following the end of the Cold War, the Security Council adopted twice as many resolutions as in the preceding 45 years. Schrijver, *supra* (fn. 82) 455.

255 Neuhold, *The United Nations as a Security Organization: The 'Balkan Laboratory'* (2007); idem, 'The Return of History in the Balkans after the Cold War: International Efforts at Crisis Management and Conflict Resolution', in: Bischof and Karlhofer (eds.), *Austria's International Position after the end of the Cold War* (2013) 167.

256 This term usually denotes a period in the history of the United States after the War of 1812 against the United Kingdom. It was marked by a desire for reconciliation between rivalling political parties and national unity and is associated, in particular, with the Presidency of James Monroe.

action may also be taken with the prior agreement of those against whom force may eventually be employed.[257]

An early spectacular example of the first type of authorization was provided by the Security Council in the wake of the invasion of neighbouring Kuwait by Iraqi troops in August 1990. This authorization was preceded by several other resolutions in which the Council took action against the breach of the peace by the regime of President Saddam Hussein. Still on the day on which Iraqi troops moved into Kuwait, the Security Council adopted Resolution 660 (1990) in which it demanded, above all, the immediate and unconditional withdrawal of all Iraqi forces from Kuwait. In Resolution 661 (1990), the Council imposed a trade and financial embargo against Iraq; in Resolution 665 (1990), it called upon member states to ensure the strict implementation of these economic sanctions through inspections by their maritime forces. A ban on flights to and from Iraq and occupied Kuwait was added in Resolution 670 (1990).

When these essentially non-military measures failed to produce the desired result, the Security Council authorized on 29 November, in Resolution 678 (1990), member states cooperating with the Kuwaiti government 'to use all necessary means to uphold resolution 660 (1990) and all subsequent resolutions and to restore international peace and security in the area'. On the basis of this resolution, a U.S.-led coalition of able and willing states launched 'Operation Desert Storm' and quickly drove the Iraqi forces out of occupied Kuwait.

This operation and its legal foundation set a precedent which the Security Council subsequently followed in various parts of the world, in particular in Africa.[258] The Council also authorized the use of force in the 'Balkan laboratory'. For instance, in its Resolution 781 (1992) of 9 October 1992 it imposed a ban on military flights in the airspace of Bosnia-Herzegovina where the post-Yugoslav conflicts took their heaviest toll. This prohibition was to be monitored by UN peacekeepers, the United Nations Protection Force (UNPROFOR). However, UNPROFOR proved unable to prevent numerous violations of the flight ban by Serbian military aircraft.

Thereupon the Security Council adopted Resolution 816 (1993) of 31 March 1993. Determining that the grave situation in Bosnia and Herzegovina continued to be a threat to international peace and security and acting under Chapter VII of the UN Charter, the Council authorized member states, acting nationally

---

257 The NATO operations in Bosnia and Herzegovina and Kosovo as well as the military mission led by Australia in Timor-Leste are examples of such 'enforcement-by-consent' missions. See *infra* 81.

258 For a comprehensive overview until 2007 see Gray, *supra* (fn. 27) 327.

or through regional organizations or arrangements, to take, under the authority of the Security Council, all necessary measures to ensure compliance with the flight prohibition.

NATO decided to make use of this authorization as the legal basis for its 'Operation Deny Flight' launched on 12 April 1993. It led to the first combat engagement in the history of the alliance, in which U.S. Air Force F-16s shot down several Serb jets over Banja Luka. While the operation was rather successful in stopping flights of fixed-wing aircraft, NATO found it more difficult to stop violations of the flight ban by helicopters.

'Operation Sharp Guard' conducted in the Adriatic Sea by NATO and the Western European Union (WEU), in which 14 states participated, from 1993 to 1996, may also be mentioned in this context.[259] The purpose of this blockade supported by patrol aircraft was to enforce sanctions imposed by the Security Council in the course of the violent disintegration of Yugoslavia: an arms ban on the SFRY[260] and a comprehensive embargo on the FRY.[261] The legal basis for the operation was provided by Security Council Resolution 787 (1993).[262] No successful efforts to run the blockade were reported.

The Atlantic Alliance, which after the loss of its initial enemy after the end of the Cold War faced the choice between 'going out of area or out of business',[263] preferred the first option.[264] This meant that NATO embarked on activities beyond the collective self-defence of its member states outside the territories of the latter. One of the new functions was to help the Security Council to enforce its decisions. The alliance also became active in the area of cooperative security, notably by offering the 'Partnership for Peace' project to CSCE/OSCE participating states which were not members of the alliance.

259 On the WEU, a military alliance of Western European states, see *infra* fn. 592.

260 SC Resolution 713 (1991).

261 SC Resolution 757 (1992). The measures taken by the SC included a trade and financial embargo, as well as bans on flights, participation in sporting events, scientific and technical cooperation and cultural exchanges by all states (and not only UN) members. The Council also decided a reduction of the level of the staff of diplomatic missions and consular posts.

262 In paragraph 12 the Council, acting under Chapters VII and VIII of the UN Charter, called upon states, 'acting nationally or through regional agencies or arrangements, to use such measures commensurate with the specific circumstances as may be necessary under the authority of the Security Council to halt all inward and outward maritime shipping in order to inspect and verify their cargoes and destinations and to ensure strict implementation of the provisions of Resolutions 713 (1991) and 757 (1992).'

263 As U.S. Senator Richard Lugar put it.

264 Neuhold, *supra* (fn. 255) 179.

It also conducted peacekeeping operations in Macedonia. Moreover, NATO launched major 'enforcement-by-consent' operations in Bosnia and Herzegovina and Kosovo.[265] Benefiting from its military superiority, it also took offensive military action without authorization by the Security Council.[266]

The 'sub-contracting' system of enforcement measures illustrated by the above NATO operations in the former SFRY is based on a division of labour between the Security Council and the states or international organizations taking action. The involvement of the Council remains indispensable.

1) Firstly, it must determine the existence of an Article 39 situation as the foundation of Chapter VII action.
2) Secondly, the Security Council has to provide the mandate for action, including, at least implicitly, resort to armed force. As a rule, the authorization by the Council is couched in general terms, such as the taking of all necessary measures or the use of all necessary means in order to achieve a given objective. Exceptionally, however, the use of force is expressly mentioned, as in Resolution 836 (1993) on the protection of safe areas in Bosnia and Herzegovina by a UN peacekeeping operation.[267] Similarly the Security Council prefers not to name the states or international organizations to which its authorization is primarily addressed.[268] However, normally the Council knows the actors who are ready to take action. The Council's authority would be further eroded if it issued an authorization which remained a dead letter.[269]
3) Thirdly, the Security Council determines the duration and the termination of an operation based on its authorization.[270]
4) Fourthly, it retains overall control over military action authorized by it.

265 See *infra* 151.

266 On 'Operation Allied Force' see *infra* 101.

267 See *infra* fn. 304.

268 However, it did so, for instance, in Resolution 1132 (1997) in the case of the Economic Community of West African States (ECOWAS) which was authorized to enforce sanctions in the civil war in Sierra Leone. For details see Gray, *supra* (fn. 27) 411.

269 Yet for some time there was a general reluctance to use the authorization of the extension of the fight against the Somali pirates from naval to operations on the ground in the territory of Somalia in accordance with Resolution 1851 (2008). Neuhold, 'The Return of Piracy: Problems, Parallels, Paradoxes', in: Hestermeyer et alii (eds.), (fn. 251) 1239.

270 For instance, the Security Council terminated the authorization on which the NATO-led 'Operation Unified Protector' in Libya in 2011 was based in its Resolution 2016 (2011). See *infra* 112.

The remaining decisions are left to the states acting on the basis of the Council's authorization. If they take collective action, they may do so as members of an existing international organization like NATO or form an ad hoc coalition of the able and willing as for the above-mentioned 'Operation Desert Storm'. It is up to states first to decide whether to take part in a mission authorized by the Security Council at all, and if they are willing to do so, how many troops, items of military equipment and other resources they will contribute. Other important aspects of an operation are the agreement on the point in time where the authorization of the Security Council will actually be implemented and military operations start, the type of operation – for example an air campaign or also ground and naval offensives–, the strategy and tactics to be used, the logistics, the chain of command, and, last but not least, the costs of a military campaign. The latter are governed, as a rule, by the principle 'the costs lie where they fall', i.e., each participating state pays for its own expenses.

The debate on the legal basis of authorizations especially without the consent of the state concerned, on which no express provision can be found in the UN Charter, is by now of primarily academic interest.[271] In the opinion of some writers they merely reiterate the right of collective self-defence enshrined in Article 51. Others object that an authorization to exercise an inherent right does not make sense. The term 'recommendation' would be more appropriate for this purpose. Moreover, the Security Council may authorize the use of force beyond the thresholds of proportionality and necessity that limit the right of self-defence.[272] Thus the above-mentioned Resolution 678 empowered the states participating in 'Operation Desert Storm' to use all necessary means to restore international peace and security in the – undefined – 'area'. This could have meant the forcible ousting of the regime of President Saddam Hussein,

---

271 Franck and Patel, 'UN Police Action in Lieu of War: "The Old Order Changeth"', 85 *AJIL* (1991) 63; Schachter, 'United Nations Law in the Gulf Conflict', ibid. 452; Rostow, 'Until What? Enforcement Action or Collective Self-Defence?', ibid. 506; Weston, 'Security Council Resolution 678 and Persian Gulf Decision Making: Precarious Legitimacy', ibid. 516; Weckel, 'Le chapitre VII de la Charte et son application par le Conseil de Sécurité', 37 *AFDI* (1991) 165; Kaikonen, 'Self-Defence, Enforcement Action and the Gulf Wars', 33 *BYIL* (1992) 299; Freudenschuß, 'Between Unilateralism and Collective Security: Authorization of the Use of Force by the UN Security Council', 5 *EJIL* (1994) 492; Zemanek, 'The Legal Foundations of the International System: General Course on Public International Law', 266 *RCADI* (1997) 23 (300); Blocker, 'Is the Authorization Authorized? Powers and Practice of the UN Security Council to Authorize the Use of Force by "Coalitions of the Able and Willing"', 11 *EJIL* (2000) 541; Sicilianos, 'L'autorisation par le Conseil de sécurité de recourir à la force: une tentative d'évaluation', 106 *RGDIP* (2002) 5; Dinstein, *supra* (fn. 27) 299.

272 See *infra* 144.

the main instigator of armed conflict in the region. Furthermore, in any event, the enforcement of Security Council measures like embargoes against all conflicting parties, aggressors as well as victims,[273] cannot be defined as the exercise of the right of collective self-defence. The same is true of 'enforcement-by-consent' operations discussed below.

Like for peacekeeping operations,[274] the legal foundation of the authorization to use armed force beyond a state defending itself against an armed attack should therefore be sought in the implied powers of the UN, by now also in customary law, and the *argumentum a maiore ad minus*.[275]

From the political point of view, effective military action on the basis of an authorization of the Security Council depends on two conditions that are not easily met. On the one hand, the necessary consent within the Security Council; on the other, the readiness of states to incur the costs of the resort to armed force. Understandably, governments are not willing to accept human casualties and the financial burdens of military operations in each and every case where such action appears necessary. However, this selective approach has led to accusations that especially Western powers only act if their major political and economic interests are at stake, for example in the Balkans or the oil-reach Middle East, but not in Rwanda or Somalia.

It should be added that the UN Charter does provide for the authorization by the Security Council of enforcement action taken by regional arrangements or agencies under its authority in Article 53(1). The use of armed force by the Economic Community of West African States (ECOWAS) in order to stop humanitarian disasters in the civil wars in Liberia and Sierra Leone in the 1990s and early 2000s raised two questions in this context. Firstly, does a military operation by a regional organization have to be authorized by the Council in advance, or may the authorization also be given retroactively? And, secondly, must the authorization be express or may it also be implicit? In those two conflicts in Africa, the Security Council commended military action taken by the ECOWAS Monitoring Group (ECOMOG) without its previous authorization and only much later assumed the role it was supposed to play as the key organ of

273 Such as the above-mentioned 'Operation Sharp Guard'. See *supra* 69.

274 See *supra* 57.

275 Since under Article 42 the Security Council may decide to take military action in which member states would be obligated to participate after concluding an Article 43 agreement, it must be deemed also to have the lesser power to authorize the use of force. Moreover, pursuant to Article 48, the Council may decide which – all or some – member states have to carry out its decisions; consequently, it ought to have the power to authorize some of them to take action.

collective security. The lack of objection to ECOMOG's activities could indicate that the less strict interpretation of Article 53(1) has prevailed.[276]

3.8.3 *Non-Military Enforcement Measures*

3.8.3.1 Problems Caused by Comprehensive Non-Military Sanctions

The Security Council has imposed non-military, in particular economic, sanctions under Article 41 of the Charter much more frequently after than during the Cold War. The list of the targeted states is long indeed; moreover, enforcement action was also taken against non-state actors.[277] The targets included the FRY and Iraq, Libya and Liberia, Angola and Rwanda, Ethiopia and Eritrea, Sudan and Afghanistan, and more recently Iran, North Korea, Sudan, and again Libya.

The primary purpose of such sanctions is not to punish the state against which they are taken but rather to make it cease its unlawful behaviour and accept the consequences of the latter under the law of state responsibility, such as the payment of reparations. This goal is to be reached by making the costs of continued breaches of legal obligations higher than compliance with them. If this objective cannot be reached, then enforcement measures should at least weaken the ability of the target state to cause further harm and delay progress in a prohibited activity, for example the development of weapons of mass destruction.[278]

The Security Council has different types of non-military sanctions at its disposal. It can choose between economic (for instance, trade restrictions) and non-economic measures (for example, the suspension of cultural and sports relations). The Council may prefer comprehensive (designed to isolate the target state as completely as possible)[279] or opt for selective sanctions (such as a

276 According to Franck, a reinterpretation of Article 53 has taken place. Franck, *supra* (fn. 225) 162. In contrast, Gray concludes that not too much should be read into general statements by the Security Council. She argues that the Council expressed its approval in general terms and that ECOWAS did not claim a wide right to use force, and points to subsequent practice, in particular in Côte d'Ivoire and the Central African Republic, supporting her restrictive view. Gray, *supra* (fn. 27) 418, 422, 426. Emphasizing the need for the Security Council to control an authorized military operation at all times, de Wet insists on the requirement of a clear prior mandate from the Council. She adds that an *ex post facto* authorization cannot be excluded but would have be given in unambiguous terms under Chapter. VII of the Charter. De Wet, *supra* (fn. 162) 294, 308.

277 For instance, against the Bosnian Serbs in Resolution 942 (1994).

278 As in the case of Iran. See Addis, 'Economic Sanctions and the Problem of Evil', 25 *Human Rights Quarterly* (2003) 573.

279 For instance, SC Resolution 757 (1992) against the FRY. See *supra* fn. 161.

ban on luxury goods). Such measures may also be comprehensive or selective with regard to the persons affected, be aimed at either the entire population or only certain individuals, juridical persons or groups of persons.[280]

In practice, non-military sanctions raised political as well as legal problems. As regards their effectiveness, they may not, at least for some time, produce their desired results. Although circumvention of binding Security Council resolutions is unlawful, it may nevertheless be tempting, in particular because of the profits that can be made through smuggling or selling embargo goods on the black market.

If and when comprehensive sanctions against the entire population become effective, they tend to hurt the wrong addressees, the average citizens, and not the ruling elites responsible for the breach by their state of its international duties. As in the case of Iraq and the FRY, indiscriminate, especially economic, measures could lead to malnutrition and starvation, declining health standards, causing, *inter alia*, higher infant mortality and epidemics, large-scale unemployment and poverty. The overall consequence may be lower average life expectancy in the country concerned.

To make matters worse, sanctions under Article 41 may even be counterproductive.[281] For, they could, at least temporarily, strengthen the hand of the regime in power instead of making it change course or bringing it down. The government of a state 'under siege' may call for national unity and solidarity against a common external enemy. Those who still oppose it can be denounced as traitors. To expect that the people will quickly rise against and oust their oppressors under the impact of international sanctions has proven unrealistic, given the instruments of repression and disinformation at the disposal of the regime.

Moreover, effective sanctions that hurt the population may lead the regime of the targeted state to adopt a more rigid position. It could regard concessions as a sign of weakness and an unacceptable loss of face in the eyes not only of the rest of the world but also of its own citizens. For less fear may result in increasing popular resistance and indeed bring about the downfall of the governing elite, which initially appeared unlikely.

Finally, it should be borne in mind that economic enforcement measures may also have a negative impact on those taking part in them. In particular, a trade embargo could mean the loss of market shares in the commercial relations with the target country.[282]

---

280 On these so-called targeted sanctions see *infra* 76.

281 Leigh, 'The Political Consequences of Economic Embargoes', 89 *AJIL* (1995) 74.

282 Under Article 49 of the UN Charter, member states have to afford mutual assistance to each other in carrying out the measures decided upon by the Security Council, but this

The effects of the far-reaching economic sanctions imposed on Iraq, which could also be observed in the FRY and Haiti, in particular raised the additional legal issue of possible limits to the powers of the Security Council under Chapter VII of the Charter. Those who answered the question in the negative could argue that the Council as a political organ was given a 'blank cheque', which it was free to fill in at its discretion when it decided upon enforcement action. However, a closer look at the Charter shows that Article 24(2) obligates the Security Council to act in accordance with the Purposes and Principles of the UN. Article 1(3) lists the promotion and encouragement of respect for human rights and fundamental freedoms among the purposes of the World Organization.[283]

The most fundamental of these rights evidently is the right to life because if it is violated the other rights cannot be exercised. Sanctions resulting in lower life expectancy affect this right. The right to life is enshrined in several major human rights treaties and international instruments, first and foremost in Article 6 of the 1966 International Covenant on Civil and Political Rights and, on the regional level, in Article 2 of the 1950 Convention for the Protection of Human Rights and Fundamental Freedoms concluded under the auspices of the Council of Europe, as well as its American and African counterparts, in Article 4 of both the American Convention on Human Rights and Article 4 of the African Charter on Human and Peoples' Rights.

Other human rights on which economic sanctions could encroach are the rights to an adequate standard of living, including adequate food, clothing and housing, and the right to the enjoyment of the highest attainable standard of physical and mental health, laid down, above all, in Articles 11 and 12 of the 1966 International Covenant on Economic, Social and Cultural Rights.

---

assistance is to be provided in the event that military action is taken. Under Article 50, states confronted with special economic problems arising from the carrying out of preventive or enforcement measures taken by the Security Council have the right to (merely) consult the Council with regard to a solution of those problems. In practice, members particularly hurt by the sanctions imposed on Southern Rhodesia, Iraq and the FRY were granted some assistance, in particular by the International Monetary Fund and the Bank for International Reconstruction and Development. Carver and Hulsman, 'The Role of Article 50 of the UN Charter in the Search for International Peace and Security', 49 *ICLQ* (2000) 528; Klein, 'Article 49', in: Cot, Pellet et Forteau (eds.), *supra* (fn. 82) 1302; Klein, 'Article 50', ibid. 1313; Reinisch and Novak, 'Article 49', in: Simma et alii (eds.), *supra* (fn. 82) 1385; Reinisch and Novak, 'Article 50', ibid. 1389.

283 For details see de Wet, *supra* (fn. 162) 217.

3.8.3.2 'Targeted Sanctions'

In order to avoid these negative effects the Security Council has switched to so-called targeted sanctions.[284] These measures are designed not to hurt the innocent and specifically aimed against persons or groups of persons like governments,[285] rebels,[286] or terrorists[287] who are directly responsible for grave breaches of international law, either as decision makers or those perpetrating unlawful acts. Examples of this type of sanction include travel restrictions, the freezing of financial assets abroad or bans on luxury goods.[288] The UN General Assembly also endorsed the concept in the above-mentioned concluding document of its 2005 meeting at the level of Heads of State and Government, the 'World Summit Outcome'.[289]

Targeted sanctions may be combined with other measures of a more general nature which are not directed against specific persons but also do not negatively affect the population as a whole, such as arms embargoes or the ban on material, technological or financial assistance to prohibited projects like nuclear enrichment or ballistic missile programmes.

Yet, the application of this new type of enforcement measure has in turn run into new political and legal difficulties. On the one hand, targeted sanctions have so far remained ineffective. Targeted persons at whom they are aimed may not be impressed by travel bans, if they prefer to stay within the borders of their

---

284 Reisman and Stenvick, 'The Applicability of International Law Standards to United Nations Economic Sanctions', 9 *EJIL* (1998) 86; Reinisch, 'Developing Human Rights and Humanitarian Law Accountability of the Security Council for the Imposition of Economic Sanctions', 95 *AJIL* (2001) 851; Craven, 'Humanitarianism and the Quest for Smarter Sanctions', 13 *EJIL* (2002) 43; Farrall, *United Nations Sanctions and the Rule of Law* (2007); Eriksson, *Targeting Peace: Understanding the UN and EU Targeted Sanctions* (2011); Carter, 'Economic Sanctions', MPEPIL.

285 For example, the Taliban targeted by SC Resolution 1267 (1999).

286 As in Sudan by SC Resolution 1556 (2004). See *supra* 47.

287 For instance, members of Al Qaeda.

288 Targeted sanctions may also be seen in the wider context of a structural shift from inter-state law to a new focus of international law on the individual which is reflected in the development of human rights and individual instead of collective responsibility for violations of international law.

289 'We…resolve to ensure that sanctions are carefully targeted in support of clear objectives…and are implemented in ways that balance effectiveness to achieve the desired results against the possible adverse consequences, including socio-economic and humanitarian consequences, for populations and third States' (paragraph 106). The concept had also been contained in the report of the High-level Panel on Threats, Challenges and Change (paragraphs 178–182) and that of Secretary-General Kofi Annan to the General Assembly (paragraph 110). See *infra* 106.

country and leave it as little as possible, or may be ready to run the risk of traveling abroad with false passports. Bank accounts have to be identified, and their secrecy may be protected by the country to which the money has been moved; or middlemen could be used for access to financial assets. Embargoes on luxury goods fail to influence people who denounce luxury for religious or other reasons or already possess the prohibited items. In any event, such sanctions which the Security Council adopted against Iran and North Korea in 2006 and has subsequently extended have so far not produced the desired effects.[290]

On the legal level, ironically, the laudable efforts to avoid violations of certain fundamental human rights by switching from indiscriminate to targeted sanctions have given rise to new problems with other, equally important human rights. Physical and legal persons were placed on 'black lists' as the addressees of such measures without offering them the guarantees of a fair trial, including their participation, the right to defend themselves and to legal counsel, and the presumption of innocence, in the proceedings of the Security Council's sanctions committees.[291] What if a person was placed erroneously on such a list or no longer meets the criteria for enforcement measures?[292]

A first remedy leading to possible delisting was provided by Security Council Resolution 1730 (2006) concerning a so-called focal point to be established within the UN Secretariat.[293] However, this institution was essentially just a kind of post office forwarding requests for removal from the 'black lists' to the interested governments.

---

290 For details see Neuhold, *supra* (fn. 180) 225.

291 As Canadian Federal Court Judge Russel W. Zinn put it in 2009: 'The 1267 Committee regime…is a situation not unlike that of Josef K. in Kafka's *The Trial*, who awakens one morning and, for reasons never revealed to him or the reader, is arrested for an unspecified crime'. *Abousfian Abdelrazik v The Minister of Foreign Affairs and the Attorney General of Canada*, 2009 FC 580, paragraph 53. Mr. Abdelrazik was a Sudanese and Canadian national placed by the United States as a terrorist on the sanctions list against the Taliban under SC Resolution 1267 (1999) and denied his constitutional right to return to Canada. His name was removed from the list in 2011. In another case Canadian lawyer Lawrence Greenspan, who defended a suspected terrorist and objected to the right of the judge to decide to keep evidence secret, had said earlier 'Kafka is rolling in his grave as we speak'. *Ottawa Citizen*, 22 March 2007.

292 The *Kadi* and *Al Barakaat* cases increased awareness of the above-mentioned legal problems. *Zgonec-Rožej, Yassin Abdullah Kadi & Barakaat International Foundation v. Council and Commission*, 103 *AJIL* (2009) 305; Feinäugle, '*Kadi* Case', MPEPIL.

293 In the 'World Summit Outcome', the political leaders of UN member states called 'upon the Security Council, with the support of the Secretary-General, to ensure that fair and clear procedures exist for placing individuals and entities on sanctions lists and for removing them, as well as for granting humanitarian exemptions' (paragraph 109).

Three years later, through Resolution 1904 (2009), the Security Council created an Ombudsperson replacing the focal point with regard to members and associates of the terrorist networks Al Qaeda and the Taliban.[294] This new organ has more competences than its predecessor.[295] It actively participates in the process of dealing with delisting petitions as a conciliator.[296] According to its initial mandate, its main activities consist in collecting relevant information and dialogue with the parties concerned, including the Sanctions Monitoring Team established by Security Council Resolution 1526 (2004). The Ombudsperson finally submits a report to the Council's Sanctions Committee which contains the principal arguments concerning the delisting request.

Security Council Resolution 1989 (2011) introduced some further improvements. In particular, the Ombudsperson shall now present to the committee not just observations but also a recommendation on the delisting of those requesting it. Moreover, if the Ombudsperson recommends delisting, the measures taken against the individual, group, undertaking or entity are to be terminated unless the committee decides by consensus in favour of maintaining the sanctions within 60 days. If no consensus is reached and a committee member so requests the Security Council is to decide the issue.

However, the basic flaws of the regime remain. Petitioners still are not granted a fair and public hearing by an independent and impartial tribunal established by law and the minimum guarantees of a fair trial;[297] they do not have access to a political body which is judge in its own cause and decides behind closed doors.

3.8.4 *'Second-Generation' Peacekeeping Operations*

Better cooperation within the Security Council, above all among its permanent members, also made it possible to extend the tasks of 'one-dimensional' UN peacekeeping operations beyond monitoring ceasefires and inter-positioning and to develop participation in non-military tasks. However, the record of some of these complex, multidimensional 'mega-missions', in which large numbers of soldiers, police officers and civilians are involved, proved problematic, to say the least.[298]

---

294 The focal point shall continue to receive requests for delisting from other sanctions lists.

295 The current Ombudsperson is the former Canadian judge Kimberly Prost.

296 On conciliation see *infra* 184.

297 As required, for example, by Article 14 of the 1966 UN Covenant on Civil and Political Rights.

298 For instance, the United Nations Protection Force (UNPROFOR) described below was composed of almost 40,000 personnel. See *infra* 79.

UN peacekeepers participating in these operations were mandated to use force not only for their own self-defence but also for the safety of other international personnel, for keeping supply routes open, securing disarmament of the forces of the conflicting parties, as well as the protection of so-called safe areas. Furthermore, their functions included helping to maintain law and order, primarily the task of the police for which soldiers are not well trained; contributions to 'state-building' and 'nation-building', in particular to the preparation, organization and supervision of democratic elections; and assisting the delivery of humanitarian aid by intergovernmental and non-governmental organizations (IGOs and NGOs).

These operations did not always follow the above-mentioned principles of the 'first generation'.[299] The mandate to use non-defensive force if necessary could lead to a serious dilemma. If UN forces fulfilled their tasks, they risked losing their crucial impartiality and being treated as enemies by those against whom they used their weapons. If 'the blue helmets' did not resort to armed force, they lost their equally important credibility in the eyes of the conflicting parties. But if they opted for the first alternative, the mission changed its character. A mission based on the consent of all parties involved along the lines of traditional peacekeeping became enforcement action without the consent of the party against which it was directed in order to make it comply with Security Council decisions. This also meant that in order to be successful, the peacekeepers transformed into peace enforcers needed military resources superior to those of the party against which force was to be used.[300]

Four such operations, examples on three different continents may be mentioned: the United Nations Transition Assistance Group (UNTAG) in Namibia as the first mission of this type (1989–1990); the United Nations Transitional Authority in Cambodia (UNTAC) (1992–1993); the two United Nations Operations in Somalia (UNOSOM I and II), 'bridged' by the U.S.-led Unified Task Force (UNITAF),[301] (1992–1995); and UNPROFOR in the former Yugoslavia (also 1992–1995).[302] The last provided a particularly dramatic illustration of 'mission creep', i.e., the continuous

---

299 See *supra* 56.

300 In addition to the use of force beyond self-defence, 'second-generation' peacekeeping operations also differed from the 'first generation' as a result of the participation of troops of the 'P 5'.

301 Ironically, given its poor performance, code-named 'Operation Restore Hope'.

302 Hufnagel, UN-Friedensoperationen der zweiten Generation: Vom Puffer zur neuen Treuhand (1996); Mayall (ed.), *The New Interventionism 1991–1994: United Nations experience in Cambodia, former Yugoslavia and Somalia* (1996).

extension of the mandate of the force by the Security Council without providing the necessary, above all military, means.

UNPROFOR was initially tasked with maintaining security in UN Protected Areas, monitoring and some border control after the entry into force of a ceasefire in a relatively stable environment in Croatia.[303] The force was subsequently also deployed in Bosnia and Herzegovina where fighting between the three main ethnic groups escalated. The mandate of UNPROFOR was extended as well and culminated in the protection of the capital, Sarajevo, and five other cities which the Security Council had declared safe areas.[304] The weak international force was humiliated, with some of the soldiers taken hostage by Serbian forces and used as human shields against NATO air strikes. The vulnerability of UNPROFOR on the ground prevented NATO from conducting effective air attacks for the protection of the safe areas, which were also authorized by the Security Council.[305] In July 1995 a Dutch UNPROFOR contingent could not prevent the conquest of one of those safe areas, the city of Srebrenica, and the massacre of the entire male population, some 8,000 men and boys, by militarily superior forces under the command of Serb General Ratko Mladić, an act of genocide according to the International Criminal Tribunal for the Former Yugoslavia (ICTY)[306] and the ICJ.[307] It took military action by NATO to turn the tables against the Serb side and force the three parties to the negotiating table at the Wright-Patterson Air Force Base near Dayton, Ohio.

In order to overcome the resulting crisis of UN peacekeeping, Secretary-General Kofi Annan appointed the Panel on United Nations Peace Operations chaired by the former Algerian Foreign Minister, Lakhdar Brahimi. In its report

---

303 SC Resolution 743 (1992).

304 In paragraph 9 of Resolution 836 (1993) the Security Council authorized UNPROFOR '…,acting in self-defence, to take the necessary measures, *including the use of force* (italics added), in reply to bombardments against the safe areas by any of the parties or to armed incursion into them or in the event of any deliberate obstruction in or around those areas to the freedom of movement of UNPROFOR or of protected humanitarian convoys'. See *supra* 70.

305 Under paragraph 10 of Resolution 836 (1993), the Security Council decided that 'Member States, acting nationally or through regional organizations or arrangements, may take,… all necessary measures, through the use of air power, in and around the safe areas in the Republic of Bosnia and Herzegovina, to support UNPROFOR in the performance of its mandate set out in paragraphs 5 and 9 above.'

306 In their judgments in the *Krstić* case by the Trial Chamber in 2001 and the Appeals Chamber in 2004. Radislav Krstić was a high-ranking Serb officer involved in the Srebrenica massacre. Bigi, '*Krstić* case', MPEPIL.

307 In its 2007 judgment in the *Application of the Convention on the Prevention and Punishment of the Crime of Genocide* (*Bosnia and Herzegovina v Serbia and Montenegro*) case, paragraph 297.

presented in August 2000, the panel drew some lessons from the failures of recent operations. While it reiterated three 'bedrock principles' of such missions, namely the consent of the local parties, impartiality, and the use of force only in self-defence, it also emphasized that equal treatment was out of the question if one party clearly violated the terms of a peace agreement. This in turn required robust rules of engagement backed by sufficiently strong military forces. Moreover, there was a need for clear, credible and achievable mandates from the Security Council. Traditional operations should be deployable within 30, complex missions within 90 days. The Security Council endorsed some of the Panel's recommendations in its Resolutions 1318 (2000) and 1327 (2000).

3.8.5 *'Enforcement-by-Consent' Operations*

A major improvement over the ill-fated UNPROFOR was achieved with the Implementation Force (IFOR) in Bosnia and Herzegovina: decisive military superiority over the troops of the local conflicting parties. The mandate of IFOR, which was not under UN but NATO command, was to enforce the military provisions of the Dayton/Paris Peace Agreement.[308] The operation differed from 'Operation Desert Storm' and similar missions, since the international force was deployed with the specific consent of the conflicting parties to its mandate. This agreement was given, albeit under international pressure, by the leaders of the three ethnic groups in Bosnia and Herzegovina (only one of them from the country itself), Presidents Alija Izetbegović, Slobodan Milošević and Franjo Tuđjman.[309] This type of military mission could be regarded as another 'generation' of peace operations.

In its Resolution 1031 (1995) the Security Council welcomed and supported the Peace Agreement and authorized IFOR to take all necessary measures to effect the implementation of and ensure compliance with the relevant Annex 1-A, noting that the parties had consented to IFOR's taking such measures.[310] The Force was thereby tasked with enforcing the ceasefire, the withdrawal of foreign forces from the country, the redeployment of local forces behind given zones of separation and the storage of heavy weapons at fixed sites. At the outset, IFOR totalled approximately 60,000 troops, one third of them U.S. soldiers. The local parties were therefore ill-advised to challenge the international force and refrained from military showdowns. In 1996, the Stabilization Force

308 The Agreement was initialled at the end of the negotiations at Dayton and signed in Paris.

309 U.S. Assistant Secretary of State Richard Holbrooke, who acted as mediator, exerted considerable pressure on the three Presidents during the negotiations leading to the Dayton/Paris Peace Agreement.

310 Paragraph 15.

(SFOR) succeeded IFOR, with its size reduced by about one half of the original personnel number, until it was in turn replaced with 'Operation Althea' conducted by the EU in 2004.

Kosovo became the site of a similar operation in 1999. President Milošević gave his crucial consent at the end of NATO's 'Operation Allied Force' undertaken in order to end the 'ethnic cleansing' of the Albanian population by Serbian forces in Kosovo.[311] In its Resolution 1244 (1999), the Security Council decided that the responsibilities of the 'security presence' in Kosovo would include maintaining and, where necessary, enforcing a ceasefire, ensuring the withdrawal and preventing the return of FRY military, police and paramilitary forces, demilitarizing the Kosovo Liberation Army and other armed Kosovo Albanian groups and establishing a secure environment.[312] The Kosovo Force (KFOR) was equally led by NATO and initially comprised about 50,000 troops. Although it successfully fulfilled its mandate in general, it did not prevent nor stop the bloody riots against the Serb minority in 2004. A considerably reduced KFOR remains in Kosovo after the declaration of independence in 2008.[313]

A similar peacekeeping mission was dispatched to Timor-Leste in 1999. Atrocities against the local population were perpetrated by Indonesian forces after a majority of the voters in the former Portuguese colony had declared itself in favour of independence. Indonesian President Jusuf Habibie eventually agreed to a peace plan which provided for the deployment of a multinational force. In its Resolution 1264 (1999) the Security Council authorized the force, *inter alia*, to take all necessary measures in order to restore peace and security and facilitate human assistance operations.[314] This International Force in East Timor (INTERFET) led by Australia was to be replaced as soon as possible by a UN peacekeeping operation.[315]

---

311 For the background of this operation see *infra* 101.

312 Paragraph 9. However, the Resolution did not contain the usual authorization to use all necessary means or take all necessary measures to accomplish the mandate. Instead, the Security Council authorized, in paragraph 7, member states and relevant international organizations to establish the international security presence in Kosovo with all necessary means to fulfil its responsibilities under paragraph 9. This was apparently a compromise formula into which Western states could read enforcement action while for reluctant Russia and China it did not expressly authorize the use of force. Gray, *supra* (fn. 27) 342.

313 See *infra* 91.

314 Paragraph 3.

315 Paragraph 10. After INTERFET had restored order in the country, the temporary United Nations Transitional Administration in East Timor (UNTAET) was established by SC Resolution 1272 (1999). After Timor-Leste became fully independent in

3.8.6 *Preventive Peacekeeping Operations*

Another, rather unique variant of peacekeeping mission was equally tested in the 'Balkan laboratory' after the Cold War: the deployment of an international force in order to preserve peace before conflicting parties resort to armed force or hostilities spill over from neighbouring crisis areas. In November 1992, Kiro Gligorov, the President of the Former Yugoslav Republic of Macedonia (FYROM), who worried about the impact of fighting in the vicinity, requested the dispatch of UN observers to his country. The Security Council complied with the request and authorized, in its Resolution 795 (1992), the Secretary-General to establish a presence of UNPROFOR in FYROM and so to inform the authorities of Albania and the FRY.[316] The force of approximately 800 military and civilian personnel was reinforced by some 300 U.S. troops in 1993.[317] Two years later, the mission was renamed United Nations Preventive Deployment Force (UNPREDEP) and became an independent operation in 1996 in accordance with Security Council Resolution 983 (1995).[318] It helped to prevent a spill-over of hostilities from abroad and stabilize FYROM by patrolling its borders.

Ironically, however, the operation was terminated when its services were most urgently needed. In February 1999, China voted against the extension of UNPREDEP's mandate in the Security Council. The Chinese delegate asserted that the situation in FYROM had sufficiently stabilized and its relations with neighbouring countries improved – at a time when the crisis in adjacent Kosovo was reaching its climax.[319] Despite a denial, the real reason for China's opposition apparently was to punish the Macedonian government for opening diplomatic relations with Taiwan in exchange for much needed economic assistance.

Effective preventive missions would be the most desirable type of peacekeeping mission since they can help to avoid human casualties and material damage altogether or keep these unwelcome consequences to a minimum by nipping a crisis in the bud. However, governments are reluctant to resort

---

2002, the new government was assisted by further UN operations: the United Nations Mission of Support in East Timor (UNMISET) under SC Resolution 1410 (2002) (2002–2005) and the United Nations Integrated Mission in Timor-Leste (UNMIT) under SC Resolution 1704 (2006–2007).

316 Paragraph 2.

317 Pursuant to SC Resolution 842 (1993).

318 In its Resolution 1046 (1996), the Security Council authorized an increase in the strength of UNPREDEP by 50 military personnel in order to provide for a continued engineering capability.

319 Gray, *supra* (fn. 27) 284.

to such operations and ask other states or international organizations for assistance at an early stage of internal or international tensions. For such a request is bound to be seen as a tacit but clear admission of the inability to maintain law and order within one's own borders or to handle a conflict with another state. Preventive peacekeeping therefore constitutes the rare exception to the rule of consenting to the presence of foreign forces only after, and not before, recourse to armed force with its negative effects. In general, conflicting parties accept the services of peacekeepers only when they realize that they cannot defeat and impose their will on their adversary and must settle for a compromise, including a ceasefire.

3.8.7 *ISAF: From Security Assistance Based on Consent to 'Enforcement without Consent'*

Another major operation authorized to use force by the Security Council, based on the agreement of the major anti-Taliban parties at a meeting in Bonn in December 2001, was the International Security Assistance Force (ISAF) in Afghanistan.

The authorization in Resolution 1386 (2001) was initially limited to assisting the Afghan Interim Authority in the maintenance of security in the capital Kabul and its surrounding areas, enabling the Interim Authority and UN personnel to operate in a secure environment.[320] Two years later, in its Resolution 1510 (2003), the Council extended the mandate of the Force 'as resources permit', to support the Afghan authorities in the maintenance of security in areas of Afghanistan outside of Kabul and its environs.[321] In 2007 the Security Council, in Resolution 1746 (2007), welcomed the completion of ISAF's expansion throughout Afghanistan.[322]

At the outset, it was generally assumed (wrongly, as it turned out) that the mission was launched with the consent of all major political and military forces in the country, and that, if sufficiently reinforced, the international troops would enjoy military superiority. Initially, it seemed that the U.S.-led 'Operation Enduring Freedom' had decisively defeated the Taliban and the Al Qaeda terrorists.[323] However, both had only temporarily withdrawn or gone underground and soon mounted attacks on the two foreign forces. What at first looked like an 'enforcement-by-consent' mission more and more became an 'enforcement-without-consent' operation.

320 Paragraphs 1 and 3.

321 Paragraphs 1 and 4. The United States initially hesitated to accept ISAF operations outside Kabul lest they interfere with those of 'Operation Enduring Freedom'. Gray, *supra* (fn. 27) 204, 344.

322 Paragraph 25.

323 See *infra* 119.

In addition, the UN launched a political mission at the request of the Afghan government. The United Nations Mission in Afghanistan (UNAMA) was created by Security Council Resolution 1401 (2002). It was designed to contribute to peacebuilding in the war-torn country by helping with recovery and reconstruction.[324] The mandate of the mission was also modified over time. Security Council Resolution 1974 (2011) charged UNAMA with leading international civilian efforts in Afghanistan, focusing, *inter alia*, on human rights and the rule of law, the Afghan-led peace and reconciliation process, the organization of elections, the fight against corruption and counter-narcotics activities.[325]

Leadership of ISAF first rotated among individual NATO member states. In 2003, the Atlantic Alliance assumed the permanent command of the force. NATO has tried to avoid the mistakes of past 'second-generation' peacekeeping missions[326] and kept sending reinforcements to Afghanistan in the face of increasing challenges by its adversaries in order successfully to fulfil the extended mandate of the force. However, Western military high technology and numerical strength have proven of limited value in asymmetrical warfare which favours the other side.[327]

In the meantime, the United States and its partners in 'Operation Enduring Freedom' as well as NATO concluded that a decisive military victory over the Taliban and other adversaries who practice a guerrilla strategy is not within reach; they nevertheless decided to gradually withdraw their combat troops from the Hindu Kush by the end of 2014 and leave the maintenance of security in the country to the Afghan government forces which they will continue to help train and equip.[328]

3.8.8 *International Administration*

The exercise of all or some of the relevant state powers in a state or territory by one or several other states or an international organization is not an innovation that had to wait for the end of the Cold War. It was already applied to protectorates in the colonial era, under the Mandate system of the League of Nations, as well as the Trusteeship system of the UN. Moreover, for example, the League of Nations administered the Saarland after World War I and the UN West Irian in 1962–1963.

---

324 See *supra* 54 and *infra* 87.

325 Paragraphs 5 and 6.

326 See *supra* 78.

327 Therefore ISAF also constitutes an example of 'mission creep'. See *supra* 79.

328 Hadley and Podesta, 'The Right Way Out of Afghanistan', 91 *Foreign Affairs* no. 4 (July/August 2012) 41.

After the end of the Cold War, in addition to UNTAC in Cambodia[329] and UNTAET in East Timor, two examples from the 'Balkan laboratory', already referred to in connection with 'enforcement-by-consent' operations, may also be mentioned in the present context and dealt with in more detail.[330]

One feature Bosnia and Herzegovina as well as Kosovo had in common was indeed their administration by several major international organizations: the UN, the OSCE, NATO, and the EU. Another similarity was the paradox of the attempt to introduce democracy by undemocratic means.[331] They also shared more than one difficult transition problem – from war to peace, from a one-party political system to pluralist democracy, from command to market economy, and from dependence to having a state of their own. These difficulties were and are aggravated by continuing conflicts along ethnic and religious lines dividing populations still traumatized by recent armed violence, bloodshed and atrocities. The economic situation is equally bleak as a result of low growth, high unemployment and insufficient foreign investment. Organized crime and widespread corruption are another scourge with which both Bosnia and Herzegovina and Kosovo continue to struggle.

The division of labour between those interlocking (and hopefully not inter-blocking) institutions followed the logic of their principal areas of activity. Each of them undertook to do what it could do best. Consequently, the OSCE focused on democratization, human rights and capacity-building, i.e., the training of local officials in various fields. The maintenance of security by military means was entrusted to NATO. The EU helped with economic recovery and reforms, and membership of the Union constitutes the principal political goal of all the countries in the region. The role of the UN varied, however. Whereas it took a back seat in Bosnia and Herzegovina, the Special Representative of the Secretary-General was the centre of power in Kosovo.

The objective of the international civilian and military presences was and is to contribute to peacebuilding.[332] The international community realized that the termination of armed hostilities by a ceasefire, which can be strengthened

329 See *supra* 79.

330 Ruffert, 'The Administration of Kosovo and East-Timor by the International Community', 50 *ICLQ* (2001) 613; Wilde, 'From Danzig to East Timor and Beyond: The Role of International Territorial Administration', 95 *AJIL* (2001) 583.

331 See *supra* 66.

332 The OSCE prefers the term 'post-conflict rehabilitation', while the EU uses the term 'post-conflict stabilization' (for instance, in Article 43[1] of the Lisbon Treaty on European Union) for the same concept – another illustration of the terminological confusion which does not help efforts to bring these organizations closer to average citizens.

by peacekeeping operations, and peacemaking, i.e., an agreement between the parties on a political solution of their conflict, with which third parties can also help,[333] are not sufficient to establish durable peace between conflicting parties. What is needed is reconciliation and political reforms in the direction of a functioning pluralist democracy based on a system of checks and balances, respect for human and minority rights, as well as the rule of law. Humanitarian assistance and economic reconstruction should be followed by reforms leading to sustainable development and an internationally competitive economy. The fruits of the resulting economic growth ought to be distributed justly.[334] After achieving these goals and national leadership and ownership in the country concerned international administration would come to an end.

However, the High Representative in Bosnia and Herzegovina was endowed with almost dictatorial competences under the Dayton/Paris Peace Agreement, which were extended by the so-called Peace Implementation Council composed of the main stakeholders, states as well as international organizations, at a meeting in Bonn in 1997. These sweeping 'Bonn powers' authorized the High Representative, for example, to annul legislation by the local authorities and to enact legislative acts himself, as well as to dismiss public officials. The persons holding this office frequently made use of these competences in practice. Since the three main ethnic groups in the country could not agree on solutions to these issues, it was the High Representative who also introduced a national currency, a national flag and a national anthem.

In Kosovo, the equivalent of the High Representative was the Special Representative of the UN Secretary-General who headed the United Nations Interim Administration in Kosovo (UNMIK) with similar far-reaching powers on the basis of Security Council Resolution 1244 (1999).

The paradox inherent in this institutional framework was the objective to establish a democratic system founded on the separation of powers by a regime based on the opposite principles. The High/Special Representative may have been indispensable to prevent the partition of the country and to ensure a modicum of political stability; at the same time, he[335] made 'self-empowerment' of the population more difficult and reinforced a mentality of dependence,

333 By offering good offices, enquiry, mediation or arbitration and adjudication. See *infra* 177.

334 In 2005 the UN created a special Peacebuilding Commission by General Assembly Resolution 60/180 and SC Resolution 1645 (2005) in order to coordinate the manifold efforts of the World Organization in this area. Schweisfurth, 'The United Nations Peacebuilding Commission's First Year', in: Fischer-Lescano et alii (eds.), *supra* (fn. 180) 297; Baetens and Kohoutek, 'United Nations Peacebuilding Commission', MPEPIL.

335 So far, only men have held these two posts.

which led people to expect that the international community would take care of their needs. It also played into the hands of the radicals who blamed the internationals for the problems in their country.

Two major problems may be highlighted in the present context, one for each country. The political situation in Bosnia and Herzegovina is complicated by the complex constitutional system agreed on at Dayton.[336] What may initially have made sense as a peace agreement did not work as a constitution. The Peace Agreement provides for one state, Bosnia and Herzegovina, with rather limited powers at the central level. The state consists of two so-called Entities, the *Republika Srpska* and the Federation of Bosnia and Herzegovina comprising the territories mainly inhabited by (Muslim) Bosniaks and Croats; these Entities hold most of the competences. The Federation is in turn composed of ten Cantons, on which some important powers are equally conferred, in addition to the District of Brčko with a special status. Finally, 142 municipalities also exercise some competences. As a result, a major share of the poor country's budget is spent on administration and bureaucracy.

The main political forces agree on the need for constitutional reform in principle, but are diametrically opposed to each other with regard to its direction. While the Bosniaks, the biggest ethnic/religious group, call for more powers for the central state, the Serbs, on the contrary, want to have some of the state competences retransferred to their Entity and threaten secession if their demands are not met. Croatians in Herzegovina want their own separate Entity, if not union with Croatia.

Discriminatory provisions in the Dayton constitution caused further legal and political difficulties. The tripartite Presidency and membership of the House of Peoples (the upper house of the national parliament) is only open to members of the three main ethnic groups, Bosniaks (Bosnian Muslims), Serbs and Croatians. A Bosnian Roma, Dervo Sejdić, and a Bosnian Jew, Jakob Finci, contested their exclusion from these high political functions and turned to the European Court of Human Rights.[337] In 2009, the Court decided in their favour, holding that the ineligibility of the applicants violated several provisions of the 1950 European Convention for the Protection of Human Rights and Fundamental Freedoms and the Protocols thereto. The EU insists on the necessary constitutional reforms as a precondition for the entry into force of the Stabilization and Association Agreement, paving the way to EU candidate status, which would open the door to accession negotiations. Since the principal political forces in the country have so far failed to agree on these revisions,

336 In Annex 4 of the Peace Agreement.

337 *Milanović*, 'Sejdić & Finci v. Bosnia and Herzegovina', 104 *AJIL* (2010) 636.

Bosnia and Herzegovina is lagging behind on the road to EU membership among the Western Balkan states not yet admitted to the Union.

The main issue in Kosovo was the final status of this Province of Serbia.[338] The relevant, already-mentioned Security Council Resolution 1244 adopted after 'Operation Allied Force' conducted by NATO member states did not resolve the controversy.[339] It reaffirmed the sovereignty and territorial integrity of the FRY and provided for the enjoyment of substantial autonomy and self-government by the people of Kosovo, pending a final settlement.[340] While for the overwhelming Albanian majority in Kosovo this final settlement could only mean independence and a state of their own, the government in Belgrade was merely ready to grant far-reaching autonomy – 'more than autonomy but less than independence'.

The basic legal issue underlying the controversy over the independence of Kosovo illustrates the fundamental problem mentioned in the introductory chapter: the 'zero-sum game' between two diametrically opposed legal principles.[341] In this case, the dilemma opposes the right of self-determination of peoples, provided that this principle also entitles a people to claim a state of its own[342] and the inhabitants of Kosovo qualify as a people,[343] on the one hand, and the sovereignty and territorial integrity of the state on whose territory the new state should be established, on the other. Each of the two principles – one

338 Neuhold, 'Kosovo: A Testing Ground for International Crisis Management and Dispute Settlement', in: Hafner, Matscher and Schmalenbach (eds.), *Völkerrecht und die Dynamik der Menschenrechte. Liber Amicorum Wolfram Karl* (2012) 324; see also Harland, 'Kosovo and the UN', 52 *Survival* no. 5 (October–November 2010) 75.

339 On this operation see *infra* 101.

340 See the preamble and paragraphs 10 and 11(a). The Security Council also decided, in paragraph 19 of the Resolution, that the international civil and security presences were established for an initial period of 12 months, to continue thereafter unless the Council decided otherwise. No criteria for the termination of the temporary international presences were specified.

341 See *supra* 5.

342 Whereas 'internal self-determination', i.e., the choice of the political, legal, economic, social and cultural system by a people is generally accepted, 'external self-determination' including the option of statehood remains controversial. See *supra* fn. 249.

343 The principle *uti possidetis,* according to which persons who live within the previously internal boundaries of a state form a people entitled to self-determination, was applied to the former SFRY. However, the relevant boundaries chosen were those of the former constituent Republics, while Kosovo was only a Province of the Republic of Serbia. *Uti possidetis* prevailed over the definition according to which ethnic and cultural similarities like a common language or religion shared by the members of a group are the relevant criteria for defining a people.

dynamic and promoting change, the other protecting the status quo – can only be implemented at the expense of the other.

The position of the international community initially was that Kosovo had to reach modern Western political and economic standards before the status issue would be addressed. However, after the 2004 riots,[344] 'standards before status' gave way to 'standards and status' and, arguably, finally 'status without standards'. Although the Special Envoy of the UN Secretary-General, the senior Norwegian diplomat Kai Eide, painted a bleak picture in his 2005 report on the situation in Kosovo, he concluded that there was a shared expectation that the status process would start. Thereupon the Security Council gave the green light for status negotiations in October 2005. Because of the irreconcilable positions of the two parties the talks soon reached a deadlock, which the mediatory efforts of the new UN Special Envoy, the experienced trouble shooter and former Finnish President Martii Ahtisaari, could not break.[345]

Ahtisaari eventually submitted his Comprehensive Proposal for the Kosovo Status Settlement in February 2007. This plan provided for the gradual independence of Kosovo under international supervision.[346] The new state was to be founded on Western values, multi-ethnic society, democracy, the rule of law and human rights, as well as an open market economy with free competition. In addition to substantial guarantees for minorities and the protection of all religious denominations, in particular the Serb Orthodox Church, Ahtisaari's proposal also included decentralization, i.e., local self-government by the municipalities.

An International Steering Group consisting of the principal international stakeholders was to supervise the implementation of the Proposal, with powers similar to those of the UN Special Representative entrusted to the International Civilian Representative, who at the same time was to serve as EU Special Representative. While a NATO-led International Military Presence was charged with ensuring external and internal security and the OSCE with continuing its activities, the EU was to conduct a major rule of law mission.

---

344 See *supra* 82.

345 Ahtisaari also served as UN Commissioner for Namibia from 1977 to 1981. After leaving office as President of Finland in 2000, he successfully mediated between the rebels of the Free Aceh Movement and the Indonesian government in 2005. In 2008 he was awarded the Nobel Peace Prize.

346 UN Doc. S/2007/168/Add. 1. Ahtisaari did not expressly mention independence in the Proposal itself but did so in the letter to the Security Council which he attached to the Proposal.

On the basis of the Ahtisaari Proposal an Albanian Assembly declared the independence of Kosovo on 17 February 2008. Interestingly, the document did not refer to any legal basis, in particular not to the right-of self-determination of peoples, but only to moral and political justifications, 'Recalling the years of strife and violence in Kosovo, that disturbed the conscience of all civilized people'. Kosovo was quickly recognized as an independent state mainly by Western states, the United States as well as most, but not all, members of the EU,[347] while many other states, above all Serbia and Russia, strongly objected to the unilateral declaration of independence.

The confrontation between the supporters and opponents of independent Kosovo was fought not only in the political arena but also on the legal front. Serbia obtained the necessary majority in the UN General Assembly for addressing a request to the ICJ for an advisory opinion on the following question: 'Is the declaration of independence by the Provisional Institutions of Self-Government of Kosovo in accordance with international law?'[348]

In its advisory opinion of 22 July 2010, the ICJ answered the question in the affirmative.[349] The Court pointed out that general international law did not prohibit the promulgation of declarations of independence, without clarifying by whom such declarations may be made. Furthermore, the ICJ stated that Security Council Resolution 1244 was still in force and constituted the applicable *lex specialis*. Yet in the view of the majority of the judges the declaration of independence did not violate this special legal regime either.[350]

However, the arguments of the dissenting judges carried some weight, and some of them may therefore also be mentioned. They raised the problem of

347 Cyprus, Greece, Romania, Slovakia and Spain have not recognized the independence of Kosovo.

348 General Assembly Resolution 63/3.

349 *Accordance with International Law of the Unilateral Declaration of Independence in Respect of Kosovo.* Oellers-Frahm, 'Problematic Question or Problematic Answer? Observations on the International Court of Justice's Advisory Opinion Concerning Kosovo's Unilateral Declaration of Independence', 53 *GYIL* (2010) 793; Falk, 'The *Kosovo* Advisory Opinion: Conflict Resolution and Precedent', 105 *AJIL* (2011) 50.

350 For the authors of the declaration had not acted as the (parliamentary) Assembly of Kosovo, one of the Provisional Institutions of Self-Government within the Constitutional Framework of UNMIK, but as a different body. This resulted from the language used in the declaration and the fact that it was also signed by the President and Prime Minister of Kosovo. Moreover, the Court also pointed out that the Special Representative had not annulled the declaration of independence as an *ultra vires* act, as he had done earlier with regard to other such acts between 2002 and 2005.

the difference between acting outside a legal order and violating it.[351] The failure of the Special Representative to take action against the declaration of independence may have been due to the 'reverberating effect' of the differences of opinion within the Security Council.[352]

In 2012, at a meeting in Prishtina, the members of the International Steering Group terminated the international supervision of the independence of Kosovo and closed the International Civilian Office. However, the presence of a reduced KFOR and the EU rule of law mission EULEX Kosovo, as well as of the OSCE and UN, will continue.

Politically, time is working for Kosovo; more than half of the member states of the UN have already recognized it as an independent state. Since admission to the EU is a political priority of the Serbian government, the Union successfully urged Serbia to normalize its relations with Kosovo.

Thus, with the EU High Representative for Foreign and Security Policy, Catherine Ashton, acting as mediator, the Serbian Prime Minister Ivica Dačić and his Kosovo counterpart Hashim Thaçi reached an agreement to this effect in 2013.[353] It provides, *inter alia,* for the establishment of an Association/Community of Serb majority municipalities in Kosovo[354] with competences in the areas of economic development, education, health and urban and rural planning. The Police Regional Commander shall be nominated from a list provided by the four mayors on behalf of the Association/Community. Special panels composed of a majority of Kosovo Serbs are to be created within the judicial system. At the same time, the existing Serb parallel police and judicial structures will be integrated into the respective Kosovo systems. Neither party will block the other side's progress on its respective EU path.

3.8.9 *Individual Criminal Responsibility*

Perhaps surprisingly at first sight, a milestone on the road towards individual criminal responsibility for major violations of international law was also accomplished by the Security Council in the framework of Chapter VII of the

351 Dissenting opinions of Judge Skotnikov, paragraph 15, and Judge Bennouna, paragraph 53.

352 Dissenting opinion of Judge Bennouna, paragraph 55. Moreover, in 2005 the Security Council had endorsed the Guidelines of the Contact Group composed of six major powers with special interests in the Balkans (France, Germany, Italy, Russia, United Kingdom and United States) for Special Envoy Ahtisaari; they provided for the endorsement of the final status of Kosovo by the Security Council. The above-mentioned paragraph 19 of Resolution 1244 pointed in the same direction. See *supra* fn. 340.

353 English text http://www.b92net/eng/news/politics-article.php?yyyy=2013&mm=04&dd=19&nav; accessed on 21 April 2013.

354 The Serbs constitute the largest minority in Kosovo.

UN Charter, and also in the 'Balkan laboratory'.[355] One of the main deficiencies of the international legal order was thereby remedied at least partially and the 'individualization' of international law increased.[356] The corollary of the recognition of the individual as a subject of international law entitled to the respect of his/her human rights is to also hold him/her accountable for unlawful acts.

Under traditional international law, the negative consequences of the breach of a legal obligation affect the entire population and not just the individuals responsible, i.e., the decision makers and those carrying out their decisions or otherwise committing unlawful acts.[357] Indeed, the average citizens usually suffer more than the ruling elites and their agents from sanctions applied by the state whose rights are directly violated[358] and from action taken by other states or international organizations.[359] One remedy for this unsatisfactory state of affairs was provided by the switch of the Security Council to targeted sanctions.[360] Considerations of justice and legal policy also demand that at least persons who order and perpetrate acts that constitute serious violations of international law be held directly and individually responsible for them.

The concept of individual criminal responsibility for what today are regarded as breaches of international humanitarian law is not new as such but can be traced back, for instance, to the Hagenbach trial in 15th century Germany. Peter von Hagenbach was sentenced to death by an ad hoc tribunal in 1474 for

---

355 It could be argued that persons responsible for violations of international humanitarian law in the course of an armed conflict will, as a rule, only be tried after armed hostilities have come to an end. At this point in time, the situation will therefore usually have ceased to constitute, under Article 39 of the UN Charter, even a 'mere' threat to the peace as commonly understood. Moreover, it may be objected that the Charter, including its system of collective security, focused on states and not individuals. Critics of the establishment of ad hoc criminal tribunals by the Security Council also underlined the immunity of state officials. However, the concept of individual criminal responsibility enforced by appropriate institutions soon met with general principled approval.

356 Hafner, 'The Emancipation of the Individual from the State under International Law', 358 *RCADI* (2013) 275.

357 See *supra* 74.

358 In particular reprisals/countermeasures and retorsions. Reprisals or, as they tend to be called more recently, countermeasures are responses that are unlawful in principle but justified by the previous illegal behaviour of the subject of international law against which they are directed. In contrast, retorsions are lawful but 'unfriendly' reactions by the victim to a breach of international law. Giegerich, 'Retorsion', MPEPIL. See also Neuhold, 'The Foreign-Policy "Cost-Benefit-Analysis" Revisited', 42 *GYIL* 1999 (2000) 84.

359 For instance, sanctions imposed by the UN Security Council. See *supra* 73.

360 See *supra* 76.

atrocities perpetrated by his troops against the inhabitants of the city of Freiburg im Breisgau.[361]

Two much more prominent persons who shaped European and world history, Napoleon Bonaparte and the German Emperor Wilhelm II, were also held personally responsible for their wartime record by the Congress of Vienna in 1815 and under Article 227 of the Peace Treaty of Versailles, respectively. While Napoleon was exiled to Saint Helena, the Netherlands refused to extradite the German Emperor who had fled to this neighbouring country. The original proposals for the PCIJ also included a High Court of International Justice designed to try individuals for international crimes, which, however, was not established.[362]

More recently, the main war criminals responsible for World War II were tried by the Nuremberg and Tokyo International Military Tribunals after the war. However, these trials not only smacked of victor's justice but for decades were not followed by the establishment of other international tribunals or courts to prosecute persons who committed similar crimes.

The decisive step was again taken in the 'Balkan laboratory' when the Security Council created the ICTY by its Resolution 827 (1993). It was followed by the establishment of similar tribunals for the conflicts in Rwanda a year later, for Sierra Leone (2000), Timor-Leste (2000), Cambodia (2006) and Lebanon (2007).[363] This process also led to the creation of the ICC under the 1998 Rome Statute which entered into force in 2002.

These new institutions share several important similarities. Their jurisdiction does not encompass all unlawful acts but is limited to serious violations of international humanitarian law. However, if a choice among the areas of international law for introducing individual criminal responsibility were to be made, humanitarian law should be picked because of the particularly heinous crimes committed in this field. More specifically, grave breaches of the 1949 Geneva Conventions, the laws or customs of war, genocide and crimes against humanity are listed in the instruments establishing the tribunals and the ICC.[364] Provisions stating that his or her official position, whether as Head of State or Government or responsible government official, do not relieve a person

361 The tribunal rejected Hagenbach's argument that he had merely carried out orders of his superior, Duke Charles the Bold (or Rash) of Burgundy.

362 Hafner, *supra* (fn. 356) 431.

363 Schabas, *The UN International Criminal Tribunals: The former Yugoslavia, Rwanda and Sierra Leone* (2006).

364 On the addition of aggression in Article 5 of the Statute of the ICC and the Kampala definition see *supra* 65.

of criminal responsibility nor mitigate punishment are to be welcomed,[365] as is the limitation of punishment to prison terms, excluding the death penalty.

From a comparative perspective, both ad hoc tribunals and the ICC have their strengths as well weaknesses and constraints. On the one hand, the jurisdiction of the tribunals is limited by territorial and temporal restrictions, i.e., to specific conflicts in specific countries within a specific time frame.[366] On the other, since these tribunals are based on a binding resolution of the UN Security Council, all states are obligated to cooperate with them, including in the arrest and extradition of indicted persons. Furthermore, their jurisdiction has primacy over that of national criminal courts.

In contrast, the ICC is a permanent court with general jurisdiction. Yet, since it was established by a treaty only the states that have ratified the Rome Statute are subject to the Court's jurisdiction. As was to be expected, states that have to fear proceedings against their nationals before the ICC have not become parties to the treaty. However, under Article 13(2) of the Statute, the Security Council may refer a situation, also involving a non-party to the Statute, to the ICC. Moreover, under Article 17 the Court's role is subsidiary, since it may deal with a case only if a contracting party with jurisdiction over it is either unwilling or unable genuinely to carry out the investigation or prosecution.

The breakthrough towards individual criminal responsibility under international law has also produced tangible results. In particular, the ICTY has not remained a 'paper tiger' but handed down numerous judgments; moreover, its jurisprudence has contributed to the clarification of major issues of international law.

The Tribunal also tried and sentenced high-ranking political and military leaders. For instance, the former Serbian President Slobodan Milošević was extradited to The Hague and died in prison before the end of his trial; his Bosnian counterpart Radovan Karadžić is currently standing trial before the ICTY judges. The military commander held responsible for the Srebrenica massacre, General Ratko Mladić,[367] and the leader of Croatian Serbs, Goran Hadžić, were at last arrested and extradited to the Tribunal in 2011. The ICTY has already

365 This provision was already included in Article 7 of the 1945 Charter of the International Military Tribunal annexed to the London Agreement of the four main victorious powers (the United States, the United Kingdom, the Soviet Union and France) for the Establishment of an International Military Tribunal which set the stage for the Nuremberg trial of the major German war criminals.

366 The Lebanon tribunal was appointed for only one case, the assassination of the former Prime Minister Rafiq al-Hariri.

367 See *supra* 80.

sentenced the former President of the *Republika Srpska*, Biljana Plavšić, and the former President of the Parliament of the *Republika Srpska*, Momčilo Krajišnik, as well as several generals, to long prison terms.

However, in November 2012, the Appeals Chamber of the ICTY acquitted, for lack of sufficient evidence, the Croatian Generals Ante Gotovina and Mladen Markač, who in 2011 had been sentenced to 24 and 18 years of imprisonment, respectively, by the Trial Chamber for their involvement in the reconquest of the Krajina, a region of Croatia controlled by Croatian Serbs at the time. Towards the end of the same month, the Appeals Chamber also acquitted, for the same reason, one of the leaders of the Kosovo Liberation Army (KLA – *Ushtria Climintare e Kosoves* – UCK) and former Prime Minister of Kosovo, Ramush Haradinaj. The Trial Chamber had initially acquitted him in 2008, but the Appeals Chamber had ordered a partial retrial in 2010. In 2013, further acquittals followed, including that of the former Chief of Staff of the FRY Army, Momčilo Perišić, who had been sentenced to 27 years in prison by the Trial Chamber in 2011.

The other tribunals and the ICC have also been active. In particular, the Court made headlines when it issued an arrest warrant against the President of Sudan, al Bashir, who was accused of atrocities committed in Darfur.[368] Moreover, in 2011, the Security Council referred the situation in Libya to the Prosecutor of the ICC in accordance with Article 13(2) of the Rome Statute.[369]

With regard to the response of public opinion to proceedings against persons indicted for violations of international humanitarian law, views on the ICTY differed considerably. According to a Gallup Balkans Monitor opinion poll conducted in 2008, almost seven out of 10 respondents in Albania (69%) and Kosovo (68%) felt that the tribunal helped reconciliation and strengthened peace. In contrast, majorities in Croatia (53%) and Serbia (64%) thought that the ICTY did not serve the interests of the region and simply fuelled past conflicts.[370]

These divergent assessments raise the general question of the most adequate method for achieving political stability and reconciliation between the parties after an armed conflict, in particular a civil war: criminal proceedings by a court or tribunal leading to punishment of the persons found guilty by the

---

368 However, President al Bashir is still at large at this writing. In 2012 the ICC handed down its first sentence against the Congolese warlord Thomas Lubanga. He was found guilty of recruiting and using child soldiers under the age of 15 in the Democratic Republic of the Congo in 2002–2003 and sentenced to 14 years in prison.

369 In paragraph 4 of Resolution 1970 (2011). See *infra* 111.

370 http://www.turkishweekly.net/news.php?id=61409, accessed on 24 November 2008.

judges in pursuit of retributive justice, or truth and reconciliation commissions based on restorative justice?[371]

The latter institutions, whose mandates vary, may be created by domestic or international legal acts, such as peace treaties.[372] These commissions are a rather recent phenomenon. They were first developed in Latin America in the 1980s after the collapse of military regimes, notably in Argentina and Chile. In the meantime, their number has risen to about 30. Their common denominator is the task to investigate and establish facts about past abuses and not to sentence and punish the perpetrators. Victims are given a voice, and at least some of them can tell their stories in public. Perpetrators can also present their versions of the crimes of which they are accused and ought to express regrets and apologize for crimes they committed.

Establishing the truth about the past for all parties involved, in particular atrocities perpetrated by them, should not be underrated. The alternative of shoving the past under the carpet usually does not mean that it will be forgotten but rather that each side sticks to its selective narrative, seeing itself as the victim and ignoring its own criminal record.[373] Similarly, prosecuting only members of the defeated parties but not the victors is bound to lead to resentment and complaints by the former about selective justice. In both cases, genuine reconciliation enabling the parties to turn a new, positive page in their relations is made difficult.

Truth and reconciliation commissions may also be authorized to attribute responsibility, to recommend to rehabilitate victims and to grant them reparations. Furthermore, accused perpetrators may be amnestied as the prize for revealing the truth. An amnesty may lead to the disclosure of facts the person concerned would not admit if he or she had to fear criminal or civil proceedings.[374]

---

371 Bisset, *Truth Commissions and Criminal Courts* (2012).

372 Hayner, 'Fifteen Truth Commissions 1974 to 1995: A Comparative Study', 16 *Human Rights Quarterly* (1994) 597; Zehr and Gohar, *The Little Book of Restorative Justice* (2003); O'Shea, 'Truth and Reconciliation Commissions', MPEPIL; Verdoolaege, *Reconciliation Discourse: The Case of the Truth and Reconciliation Commission* (2008); Hayner, *Unspeakable Truths: Transitional Justice and the Challenge of Truth Commissions* (2nd ed., 2011).

373 The practice of forgetting rather than remembering was already recorded by Aristotle in ancient Athens and was also laid down in Article II of the Westphalian Treaty of Münster in 1648, in which the parties agreed on perpetual Oblivion, Amnesty or Pardon. O'Shea, *supra* (fn. 372) paragraph 3.

374 Truth and reconciliation commissions may therefore contribute to criminal prosecution by providing relevant information or hinder it if amnesty is granted. The simultaneous or subsequent application of the two methods may indeed lead to difficulties. The prospect

The Truth and Reconciliation Commission chaired by the 1984 Nobel Peace Prize laureate, Archbishop Desmond Tutu, which was established in South Africa in 1995 after the abolition of the apartheid regime in the country, provided a comprehensive application of this method, with its Human Rights Violations Committee, Reparation and Rehabilitation Committee and Amnesty Committee.[375] It achieved some of its objectives, although it could not completely end violence in the country.

After the civil war in Sierra Leone, the two methods were combined with the creation of a Special Court, which indicted only 13 individuals, who previously had held leading positions, and a truth and reconciliation commission, which despite its limited resources also made a useful contribution to national reconciliation.[376]

Both methods have their advantages and shortcomings, so that neither is inherently superior. Truth and reconciliation commissions aim at healing the wounds of the past and open the door to a brighter future for the former adversaries. On the downside, they may not satisfy those victims who insist on justice and punishment of the guilty. Future perpetrators may be encouraged if they expect that they will not be prosecuted. For some people, public proceedings may bring back the horrors of the past and prove another traumatic experience.

In contrast, justice is served by proceedings by courts and tribunals. Punishment of the perpetrators satisfies victims and their relatives and supporters. The probability of standing trial should have a deterrent effect. But this method may also perpetuate and not solve conflicts and further divide the parties.[377]

A choice between the two methods ought to be made on the merits of each specific case. Thus criminal proceedings leading to a sentence should be preferred if the perpetrators are a few individuals who enjoy little popular support. They may never have had many supporters, as in the case of an oppressive

---

of subsequent trials may make perpetrators hesitate to admit to their crimes. Conversely, granting amnesty to those who committed human rights abuses in order to establish the full truth in the framework of a truth commission may be problematic from the point of view of retributive justice.

375 Boraine (ed.), *Dealing with the Past: Truth and Reconciliation in South Africa* (1997); Chapman and van der Merwe, *Truth and Reconciliation in South Africa: Did the TRC Deliver?* (2008).

376 Schabas, 'The Relationship between Truth Commissions and International Courts: The Case of Sierra Leone', 25 *Human Rights Quarterly* (2003) 1035.

377 It may also serve the purpose of incapacitation, i.e., prevent the perpetrators of the most heinous crimes from inflicting further harm for the rest of their lives; however, it may be objected that even the worst criminals should be offered the chance of catharsis, of realizing the wrongfulness of their past acts and changing their behaviour, and reintegration into society.

dictatorial regime; or their previous supporters may have recognized their errors and repented or read the writing on the wall correctly and joined the opposition camp in time. Criminal courts and tribunals are more problematic if a society is split down the middle, even if members of all conflicting parties have to stand trial. Different traditions should also be taken into account, since the desire for justice and punishment is stronger in some, especially Western, civilizations than in others with a preference for reconciliation.

3.8.10 *The Security Council as Legislator*

The Security Council, the central organ of the UN system of collective security, ventured into another legal area not included in the Charter but related to its main task: the maintenance of international peace and security. In order to cope with two of the main threats in the post-Cold War world, terrorism on an unprecedented scale and the proliferation of weapons of mass destruction, in particular their development or acquisition by terrorists, the Council went beyond dealing with specific Article 39 situations.[378] It imposed general rules that were meant to be binding on all states, irrespective of their consent, for an indefinite period of time.

The Council thereby avoided the shortcomings of the traditional norm creation processes in international law through customary law and treaties. The rules stemming from both sources are binding only on states that have freely agreed to them. This prerequisite may prevent adequate responses to an increasing number of global challenges that require action by all members of the international community. 'Free riding', the refusal to contribute to the solution of such problems and the benefits of non-cooperation, not only in the area of security but also, for instance, the protection of the environment, should be excluded.

Moreover, the necessary rules ought to be established as quickly as possible. Yet, the development of international practice, coupled with *opinio juris*, which is required for the emergence of customary rules, may take time, as does the 'long march' to the entry into force of a treaty. The negotiations leading to the adoption of the text may already be time-consuming, even if they merely result in the lowest common denominator of the positions of the parties involved. Still more time may expire until the number of expressions of consent to be

378 Aston, 'Die Bekämpfung abstrakter Gefahren für den Weltfrieden durch legislative Maßnahmen des Sicherheitsrates – Resolution 1373 (2001) im Kontext', *ZaöRVR/HJIL* (2002) 257; Marschik, 'Legislative Powers of the Security Council', in: Macdonald and Johnston (eds.), *Towards World Constitutionalism: Issues in the Legal Ordering of the World Community* (2005) 457.

bound required under the treaty for its entry into force is reached. Reservations may subsequently further erode the substance of the adopted text and prevent uniform action by the parties.

Although numerous treaties designed to curb terrorism[379] and the spread of weapons of mass destruction[380] existed, they obviously failed adequately to cope with these two threats, due to the refusal of important states to become bound by them and because of weak enforcement mechanisms. Therefore the Security Council, acting under Chapter VII of the Charter, unanimously adopted two resolutions designed to ensure rapid, effective and universal action by the international community as a whole.

Resolution 1373 (2001) aimed at depriving international terrorists of their crucial financial resources, in particular by criminalizing the provision or collection of funds and freezing the financial assets or economic resources of terrorists and persons participating in or facilitating the commission of terrorist acts.[381] Moreover, all states were obligated to refrain from supporting terrorists, for example by supplying weapons or providing safe havens to them.[382] The resolution contains no 'sunset clause' but remains in force until revoked by the Security Council. Key provisions of the resolution were taken from the 1999 International Convention for the Suppression of the Financing of Terrorism which at the time had been ratified by only four states and not yet entered into force.

In its Resolution 1540 (2004) the Security Council decided that all states shall refrain from supporting non-state actors that attempt to develop, acquire, manufacture, possess, transport, transfer or use nuclear, chemical or biological weapons or their means of delivery[383] and take effective control measures to prevent the proliferation of such weapons,[384] specifically referring to terrorist purposes.

Whereas Resolution 1373 met with general support, Resolution 1540 was criticized by some, above all non-aligned, states since non-members of the

---

379 Since 1963, 14 conventions, some of them supplemented by protocols, on various aspects of terrorism, but no comprehensive convention, have been concluded on the global level, in addition to regional treaties.

380 Above all, the 1968 Treaty on the Non-Proliferation of Nuclear Weapons, the 1972 Convention on the Prohibition of the Development, Production and Stockpiling of Bacteriological (Biological) and Toxin Weapons and on their Destruction, and the 1993 Convention on the Prohibition of the Development, Production, Stockpiling and Use of Chemical Weapons and on their Destruction.

381 Paragraph 1.

382 Paragraph 2.

383 Paragraph 1.

384 Paragraph 3.

Security Council had not been involved in its adoption but were nevertheless bound by it.

As stated above, both resolutions undermined the principle that no state is bound by a rule of international law without its consent, a consequence of sovereign equality on which the traditional international legal order is built. However, although the Charter does not expressly confer on the Security Council the competence to impose such general norms on member states, the Council's implied powers could arguably provide the legal basis for this activity, as could the above-mentioned *argumentum a maiore ad minus* in light of the far-reaching powers of the Security Council under Chapter VII.[385] In any event, those two resolutions do not seem to have set a trend towards a major legislative role of the Security Council, since they were adopted several years ago and have not been followed by other similar decisions.

3.8.11 *A 'Slap in the Face' of the Security Council: 'Operation Allied Force'*

It was also in the 'Balkan laboratory' that the UN, in particular the Security Council as the main pillar of the international security architecture, suffered a severe blow. In 1999 NATO member states, without authorization by the Council, conducted 'Operation Allied Force' in order to stop 'ethnic cleansing' of the Albanian majority by Serb forces in Kosovo.

The Kosovo crisis which culminated in 1999 was caused by the abolition of the autonomy of the Province by the regime of President Milošević ten years earlier. At first, the Kosovo Albanians led by Ibrahim Rugova, 'the Gandhi of the Balkans', practiced non-violent passive resistance which was ignored by both the authorities in Belgrade and the international community. Thereupon the KLA which resorted to armed violence was formed.[386] The response to its attacks was increased brutality and repression by Serb forces, including atrocities against Albanian civilians, which led to a wave of refugees. Under international pressure, the conflicting parties held negotiations at Rambouillet near Paris and in the French capital itself in February/March 1999. The Albanians finally accepted a peace plan elaborated by the Contact Group[387] which the Serb side continued to reject. The Milošević regime was also not impressed by two ultimata issued by NATO.

At a time when Western powers dominated in an essentially unipolar international system, members of the Atlantic Alliance thereupon launched an air campaign against targets in the FRY, including the capital Belgrade. The obvious

385 See *supra* 57.

386 See *supra* 96.

387 See *supra* fn. 352.

reason for bypassing the Council was the expectation that the two non-Western permanent members, China and Russia, would oppose the use of 'all necessary means' or the taking of 'all necessary measures', also implying recourse to armed force, in order to achieve the goal of the operation. In his short speech on 24 March 1999 in which he announced 'Operation Allied Force', U.S. President Bill Clinton made no reference to its legal basis.

However, the legal aspects of the air strikes gave rise to an extensive debate among both governments and scholars.[388] Those in favour of the lawfulness of 'Operation Allied Force' mainly justified it as 'humanitarian intervention'. This type of intervention denotes the use of armed force in order to protect the inhabitants of a state from major human rights abuses perpetrated against them by the authorities of that state.[389] However, under modern international law 'humanitarian intervention' is complicated by the prohibition of the threat or use of force. Advocates of its lawfulness emphasize that respect for human rights has evolved into one of the main cornerstones of the international legal order since its inclusion in the UN Charter. Moreover, they point out that this principle has acquired the rank of *jus cogens* with *erga omnes* effect.[390]

While this positive development ought to be welcomed, this does not necessarily mean that armed force may be employed in order to enforce human rights in another state. The legal foundation for a third exception to the prohibition in Article 2(4) of the Charter remains to be demonstrated. At the time NATO conducted 'Operation Allied Force' no treaty permitted the resort to force in order to stop grave human rights violations in another state.[391] Nor can

388 See the literature quoted by Neuhold, *supra* (fn. 158) 98. For more recent views on the legal aspects of 'humanitarian intervention' see, for example, Holzgrefe and Keohane (eds.), *Humanitarian Intervention: Ethical, Legal, and Political Dilemmas* (2003); Zemanek, 'Human Rights Protection vs. Non-Intervention: A Perennial Conflict?', in: Chand et alii. (eds.), *Man's Inhumanity to Man: Essays on International Law in Honour of Antonio Cassese* (2003) 953; Breau, *Humanitarian Intervention: The United Nations and Collective Responsibility* (2005); Neuhold, 'Human Rights and the Use of Force', in: Breitenmoser et alii (eds.). *Human Rights, Democracy and the Rule of Law: Liber Amicorum Luzius Wildhaber* (2007) 479 (483); Gray, *supra* (fn. 27) 33.

389 SC Resolutions 1160 (1998), 1199 (1998) and 1203 (1998) were also invoked. They condemned the use of force by Serb forces and Kosovar terrorism, and the last two resolutions qualified the situation in Kosovo as a threat to peace and security in the region. Moreover, while the first two resolutions mentioned the consideration of further action and additional measures, Resolution 1203 (1998) contained no such warning. However, to interpret this as implicit authorization to use force is going too far. Neuhold, *supra* (fn. 158) 95.

390 See *supra* 25.

391 Under Article I of the 1948 Convention on the Prevention and Punishment of the Crime of Genocide, the contracting parties undertake to prevent and to punish genocide.

'humanitarian intervention' be justified under customary international law. Precedents from the 19th and first half of the 20th centuries are not relevant after the entry into force of Article 2(4) of the UN Charter. State practice after 1945 comprises only a few precedents,[392] which, moreover, were not backed by sufficient *opinio juris* but met with widespread protests.[393] Moreover, the states which claimed to pursue humanitarian objectives also relied on other justifications such as the right of self-defence and resolutions of the UN Security Council which they interpreted as implicit authorizations to use force.[394] Even if a general principle of law can be proven by comparing domestic legal systems, it must take a back seat to the provisions of the UN Charter. Furthermore, the critics of the NATO bombing campaign could point out that the prohibition of the threat or use of force is equally one of the few peremptory norms of international law.[395]

As already stated, there is no rule on which of two principles of international law that conflict with each other ought to have primacy.[396] Once again, regardless of whether the protection of human rights or the interdiction of force is chosen, far-reaching negative consequences must be expected. On the one hand, prohibiting the use of force for stopping atrocities in another

---

However, pursuant Article VIII, any party may call upon the competent UN organs to take such action as they consider appropriate for the prevention and suppression of acts of genocide. Moreover, the compromissory clause (see *infra* 187) in Article IX provides for the compulsory jurisdiction of the ICJ in disputes between the parties on the interpretation, application or fulfilment of the Convention, including the responsibility of a state for genocide. Consequently, it is for the UN and not individual or several states to take action, in particular forcible action, against genocide. Dinstein, *supra* (fn. 27) 74. For subsequent developments in Africa see *infra* 107.

392 Notably military action by India in East Pakistan, which helped the secessionist forces to establish the new state of Bangladesh in 1971; by Vietnam in Cambodia against the genocide regime of the Khmer Rouge in 1978; by Tanzania against the human rights abuses by the regime of President Idi Amin in 1979; by the United States and the United Kingdom, and initially also France, in Iraq in order to protect the Kurds in the north and the Shiites in the south against the regime of President Saddam Hussein, as well as by ECOWAS in situations of humanitarian disaster in Liberia and Sierra Leone in the 1990s.

393 In particular by the Non-Aligned Movement that comprises the majority of UN member states. It should also be noted that Article 5(a) of the 1974 definition of aggression adopted by the UN General Assembly in 1974 provides that no consideration of whatever nature, whether political, economic, military or otherwise, may serve as a justification of aggression. See *supra* 64.

394 See *supra* fn. 389.

395 See *supra* 25.

396 See *supra* 5.

state means that they will continue and more victims will suffer. On the other hand, allowing 'humanitarian intervention' by other states is also bound to entail human casualties; moreover, there is the risk that powerful states may abuse it in situations where the conditions for the recourse to force for humanitarian purposes are not fully met. In addition, the ban on force should not be undermined in the age of weapons of mass destruction and other highly effective arms. Consequently, this author, albeit reluctantly, submits that 'Operation Allied Force' was illegal. At the same time, it may be considered legitimate, i.e., morally acceptable, and probably was politically necessary from NATO's point of view in order to prevent a severe loss of face and credibility.

3.8.12 *The 'Responsibility to Protect'*

It was against the backdrop of the debate on the lawfulness of 'Operation Allied Force', as well as the earlier genocide in Rwanda which the international community had failed to prevent and stop, that the Canadian government responded to a request by UN Secretary-General Kofi Annan and established the International Commission on Intervention and State Sovereignty (ICISS).[397] The Commission which was co-chaired by the former Australian Foreign Minister, Gareth Evans, and the Special Adviser to the Secretary-General, Mohamed Sahnoun, submitted its report entitled 'The Responsibility to Protect' in December 2001.[398]

The new concept comprised three dimensions:

a) the responsibility to prevent by addressing both the root causes and direct causes of internal conflict and other man-made crises putting populations at risk;

---

397 Evans and Sahnoun, 'The Responsibility to Protect', 81 *Foreign Affairs,* No. 6 (November/December 2002) 99; de Chazournes and Condorelli, 'De la "responsabilité de protéger", ou d'une nouvelle parure pour une notion déjà bien établie', 110 *RGDIP* (2006) 11; Winkelmann, 'Responsibility to Protect', MPEPIL; Neuhold, *supra* (fn. 388) 488; Stahn, 'Responsibility to Protect: Political Rhetoric or Emerging Legal Norm?', 101 *AJIL* (2007) 99; Brock, 'Von der "humanitären Intervention" zur "Responsibility to Protect". Kriegserfahrung und Völkerrechtsentwicklung seit dem Ende des Ost-West-Konflikts', in: Fischer-Lescano et alii (eds.), *supra* (fn. 180) 19; Evans, *The Responsibility to Protect: Ending Mass Atrocity Crimes Once and For All* (2008); Bellamy, Davies and Glanville, *The Responsibility to Protect* (2009); Peters, 'The Responsibility to Protect: Spelling Out the Hard Legal Consequences for the UN Security Council and its Members', in: Fastenrath et alii (eds.), *supra* (fn. 10) 297; Hilpold, 'From Humanitarian Intervention to Responsibility to Protect: Making Utopia True?', ibid. 462.

398 http://www.dfait-maeci.gc.ca/iciis-ciise/report2-en.asp.

b) the responsibility to react by responding to situations of compelling human need with appropriate measures, which may include coercive measures like sanctions and international prosecution, and in extreme cases military intervention;
c) the responsibility to rebuild by providing, particularly after military intervention, full assistance with recovery, reconstruction and reconciliation, addressing the causes of the harm the intervention was designed to halt or avert.[399]

The ICISS also claimed that while there was not yet a sufficiently strong basis for a new principle of customary law, international practice suggested what the Commission called an emerging guiding principle in favour of military action for human protection purposes. According to this principle, if a state is unable or unwilling to end the harm, or is itself the perpetrator, members of the broad community of states have the responsibility to protect the citizens of other states as well.[400]

The Commission laid down a number of principles for military action in the exercise of what could be called the secondary or subsidiary responsibility to protect. They include a return to the notion of just cause, i.e., the prevention of large-scale loss of life or 'ethnic cleansing'.[401] Moreover, those who use force must be guided by the corresponding right intention to halt or avert human suffering; force must constitute the last resort after all non-military options have been explored; the means used to secure the humanitarian objective in question have to be proportional in terms of scale, duration and intensity; and there must be reasonable prospects of success, so that the consequences of action are not likely to be worse than those of inaction.

Furthermore, according to the ICISS, right authority is needed, i.e., authorization of the use of force by the UN Security Council. If the Council fails to discharge its responsibility to protect, then the alternative of the endorsement of military action by the General Assembly is envisaged. Such support, especially by an overwhelming majority of member states, may increase the legitimacy of military action; however, it should be pointed out that it would not make it lawful. The Commission also referred to the role of regional or sub-regional organizations in the exercise of the responsibility to protect and noted the cases of Liberia and Sierra Leone where the Security Council gave its approval *ex post facto*, pointing to a certain leeway for future action in this respect.[402]

---

399 As formulated in the synopsis of the report.
400 Paragraphs 2.24–2.27.
401 See *supra* 12.
402 See *supra* 72.

Moreover, the ICISS warned against the possible consequences of inaction by the Council.[403] In conscience-shaking situations crying out for action, it would be unrealistic to expect concerned states to rule out other means and forms of action to meet the gravity and urgency of these situations. This would entail the risk of ad hoc coalitions or individual states resorting to force without the right reasons or without respecting the principles and criteria formulated by the Commission.

In 2003 Secretary-General Kofi Annan appointed the High-level Panel on Threats, Challenges and Change chaired by the former Prime Minister of Thailand, Anand Panyarachun.[404] The task of this group of eminent persons, which included former prime ministers and foreign ministers as well as former chief administrative officers of international organizations, was to help the Secretary-General to draft his own report to the meeting of the General Assembly at the level of Heads of State or Government on the occasion of the 60th anniversary of the UN in September 2005. The Panel included the ICISS's concept of the responsibility to protect in its report entitled 'A more secure world: our shared responsibility' submitted in December 2004.[405]

In addition to restating the guidelines for the legitimacy of the use of force proposed by the Commission,[406] it underlined the primary responsibility of each state to protect its citizens from humanitarian catastrophes. However, it also endorsed the emerging norm of a collective international responsibility to protect, exercisable by the Security Council authorizing military intervention as a last resort, in the event of genocide and other large-scale killing, ethnic cleansing or serious violations of international humanitarian law which the sovereign Governments had proved powerless or unwilling to prevent.[407] In contrast, the report did not envisage the recourse to force by states in order to ensure respect for human rights in another state without the backing of the Security Council.

Similarly, according to Kofi Annan's own report entitled 'In larger freedom',[408] which was based on that of the High-level Panel, the secondary protection against genocide, ethnic cleansing and other such crimes against humanity was up to the Security Council, since they were also threats to international peace and security.[409] Moreover, he reiterated the above-mentioned criteria

403 Paragraphs 6.36–6.40.
404 Neuhold, 'High-level Panel on Threats, Challenges and Change', MPEPIL.
405 UN documentA/59/565 (2004).
406 Paragraph 207.
407 Paragraph 203.
408 UN document A/59/2005.
409 Paragraphs 122–126.

which the Council should apply when authorizing or endorsing the resort to military force. The Secretary-General also noted that member states were deeply divided over the right – or perhaps the obligation – to use force protectively to rescue the citizens of other states from genocide or comparable crimes. He pointed out that the task was not to find alternatives to the Security Council as a source of authority but to make it work better.

In its concluding document, the 'World Summit Outcome', the meeting of the General Assembly at the highest level also endorsed the concept of the responsibility to protect.[410] Each state was declared responsible for protecting its population from genocide, war crimes, ethnic cleansing and crimes against humanity. This responsibility entailed the prevention of such crimes, including their incitement. A similar responsibility to use appropriate diplomatic, humanitarian and other means, in accordance with Chapters VI and VIII of the UN Charter, was incumbent on the international community, through the United Nations. Should peaceful means prove inadequate and national authorities manifestly fail to live up to their responsibility to protect, member states declared their readiness to take collective action, in a timely and decisive manner, through the Security Council, in accordance with the Charter, including Chapter VII, on a case-by-case basis and in cooperation with relevant regional organizations as appropriate.[411] This obviously meant non-military enforcement measures under Article 41, as well as authorizing states to use armed force.[412] The issue of whether armed force may be used for humanitarian purposes without authorization by the Security Council was again not explicitly addressed.[413]

However, a treaty basis for military action to this end was added with the conclusion of the Lomé Protocol relating to the Mechanism for Conflict

---

410 UN Document A/60/1, paragraphs 138–140.

411 Reaffirmed by the Security Council in Resolution 1674, paragraph 4, as well as paragraph 2 of the preamble to Resolution 1706 (2006). See also Implementing the responsibility to protect. Report of the Secretary-General, UN Document A/63/677.

412 For a sceptical view on the question whether the Security Council has at least a moral duty to prevent the occurrence of a humanitarian disaster or its permanent members ought to refrain from exercising the veto to this end see Pellet, 'Le recours à la force, le droit et la légitimité. Notes sur les problèmes posés par le principe de l'interdiction du recours à la force armée en cas de carence du Conseil de sécurité', in Fischer-Lescano et alii (eds.), *supra* (fn. 180) 249.

413 For the view, not shared by this author, that the 'World Summit Outcome' permits unilateral military action under certain narrow circumstances if the UN fails to protect populations against genocide and other atrocities, see Bannon, 'The Responsibility to Protect: The U.N. World Summit and the Question of Unilateralism', 115 *Yale Law Journal* (2006) 1157.

Prevention, Management, Resolution, Peace-Keeping and Security of 1999.[414] Under Article 25 of the Protocol, the Mechanism is to be applied, *inter alia*, in case of internal conflict that threatens to trigger a humanitarian disaster or in the event of a serious and massive violation of human rights and the rule of law. The options available to the ECOWAS Mediation and Security Council, for whose decisions a two-thirds majority suffices, include intervention by ECOMOG to which member states agree to make stand-by units available.[415]

The same right was recognized at the continental level a year later in the 2000 Constitutive Act of the African Union (AU) which replaced the Organization of African Unity (OAU). The treaty entered into force in 2001 after ratification by two thirds of the OAU member states in accordance with its Article 28. The long list of guiding principles in Article 4 not only comprises the prohibition of the use or threat of force and non-interference in the internal affairs of another member state. It also includes the right of AU members to request intervention from the organization in order to restore peace and security.[416] What is more, Article 4(h) adds the right of the Union to intervene in a member state pursuant to a decision of the AU Assembly in respect of grave circumstances, namely war crimes, genocide and crimes against humanity. The Assembly as the supreme organ is composed of the heads of state or government of all members. By virtue of Article 7 of the Constitutive Act, it takes its decisions by consensus or, failing which, by a thirds-majority of member states.[417]

Moreover, at its first regular session in Durban on 9 July 2002, the Assembly adopted the Protocol on the Establishment of the Peace and Security Council of the AU. This 15-member body serves as a standing decision-making organ for the prevention, management and resolution of conflicts, a collective security and early-warning arrangement of the Union to facilitate timely and efficient response to conflict and crisis situations in Africa.[418] It is supported, *inter alia*, by an African Standby Force.[419] Its powers include recommending intervention to the Assembly if the above-mentioned grave circumstances exist.[420]

414 Dinstein, *supra* (fn. 27) 122.

415 Articles 9, 27(3) and 28. Similar mechanisms have been agreed on within the Economic Community of Central African States (ECCAS) in 2000 and the South African Development Community (SADC) in 2001. For details see Neuhold, *supra* (fn. 388: 'Human Rights...') fn. 55.

416 Article 4(j).

417 Allain, 'The True Challenge to the United Nations System of the Use of Force: The Failures of Kosovo and Iraq and the Emergence of the African Union', 8 *Max Planck* YBUNL (2004) 237.

418 Article 2(1).

419 Article 13.

420 Article 7(1)(e).

Like the Assembly, the Council may make decisions by a two-thirds majority if consensus cannot be achieved.[421]

The African position on the need for authorization of the employment of armed force for humanitarian reasons by the UN Security Council was subsequently clarified or qualified by the 'Ezulwini Consensus',[422] the Common African Position on the report of Kofi Annan's High-level Panel, which the Executive Council of the AU adopted at Addis Ababa on 7–8 March 2005.[423] The Executive Council also subscribed to the concept of the responsibility to protect; furthermore, it stated 'that the intervention of Regional Organizations[424] should be with the approval of the Security Council; although in certain situations, such approval could be granted "after the fact" in circumstances requiring urgent action'.[425]

Given the importance which the relatively young African states, most of which became independent in the process of decolonization after World War II, attach to their sovereignty, their acceptance of 'humanitarian intervention' on their continent may indeed come as a surprise. However, against the backdrop of bloody civil wars marked by large-scale atrocities against the civilian population in African countries, with the danger of a spill-over to neighbouring states, support for collective action, in some cases even without previous Security Council authorization, in order to stop gross human rights abuses is easier to explain.[426] Yet, the compatibility of this position with Article 53(1) of the UN Charter remains problematic.[427] It should be recalled that under its Article 103 the obligations of the member states under the Charter prevail over their obligations under any other agreement, and that a treaty conflicting with the *jus cogens* principle in Article 2(4) is void.[428]

In any event, the new understanding of sovereignty underlying the responsibility to protect ought to be applauded. It marks a paradigm change from the rights and privileges states enjoy by virtue of their sovereignty to the duties they owe to their populations. The main task of the state is to serve its citizens, not the other way round. Previously, the emphasis was placed on the

421 Article 8 paragraph 13.

422 Named for the valley in Swaziland where the agreement was reached.

423 AU Doc. Ext/EX.CL/2 (VII), B.i.

424 According to the AU, these organizations should be empowered to take action in areas of proximity to conflicts.

425 Moreover, according to the Common African Position, 'It is important to reiterate the obligation of states to protect their citizens, but this should not be used as pretext to undermine the sovereignty, independence and territorial integrity of states'.

426 On military action by ECOWAS without prior authorization by Security Council see *supra* 72.

427 See *supra* 105.

428 Dinstein, *supra* (fn. 27) 123.

obligations of citizens towards their state, including that of sacrificing their lives, even if their leaders resorted to war recklessly, if not illegally. Now the state has, as a result of the internal dimension of the responsibility to protect as initially defined by the ICISS, to justify its existence by respecting the dignity and basic rights of all the people within its borders.[429] This perspective may be understood as entailing the duty to ensure the physical safety and well-being of the population.

3.8.13 *The Exercise by the Security Council of its Secondary Responsibility to Protect in the 2011 Libyan Civil War: Targeted Sanctions and the Authorization to Use Force*

The Security Council lived up to its secondary responsibility to protect[430] and took effective action against human rights abuses perpetrated by the regime of President Muammar Gaddafi against the civilian population after the 'Arab Spring' of 2011 had also spread to Libya.[431] Major unrest began on 15 February 2011, when some 500 demonstrators protested in front of the police headquarters in the eastern Libyan city of Benghazi against the arrest of human rights lawyer Fathi Terbil. Two days later, the opposition proclaimed a 'Day of Rage', with protesters taking to the streets throughout the country. Libyan security forces responded with extreme brutality, firing live ammunition into the crowds. Opponents of the regime took up arms, engulfing the country in a civil war/non-international armed conflict.

For several months, neither the regime, which hired foreign mercenaries mainly from Africa, nor the insurgents, who were supported by a NATO-led military operation which was authorized to use force by the UN Security Council, were able achieve a decisive military victory. The conquest of the capital city of Tripoli in August marked a turning point in favour of the anti-Gaddafi forces. Finally, on 20 October, they also took Sirte, Gaddafi's home town and last stronghold, and killed him. On 23 October, the liberation of all of Libya was proclaimed. On 31 October 2011, NATO ended its military operation.

Firstly, the Security Council adopted targeted sanctions against individual members of the Gaddafi regime in its Resolution 1970 (2011). In the preamble,

429 In addition to external responsibility resulting from sovereignty, that of respecting the sovereignty of other states. Paragraph 1.35 of the ICISS's report.

430 Neuhold, 'Secondary Responsibility to Protect: Enforcement Action by the UN Security Council in the 2011 Libyan Crisis', 16 *Austrian Review of International and European Law* (2011) 137.

431 This movement for democratic reforms had started in Tunisia and Egypt in early 2011 and led to the downfall of Presidents Zine El Abidine Ben Ali and Hosni Mubarak, respectively.

the Council expressly stated the principle, recalling the Libyan authorities' responsibility to protect its[432] population.[433]

The Security Council first decided to refer the situation in the Libya since 15 February 2011 to the Prosecutor of the ICC.[434] In principle, in accordance with the law of international treaties,[435] the jurisdiction of the Court is limited to the parties to its 1998 Rome Statute. However, under Article 13(2) of the Statute, the Security Council, acting under Chapter VII of the Charter, may refer a situation to the Prosecutor of the ICC, thus extending the latter's jurisdiction to non-parties.[436] On 29 June, the Court issued arrest warrants against Gaddafi, one of his sons and his brother-in-law.[437]

Secondly, the Security Council obligated all member states to prevent both the direct and indirect supply, sale or transfer of arms and related materiel and other assistance, to Libya. The Council also banned exports of all arms and related materiel from that state, while all UN members had to prohibit the procurement of such items from Libya by their nationals.[438] It also provided for the enforcement of the ban through inspection and the authorization to seize and dispose of prohibited items.[439]

432 Instead of 'their' – an obvious error.

433 Paragraph 9.

434 Paragraph 4.

435 According to the *pacta tertiis nec prosunt nec nocent* principle. See Articles 34–38 of the 1969 VCLT *supra* 23.

436 See *supra* 95. While it recognized that states not party to the Rome Statute had no obligation under the Statute, the Council also urged all states and concerned regional and other international organizations to cooperate fully with the Court and the Prosecutor. Paragraph 5 of the resolution.

437 Although it may be highly desirable to bring individuals responsible for atrocities to justice, the involvement of the ICC (or an ad hoc criminal tribunal) may prove a double-edged sword. Especially if the Court issues arrest warrants against the political and military leaders of a country, the latter may, in order to postpone their capture and trial, continue armed resistance as long as possible, even if they realize that eventual defeat is inevitable. This decision is bound to lead to additional human casualties, suffering and material damage. Moreover, the referral of a situation to the ICC may further complicate matters for another reason. If neither party to a conflict gains the upper hand, a compromise solution may have to be sought. Such a settlement may provide for power sharing with the persons the Court wants to see arrested, granting them immunity or allowing them to go into exile.

438 Paragraphs 9–14.

439 Since the ban applied to Libya without further specification, its wording apparently also prohibited military assistance to the anti-Gaddafi rebels. As a result, this comprehensive military embargo caused the same dilemma as in the case of the former SFRY. Although desirable in principle with a view to limiting fatalities, injuries and material destruction,

Thirdly, the Resolution included a travel ban, i.e., the prevention of entry or transit through the territories of UN member states, for persons listed its Annex I.[440] This list comprised members of the Gaddafi family, including the 'Revolution Leader' himself, and other high-ranking members of the regime.

Fourthly, the Security Council decided to freeze the funds, other financial assets and economic resources owned or controlled by the six individuals listed in Annex II of the Resolution. They were all members of Gaddafi's family and were also mentioned in Annex I.[441] In addition, member states were obligated to ensure that such funds, assets or resources were not made available to the targeted persons.

Since these non-military sanctions failed to produce the desired result of making the Gaddafi regime cease its abuses of human rights and violations of international humanitarian law, the Security Council, by a vote of 10:0:5, adopted Resolution 1973 on 17 March 2011.[442] It decided three additional enforcement measures that included the use of force and extended the already existing sanctions.[443] The preamble reiterated the reference to the responsibility of the Libyan authorities to protect their population in Resolution 1970.

Firstly, the Security Council demanded an immediate cease-fire and a complete end to violence and all attacks against, and abuses of, civilians.[444] In order to give teeth to this demand, the Council authorized member states, acting nationally or through regional organizations or arrangements, to take all necessary measures to protect civilians and civilian populated areas under

---

it played into the hands of the 'wrong' party. For, like the FRY under Milošević in the early 1990s, the Gaddafi regime that controlled the Libyan armed and security forces initially found itself in a superior military position, since its opponents lacked sufficient, especially modern, military equipment. See *supra* 47. However, the rebels succeeded in obtaining a considerable amount of military hardware, partly from conquered arms caches of the government forces, but in all probability partly also weapons supplied from abroad in violation of the arms embargo.

440 Paragraph 15.

441 Paragraphs 17–23.

442 The five member states that abstained included not only the two permanent members China and Russia, known for their reluctance to authorize the resort to force, but also the emerging powers India and Brazil, which worried that military measures could cause more casualties than protect civilians, and – surprisingly – Germany. The vote of this state could mainly be explained by considerations of domestic politics in view of forthcoming local elections, where support for military action was expected to be unpopular.

443 The Security Council strengthened the arms embargo by authorizing member states to use all measures commensurate to the specific circumstances to carry out inspections to ensure the strict implementation of the embargo. It also added new names to the list of persons targeted by the travel ban and the asset freeze.

444 Paragraph 1 of Resolution 1973.

threat of attack in Libya, while excluding a foreign occupation force of any form on any part of Libyan territory.[445]

The vague wording of this authorization gave rise to controversies. Above all, which measures were necessary for the protection of civilians under threat? Were only attacks on military targets – troops, equipment and buildings – authorized by the Security Council? Arguably, civilians, in particular the political elite giving orders to the army and the security forces and its administrative institutions, also posed at least indirect threats to the population to be protected and were the root cause of the atrocities. Moreover, was the declared objective of Western states, regime change, i.e., ousting the Gaddafi regime, also covered by the resolution?

Secondly, the Security Council imposed a specific ban on all flights in the Libyan airspace equally in order to help protect civilians against whom Gaddafi's forces had also carried out air attacks.[446] The Council similarly authorized all necessary measures to enforce compliance with the flight prohibition.[447]

Thirdly, the Security Council coupled this no-fly zone with a flight ban on Libyan aircraft outside the country, prohibiting all states from permitting any aircraft registered in Libya or owned or operated by Libyan nationals or companies to take off from, land or overfly their territory.[448]

Western states that had been the driving forces behind Resolution 1973 were ready to implement it and use the authorization of the Security Council to resort to armed force. 'Operation Odyssey Dawn' launched by the United States was succeeded by the NATO-led 'Operation Unified Protector' in which some non-members of the Atlantic Alliance, Jordan, Qatar and the United Arab Emirates, as well as Sweden, also participated.[449]

An attempt to assess the contribution of the measures taken by the Security Council to the eventual victory of the rebels in the Libyan civil war leads to the conclusion that the non-military sanctions alone would probably not have brought the Gaddafi regime to its knees within eight months, although the freeze of its assets abroad must have hurt it. In contrast, the use of force authorized by the Security Council undoubtedly had a decisive impact.[450]

---

445 Paragraph 4.

446 Paragraph 6.

447 Paragraph 8.

448 Paragraph 17.

449 The contributions of these Arab states were deemed important to demonstrate that the operations were not conducted only by Western states.

450 As early as 23 March 2011, British Air Vice-Marshal Greg Bagwell stated that the Libyan air force had been almost totally destroyed and no longer existed as a fighting force.

However, subsequent events in Libya confirmed the sobering truth that military victory does not necessary entail peace and stability in a country. On the contrary, Libya soon slid into renewed armed conflict and political chaos, leading it to the brink of becoming a failed state. The national army and Islamist and anti-Islamist militias are fighting each other, and two rival parliaments and governments are contesting the political leadership of the country. These unfortunate developments have also shown that Libya was another rather artificial state previously held together by the dictatorial rule of Gaddafi. It can only be hoped that efforts at finding a peaceful solution to those conflicts, with Libyan oil attracting the interests of other countries, will eventually succeed.

3.8.14 *Another 'Slap in the Face' of the Security Council: 'Operation Iraqi Freedom'*

An ad hoc coalition led by the United States dealt the UN as the principal global security organization another, less blatant, blow when it resorted to military force against the regime of President Saddam Hussein in 2003 without sufficient authorization by the UN Security Council. While also invoking the right of self-defence,[451] the United States claimed that 'Operation Iraqi Freedom' could equally be based on Security Council resolutions.[452] However, the arguments in favour of the lawfulness of the operation are not convincing in the eyes of this author and many of his colleagues.[453]

---

451 As President George W. Bush did in his speech to the UN General Assembly on 12 September 2002 prior to the adoption of Resolution 1441 (2002) by the Security Council. Corten, *supra* (fn. 27) 664.

452 Taft and Buchwald, 'Preemption, Iraq, and International Law', 97 *AJIL* (2003) 557. Mr. Taft was Legal Adviser, Mr. Buchwald Assistant Legal Adviser for Political-Military Affairs at the U.S. Department of State at the time. On the problems of anticipatory self-defence see *infra* 130. The United Kingdom and Australia, states contributing troops to the operation, did not invoke self-defence but only relied on Security Council authorization. Gray, *supra* (fn. 27) 219.

453 Neuhold, 'Law and Force in International Relations – European and American Positions', 64 *ZaöRV/HJIL* (2004) 263 (274); in favour of the legality of 'Operation Iraqi Freedom' in the agora on the issue in the *AJIL*, Yoo, 'International Law and the War in Iraq', 97 *AJIL* (2003) 563; Wedgwood, 'The Fall of Saddam Hussein: Security Council Mandates and Preemptive Self-Defense', ibid. 576; Gardner, 'Neither Bush nor the "Jurisprudes",' ibid. 585; Dinstein, *supra* (fn. 27) 299, 322; against the lawfulness of the operation, Sapiro, 'Iraq, The Shifting Sands of Self-Defense', 97 *AJIL* (2003) 599; Franck, 'What Happens Now? The United Nations After Iraq', ibid. 607; Farer, 'The Prospect of International Law and Order in the Wake of Iraq', ibid. 621; also against the lawfulness of the operation were the European authors Schaller, 'Massenvernichtungswaffen und Präventivkrieg

In particular, the warning in Resolution 1441 (2002) that Iraq 'will face serious consequences as a result of its continued violations of its (disarmament and inspection) obligations' was hardly sufficient to legalize military action. Not only was it up to the Security Council (and not individual member states) to determine the commission of a material breach by Iraq of its obligations, but the serious consequences referred to in the resolution also had to be specified. Most importantly, the Security Council had to authorize the resort to armed force in an additional resolution. Yet, the United States and its coalition partners failed to persuade the necessary majority of the Council members to vote in favour of an authorization. That these states sought another resolution authorizing the use of force also undermines their argument that no further Security Council decision was required.[454]

Secondly, the claim that individual member states were entitled to suspend the ceasefire established by Security Council Resolution 687 (1991), on the grounds of material breaches by Iraq of its obligations to renounce weapons of mass destruction subject to international inspection under this resolution, is not convincing. Only the Security Council had the right to take this step.

Thirdly, the contention that the authorization to use all necessary means in Resolution 678 (1990), which had provided the legal basis for 'Operation Desert Storm' in 1991,[455] had not expired but remained in force after the liberation of Kuwait was equally spurious.[456] The better view is that the above-mentioned

---

– Möglichkeiten der Rechtfertigung einer militärischen Intervention im Irak aus völkerrechtlicher Sicht', 62 *ZaöRVR/HJIL* (2002) 641; Bothe, 'Der Irak-Krieg und das völkerrechtliche Gewaltverbot', 41 *Archiv des Völkerrechts* (2003) 255; Nguyen-Rouault, 'L'intervention armée en Irak et son occupation au regard du droit international', 108 *RGDIP* (2003) 835; Tomuschat, 'Iraq – Demise of International Law?', 78 *Die Friedenswarte* (2003) 141; Weckel, 'L'usage déraisonnable de la force', 107 *RGDIP* (2003) 377; Wolfrum, 'The Attack of September 11, 2001, the Wars against the Taliban and Iraq: Is There a Need to Reconsider International Law on the Recourse to Force and the Rules in Armed Conflict', 7 *Max Planck YBUNL* (2003) 1 (11); Gray, *supra* (fn. 27), 369; Corten, *supra* (fn. 27) 555, 664.

454 Gray, *supra* (fn. 27) 358.

455 See *supra* 68.

456 The United States and the United Kingdom had earlier invoked what they regarded as implied or revived authorizations to use force by the Security Council. According to this view, Resolution 688 (1991), in which the Council demanded that Iraq stop the repression of the Iraqi civilian population, including most recently in Kurdish-populated areas, justified military action for the protection of Kurds and Shiites in the county. Resolution 1205 (1998) in which the Council condemned the failure of the regime of Saddam Hussein to cooperate with international disarmament inspectors in accordance with Resolution 687 (1991) and other relevant resolutions had revived the authorization to use force in

'ceasefire Resolution' 687 terminated it. Moreover, the situation in 2003 differed fundamentally from that in 1990/1991, when the objective was to drive out Iraqi invasion forces from Kuwait; therefore the argument that 'Operation Iraqi Freedom' could be justified as a measure to restore international peace and security in the area 12 years later is questionable.

It should also be noted that a majority of UN member states considered the operation illegal. The opposition not only included the then 116 members of the Non-Aligned Movement and the League of Arab States but also three permanent members of the Security Council: China, France and Russia.[457]

3.8.15 *The Security Council Facing a Double Legitimacy Crisis*

On balance, after promising activities in the 1990s, the record of the system of collective security of the UN has been unsatisfactory in recent years. In particular, the Security Council as the central organ of the system is confronting a twofold legitimacy crisis. Its composition is widely criticized as representative neither of the present distribution of power in international relations nor the contributions of member states to the budget of the organization, development cooperation and peacekeeping and other activities. However, as pointed out above, calls for a reform of the Council have so far fallen on the deaf ears of the 'P 5', whose consent is required for amendments to or a revision of the Charter.[458]

To make matters worse, the Security Council has not been living up to its primary responsibility for the maintenance of international peace and security under the UN Charter. The exercise of its secondary responsibility to protect in the Libyan civil war has not been repeated in similar crisis situations. The Security Council did authorize the use of force and launched peacekeeping operations, in particular in order to protect civilians in danger, for example in Mali,[459] the Central

Resolution 678 (1990) and therefore justified 'Operation Desert Fox', a major bombing campaign to reduce, to 'degrade', as U.S. Secretary of State Madeleine Albright put it, Iraq's ability to manufacture and use weapons of mass destruction. However, these positions received little international support. Gray, *supra* (fn. 27) 348.

457 Corten, *supra* (fn. 27) 665. In subsequent resolutions in which it imposed sanctions on North Korea and Iran the Security Council used language that could not be interpreted as authorizing the use of force without a further decision, in particular by basing the measures on Article 41 of the Charter providing for non-military enforcement action. Gray, *supra* (fn. 27) 367.

458 See *supra* 52.

459 Bannelier and Christakis, 'Under the UN Security Council's Watchful Eyes: Military Intervention by Invitation in the Malian Conflict', 26 *Leiden Journal of International Law* (2013) 855.

African Republic and South Sudan.[460] However, the positive impact of these measures has remained limited. Moreover, the Security Council has failed to take effective steps against the atrocities in Syria[461] and Iraq where human casualties have exceeded those in Libya. The Council has frequently imposed non-military sanctions, but, as in the case of North Korea and Iran, their effects on the behaviour of the target states remain to be seen.[462] Recent tensions between the Western members of the Security Council and Russia, in particular over Ukraine, bode ill for the future of the UN system of collective security.

3.9 Self-Defence

3.9.1 *The Basic Problem and the Evolution of the Right of Self-Defence*[463]

Even in the more developed and centralized domestic legal orders attacked persons must have the right to use force to defend themselves. Otherwise their security would require that they be accompanied all the time by armed agents allowed to use their weapons – an alternative that is neither practicable nor desirable. The right of self-defence as a form of self-help is even more important in the international legal system since, as pointed out above, the effectiveness of the existing system of collective security leaves a great deal to be desired.[464] It may also be recalled that although under 'classical' international law states had an unlimited *jus ad bellum*, they still invoked the right to self-defence, hoping to make the resort to force appear more legitimate in the eyes of their own population and other countries.[465]

---

460 A step worth mentioning in this context was the creation, under SC Resolution 1996 (2011), of an 'Intervention Brigade' within MONUSCO (Mission de l'Organisation des Nations unies pour la stabilisation en République démocratique du Congo). It was tasked with the 'neutralization' of armed groups in the country, in other words the non-defensive use of armed force.

461 The decision of the Security Council in Resolution 2118 (2013), under which the Assad regime had to permit the destruction of its chemical weapons, was a laudable but insufficient step to end armed conflict in the country.

462 See *supra* 77. However, the prediction by President George W. Bush in the context of the 2003 Iraqi crisis that the Security Council would 'fade into history as an ineffective debating society' was somewhat premature. Glennon, 'Why the Security Council Failed', 83 *Foreign Affairs*, No. 3 (May/June 2003) 16 (18).

463 In addition to the literature quoted in fn. 27, see Greenwood, 'Self-Defence', MPEPIL.

464 See *supra* 116.

465 See *supra* 14.

It was U.S. Secretary of State Daniel Webster who defined the 'classical' criteria for the exercise of the right of self-defence on the occasion of the *Caroline* incident of 1837.[466] Rebels against the British rule in Upper Canada were supported by U.S. nationals who used the steamboat *Caroline* from Fort Schlosser on the American bank of the Niagara to transport men, weapons and ammunition across the river to an island occupied by the insurgents. After the British authorities had protested in vain against these supplies, they launched a commando action at night across the Niagara and boarded the vessel. Shots were fired and several U.S. citizens killed or wounded. The *Caroline* was set on fire, cut loose from the dock, towed into the current, and went down the Niagara Falls.

The British government countered U.S. protests by invoking the right of self-defence. Thereupon Webster stated that the exercise of this right required 'a necessity of self-defence, instant, overwhelming, leaving no choice of means, and no moment for deliberation' and to show that the authorities in Canada 'did nothing unreasonable or excessive'.[467] The British special minister Lord Ashburton, who had been appointed to settle the dispute, tried to prove that these criteria had been met, but eventually presented the apologies of his government which the United States accepted.

The League of Nations Covenant, which did not abolish but merely limited the *jus ad bellum*,[468] remained silent on self-defence. In contrast, while this right was not contained in earlier drafts of the constituent treaty of the new World Organization, it was inserted in the UN Charter at the final stage of the negotiations at the San Francisco Conference in 1945. The inclusion of the right was urged by the Latin American states.[469] They wanted to ensure the lawfulness of their emerging system of collective self-defence under the 1945 Act of Chapultepec on Reciprocal Assistance and American Solidarity, which was finalized later in the 1947 Rio Treaty[470] and the 1948 Bogotá Charter of the OAS.[471] The exercise of this right should not depend on an authorization by the Security Council.

The result of this initiative was Article 51 of the UN Charter at the end of Chapter VII, which reads as follows:

---

466 'This episode has attained a mythical authority'. Gray, *supra* (fn. 27) 149; Jennings, 'The *Caroline* and McLeod Cases', *AJIL* 32 (1938) 82.

467 Ibid. 89.

468 See *supra* 18.

469 Kunz, 'Individual and Collective Self-Defense in Article 51 of the Charter of the United Nations', 41 *AJIL* (1947) 872 (872).

470 Article 3.

471 Article 25.

> Nothing in the present Charter shall impair the inherent right of individual or collective self-defence if an armed attack occurs against a Member of the United Nations, until the Security Council has taken measures necessary to maintain international peace and security. Measures taken by Members in the exercise of this right of self-defence shall be immediately reported to the Security Council and shall not in any way affect the authority and responsibility of the Security Council under the present Charter to take at any time such action as it deems necessary in order to maintain or restore international peace and security.

The text of this provision has given rise to a growing number of legal issues over the years since 1945.[472] They have been further complicated by subsequent developments, notably the rise of terrorism and more recently the advent of 'cyber force'.[473] In this context, the '9/11' attacks by members of Al Qaeda on the World Trade Center in New York City and the Pentagon in Washington, D.C., are particularly relevant. The United States responded by launching 'Operation Enduring Freedom' against Al Qaeda terrorists and the Taliban regime in Afghanistan supporting them.[474] The administration of George W. Bush based this operation on the right of self-defence which was recognized and reaffirmed in the preambles to Security Council Resolutions 1368 (2001) and 1373 (2003), as well as by NATO, which invoked the collective self-defence provision in Article 5 of the North Atlantic Treaty for the first time in the history of the alliance, and by the OAS.[475]

Although the Council would probably have authorized the United States to use all necessary means or take all necessary measures, thereby including resort to armed force, in its response to the terrorist acts, and thus, in addition to providing a solid legal basis, enhanced the legitimacy of 'Operation Enduring Freedom' by the support of the international community, the Bush administration preferred to rely on the right of self-defence. As a result, the Security

---

472 See *infra* 121.

473 See *supra* 31.

474 On this operation and ISAF see *supra* 84.

475 The initial overwhelming international support for U.S. military action in self-defence against Al Qaeda and the Taliban in Afghanistan should set aside doubts about the legal value of SC Resolutions 1368 (2001) and 1373 (2001). They were based on the fact that the references to the right of self-defence were inserted in the preambles and not the operative parts of the resolutions and that they mentioned a threat to international peace and security and not an armed attack under Article 51. References to 'Operation Enduring Freedom' in subsequent SC resolutions may also be seen as implicit acceptance of the legality of the operation. Gray, *supra* (fn. 27) 199, 206. For critical comments see Cassese, 'Terrorism is Also Disrupting Some Crucial Legal Categories of International Law', 12 *EJIL* (2001) 993.

Council had even less control over the military operation conducted by the United States than on the basis of an authorization to use force.[476]

Yet, interestingly, the United States did not accept the assistance of its NATO allies which the North Atlantic Council offered by invoking the collective defence commitment under Article 5 of the 1949 North Atlantic Treaty, which is explicitly based on Article 51 of the UN Charter, the day after the '9/11' attacks.[477] The United States obviously did not need and did not want to operate within the framework of the Atlantic Alliance. It did not need the assistance of its NATO allies because they could contribute only little to the high-tech campaign conducted by the United States. It did not want to use the collective defence system of the alliance because it wished to avoid another 'war by committee' similar to 'Operation Allied Force' in 1999. Decisions within NATO are made by consensus and can therefore be blocked by the objection of a single member, even a small state. Hence, the U.S. government decided to launch 'Operation Enduring Freedom'[478] outside the framework of the alliance, with the assistance of several partner countries, including its staunch ally, the United Kingdom, which formed an ad hoc coalition.

That Article 51 requires an armed attack, the existence of which the state claiming to exercise its right of self-defence has to prove, seems to be stating the obvious. However, practice has shown that this apparent truism raises several questions:

1) the definition of arms used for the attack
2) the scope and effects of the attack
3) the identity of the attacker

476 See *infra* 154.

477 However, this was not the first time that the right of self-defence was invoked as justification for forcible action against terrorists and states harbouring them. Israel relied on this right as the legal basis of an air attack on Beirut airport in 1968 in response to a terrorist attack on an Israeli plane at Athens airport, as well as on PLO headquarters in Tunis in 1985. The United States claimed to act in self-defence when it reacted to terrorist attacks against U.S. citizens abroad by using force against Libya in 1986, to an alleged attempt to assassinate former President George H. Bush against Iraq in 1993, and to terrorist attacks on its embassies in Kenya and Tanzania in 1998 for which Al Qaeda was held responsible. The response to the last terrorist acts was U.S. missile strikes against a training camp in Afghanistan and a pharmaceutical plant in Sudan, which was suspected of producing chemical weapons for terrorist activities. Gray, *supra* (fn. 27) 195.

478 The operation was initially called 'Operation Infinite Justice', but this name was changed in order not to offend the Muslim population in Afghanistan for whom only God exercises infinite justice.

4) the requirement of the attacker's intent to inflict harm and
5) the targets of the attack.

These and the other problems dealt with below are not just intellectually challenging and of academic interest. They also have far-reaching political and military implications. What may be at stake is the very existence of states, their population, territorial integrity and independence. The relevance of these questions is further increased by the fact that self-defence is the ground which states invoke most frequently as the legal basis for the recourse to armed force.[479]

3.9.2 *The Definition of Arms Used for an Armed Attack*

Initially, the authors of the Charter envisaged the use by a state of its regular armed forces employing so-called conventional weapons against another state. The two superpowers in particular, but other countries as well, further developed their military technologies and included new arms in their arsenals, in particular weapons of mass destruction. These weapons came to include, in addition to chemical, biological and bacteriological weapons and atomic fission bombs used by the United States against Japan in 1945, even more powerful thermonuclear fusion devices. Mention should also be made in this context of radiological weapons, the so-called dirty bombs, the 'weapons of mass disruption'.[480] Moreover, new delivery systems were invented, in particular highly accurate and rapid ballistic missiles that can also cover intercontinental distances, and cruise missiles that fly at low altitudes and thereby pose problems to defensive radar systems. Conventional weapons were also improved considerably in various respects such as accuracy and range.

However, the decisive criterion for defining the means employed in an armed attack under Article 51 of the UN Charter ought not to be technological, but rather their effect.[481] This became obvious with the '9/11' attacks for which the Al Qaeda terrorists used box cutters and flew hijacked civilian aircraft into

479 Greenwood, *supra* (fn. 463) paragraph 6; Gray, *supra* (fn. 27) 114.

480 Radiological weapons or radiological dispersion devices (RDD) consist of conventional explosives combined with nuclear material. They cause less damage than nuclear weapons but are easier to build and also have highly negative effects like spreading panic and contaminating the area where they explode.

481 As the ICJ stated in its 1996 advisory opinion on the *Legality of the Threat or Use of Nuclear Weapons:* 'These provisions (Articles 2 [4], 51 and 42 – the author) do not refer to specific weapons. They apply to any use of force, regardless of the weapons employed. The Charter neither expressly prohibits, nor permits, the use of any specific weapon, including nuclear weapons'. Paragraph 39. See also Dinstein, *supra* (fn. 27) 88 and 212.

their targets. Two of these planes caused the deaths of close to 3,000 people, the equivalent of a major attack with conventional weapons. The high number of casualties certainly was a major factor behind the general agreement, also within the Security Council, that the United States had the right to resort to self-defence under Article 51 in response to the attack.[482]

An even more complex issue has more recently been raised by the occurrence of cyber-attacks. On the one hand, as pointed out above, the havoc they could wreak may exceed that caused by '9/11' and should therefore entitle the victims to the use of force in self-defence in such cases.[483] On the other, the perpetrators and the states under whose orders or with whose support they act may be even more difficult to identify and track down than in the struggle against terrorists using 'traditional' weapons like bombs or guns.

3.9.3 *The Scope and the Effects of an Armed Attack*

Another thorny problem is due to the fact that, according to the prevalent view, not every use of a weapon amounts to an armed attack under Article 51.[484] On the one hand, a border incident in the course of which a couple of shots are fired clearly falls beyond this threshold, although it constitutes a violation of the prohibition in Article 2(4) of the Charter;[485] the Security Council may still qualify it as an Article 39 situation and take action under Chapter VII. On the other hand, an all-out invasion by the armed forces of a state undoubtedly entitles the invaded one to self-defence. As in similar cases of the 'grey-area phenomenon', there is a spectrum of conceivable scenarios. It is characterized by two 'hardcore clusters' of possible scenarios at both ends of the spectrum, which should not give rise to difficulties when it comes to determining their legality or illegality; but between them, there exists a 'grey zone' of uncertainty where controversies are likely to arise.[486] As pointed out above, in international law the problem is aggravated by the lack of effective institutions that decide whether a concrete case falls into one or the other category. For, although the Security Council should perform this function with regard to the use of force according to the concept of the Charter, in political reality disagreements among its members, especially the 'P 5', prevent it from actually doing so.

---

482 See *supra* 119.

483 See *supra* 32.

484 A similar distinction was included in Article 2 of the 1974 definition of aggression adopted by the UN General Assembly. See *supra* 64.

485 However, some writers are of the opinion that self-defence is also permitted against small-scale attacks. Kunz, *supra* (fn. 469) 878; Brownlie, *supra* (fn. 27) 366; Hargrove, 'The *Nicaragua* Judgment and the Future of the Law of Force and Self-Defense', 81 *AJIL* (1987) 135 (139); for another sceptical view see Dinstein, *supra* (fn. 27) 210.

486 See *supra* 7.

However, the ICJ did formulate two criteria for solving the problem in its judgment in the *Nicaragua* case in 1986: the scale and the effects of the attack.[487] Writers have elaborated on these rather general yardsticks.[488] It has been suggested to define scale in terms of scope, i.e., the numbers of forces involved, and/or intensity, meaning the destructive potential of the weapons used. This means that the firing of a single missile equipped with a powerful nuclear warhead without the mobilization of troops may suffice for an attack under Article 51.

As regards the effects, in other words the negative consequences, of the attack they may consist in human casualties, material damage, or the occupation of territory beyond a certain threshold.[489] These quantifiable indicators should make it easier to reduce the 'grey area' mentioned above.[490] However, the size of the attacked state – measurable by the size of its population, GDP and the extension of its territory – tends to further complicate the problem; it could be solved, however, by focusing on percentages instead of the sheer numbers of these three indicators. But in any event, disagreements are likely to remain on whether or not an armed attack in the sense of Article 51 has been committed in a concrete case.

Another question arises in the event that several attacks, each of which remains below the Article 51 threshold, cumulatively produce the required effects. This is true, in particular, of terrorist acts. According to the 'accumulation-of-events' theory, they would also constitute an armed attack entitling a state to exercise its right of self-defence. The ICJ referred to this problem in its judgments in the 1986 *Nicaragua*,[491] the 2003 *Oil Platforms*[492] and 2005 *Armed Activities in the Democratic Republic of the Congo* (*DRC*)[493] cases.

Moreover, the requirement for a minimum intensity of an armed attack to justify the use of force in self-defence under Article 51 raises the problem of the reaction to an attack below this threshold. Since the ILC's Articles on State Responsibility do not permit countermeasures contrary to *jus cogens*, which includes the prohibition of the threat or use of force,[494] a gap to the detriment of the victims of such minor attacks may result if a non-military response proves

---

487 *Military and Paramilitary Activities in and against Nicaragua* (*Nicaragua v. United States of America*), Merits, paragraph 195.

488 Constantinou, *The Right of Self-Defence and Customary Law and Article 51 of the Charter* (2000) 63; Zemanek, 'Armed Attack', MPEPIL paragraph 10.

489 Dinstein, *supra* (fn. 27) 208.

490 See *supra* 7.

491 *Military and Paramilitary Activities in and against Nicaragua* (*Nicaragua v. United States of America*), Merits, paragraph 231.

492 *Oil Platforms* (*Islamic Republic of Iran v. United States of America*), paragraphs 62, 64.

493 *Armed Activities on the Territory of the Congo* (*Democratic Republic of the Congo v. Uganda*), paragraph 146.

494 See *supra* 25.

inadequate. In this case, should the victim be allowed to resort to force, provided the criteria of necessity and proportionality, which a state acting in self-defence also has to observe, are met?[495]

The IDI adopted a Resolution on self-defence at its 2007 Santiago Session, in which it also stated that an armed attack triggering the right of self-defence must be of a certain degree of intensity.[496] Acts involving the use of force of lesser intensity may give rise to countermeasures in conformity with international law. Moreover, the target state may also take strictly necessary police measures to repel an attack of lesser intensity. The Institute did not, however, add criteria for determining the degree of intensity entitling a state to self-defence, nor did it elaborate on the police measures.

3.9.4 *The Identity of the Attacker*

Thirdly, the identity of those carrying out an armed attack has given rise to increasing difficulties. They were due to the above-mentioned strategic developments after 1945. Given the growing risks a state which used its regular armed forces in uniform incurred, a shift to 'indirect force', i.e., the employment of paramilitary forces and support to armed bands, occurred. It may be recalled that the UN General Assembly took this development into account in Article 3(g) of its 1974 definition of aggression: 'the sending by or on behalf of a State or armed bands, groups, irregulars or mercenaries'.[497] In the *Nicaragua* case, the ICJ, which considered this provision as reflecting customary international law, ruled that these activities would constitute an armed attack under Article 51 of the Charter, provided it could be proven that the state concerned had effective control of the military or paramilitary operations in the course of which they were committed.[498]

495 This question was answered – rightly, in the opinion of this writer – in the affirmative by Judge Simma in his separate opinion in the *Oil Platforms* case: 'Against such smaller-scale use of force, defensive action – by force also "short of" Article 51 – is to be regarded as lawful. In other words, I would suggest a distinction between (full-scale) self-defence within the meaning of Article 51 against an "armed attack" within the meaning of the same Charter provision on the one hand and, on the other, the case of hostile action, for instance against individual ships, below the level of Article 51, justifying proportionate defensive measures on the part of the victim, equally short of the quality and quantity of action in self-defence expressly reserved in the United Nations Charter'. *Oil Platforms (Islamic Republic of Iran v. United States of America)*, separate opinion of Judge Simma, paragraph 12. On the two principles see *infra* 144.

496 Paragraph 5.

497 See *supra* 64.

498 *Military and Paramilitary Activities in and against Nicaragua (Nicaragua v. United States of America)*, Merits, paragraph 115. The ICJ also referred to this provision in the *Armed Activities in the DRC* case. *Armed Activities on the Territory of the Congo (Democratic Republic of the Congo v. Uganda)*, paragraph 146.

The Appeals Chamber of the ICTY disagreed with the ICJ in the *Tadić* case in 1999 and deemed *overall* (italics added) control over a military or paramilitary group by a state sufficient for the purpose of attributing acts of this group to the state. This role was defined as a role in organizing, coordinating or planning the military actions of the military group, in addition to financing, training and equipping or providing operational support for it.[499]

The ICJ referred to the effective control criterion again in the *Armed Activities in the DRC* case in 2005.[500] It reiterated its position and again rejected the general control criterion in its 2007 judgment in the *Genocide* case, at least for the purpose of establishing state responsibility, while the criterion could be used for determining whether an armed conflict was international or not.[501] The ICTY stuck to its position in subsequent rulings.[502]

The '9/11' attacks raised the question whether non-state actors could also launch an armed attack in the sense of Article 51 of the Charter. The ICJ upheld its conservative view in its 1986 judgment in the *Nicaragua* case that an armed attack is limited to acts attributable to a state,[503] in the *Israeli Wall* advisory opinion in 2004[504] and the judgment in the *Armed Activities in the DRC* case in 2005.[505]

However, it may be objected that the attacker is not defined in Article 51 and consequently not necessarily a state. There is no evidence in the *travaux préparatoires* to contradict this conclusion.[506] The general wording thus covers new political and strategic developments. Moreover, Article 2(4) of the Charter imposes the prohibition of the threat or use of force on all Members, i.e., states

499 ICTY Appeals Chamber, *Prosecutor v. Tadić*, paragraphs 131, 137.

500 *Armed Activities on the Territory of the Congo (Democratic Republic of the Congo v. Uganda)*, paragraph 160.

501 *Application of the Convention on the Prevention and Punishment of the Crime of Genocide (Bosnia and Herzegovina v. Serbia and Montenegro)*, paragraphs 396–407. Cassese, 'The *Nicaragua* and *Tadić* Test Revisited in the Light of the ICJ Judgment on Genocide in Bosnia', 18 *EJIL* (2007) 649.

502 Dinstein, *supra* (fn. 27) 222.

503 *Military and Paramilitary Activities in and against Nicaragua (Nicaragua v. United States of America)*, Merits, paragraph 195.

504 *Legal Consequences of the Construction of a Wall in the Occupied Palestinian Territory*, paragraph 139. However, it could be argued that the Court did not say that the right of self-defence *only* existed in the case of an armed attack by one state against another. Gray, *supra* (fn. 27) 135.

505 *Armed Activities on the Territory of the Congo (Democratic Republic of the Congo v. Uganda)*, paragraph 146.

506 Scholz, *Staatliches Selbstverteidigungsrecht gegen terroristische Gewalt* (2006) 101; Zemanek, *supra* (fn. 488) paragraph 16.

both as perpetrators and victims, whereas Article 51 remains silent on the actor launching an armed attack, a difference that ought not to be dismissed as irrelevant. In addition, the position of the ICJ conflicts with that of the Security Council, in particular its above-mentioned Resolutions 1368 (2001) and 1373 (2001), which were also confirmed by subsequent state practice.[507]

The use of force against the Al Qaeda terrorists in Afghanistan gave rise to another legal issue: since terrorists do not have a territory of their own but operate from that of a state, may self-defence also be directed against that state? The answer is clearly in the affirmative if the persons concerned act as organs of the state in question. Otherwise the extent of the control exercised by the authorities of the state over the terrorists is relevant. If the above-mentioned criteria formulated by the ICJ and the UN General Assembly in its 1974 definition of aggression are met, military action may also be taken against the state sheltering[508] the terrorists.

In addition, states are required to comply with their due diligence or the duty of vigilance obligations already established by the arbitral tribunal in the *Alabama* case.[509] Similarly, the ICJ emphasized in the 1949 *Corfu Channel* case that it is, 'every State's obligation not to allow knowingly its territory to be used for acts contrary to the rights of other States'.[510]

With regard to 'Operation Enduring Freedom', close ties between Al Qaeda and the Taliban regime in Afghanistan undoubtedly existed. The terrorists did not act as organs of that state, but the latter was 'substantially involved' in the activities of the former. Moreover, the Security Council had previously, in its Resolutions 1214 (1998), 1267 (1999) and 1333 (2000), called on the Taliban to stop providing sanctuary and training to international terrorists and to extradite the Al Qaeda leader Osama bin Laden. The recognition of the right of self-defence in the preambles to Resolutions 1368 (2001) and 1373 (2001) in anticipation of U.S. military action against Al Qaeda in Afghanistan also corroborates the lawfulness of the use of force by the attacked state in this particular case.

---

507 Bruha and Tams, 'Self-Defence Against Terrorist Attacks. Considerations in the Light of the ICJ's "Israeli Wall" Opinion', in: Dicke et alii (eds.), *Weltinnenrecht: Liber Amicorum Jost Delbrück* (2005) 85 (95); Zemanek, *supra* (fn. 488) paragraph 16. According to paragraph 10 of the above-mentioned 2007 Resolution of the IDI, in the event of an armed attack against a state by non-state actors, Article 51 of the Charter as supplemented by customary international law applies as a matter of principle.

508 Or 'harbouring', the term used by the United States and the United Kingdom. Gray, *supra* (fn. 27) 200.

509 See *infra* 189.

510 *Corfu Channel case* (*United Kingdom v. Albania*), Merits, 22.

For military action against non-state actors within another state to qualify as lawful self-defence several prerequisites have to be met. The state from whose territory terrorist groups or armed bands, which have already attacked the state resorting to defensive force and in all probability will strike again in the future, launch their operations must be unwilling or unable to take effective action against them.[511] Only then is the victim of the attack(s) committed by the non-state actors entitled to conduct military operations within the borders of that state.[512] Moreover, such action must be in accordance with the principles of necessity and proportionality, i.e., be a means of last resort and remain proportionate to the initial attack(s) by the terrorists.[513] It may also be recalled that the *Caroline* incident, the precedent in which the prerequisites for self-defence received their 'classical' formulation, involved military measures taken by one state against non-state actors operating from across the border with another state.[514]

3.9.5 *Is an Intention to Cause Harm Required?*

The ICJ added a problematic requirement in its judgment in the *Oil Platforms* case, the 'specific intent of harming'.[515] This psychological criterion, which makes

511 In principle, the unwillingness or inability of a state to stop attacks by non-state actors from its territory ought to be established by a futile request for its consent to the use of force against them by the victim state. See also the self-defence principles proposed by Bethlehem, 'Self-Defense Against an Imminent or Actual Armed Attack by Nonstate Actors', 106 *AJIL* (2012) 769, and the ensuing debate in the *AJIL*.

512 In paragraph 10 of its 2007 Santiago Resolution, the IDI stated the obligation of the state from which an armed attack by non-state actors is launched to cooperate with the target state. See *supra* 124.

513 Greenwood, *supra* (fn. 463) paragraph 18. Dinstein calls this variant of self-defence 'extra-territorial law enforcement'. Dinstein, *supra* (fn. 27) 268.

514 See *supra* 118. For more recent examples see Lietzau, 'Old Law, New Wars: Jus ad Bellum in an Age of Terrorism', 8 *Max Planck YBUNL* (2004) 383 (418); Dinstein, *supra* (fn. 27) 272. A case that made headlines was the killing of the Al Qaeda leader, Osama bin Laden, by U.S. Navy Seals, without informing the Pakistani government, in Pakistan in 2011. The United States apparently decided to act without the consent of Pakistan out of concern that the response to the request would be negative or the plan to capture or kill Osama bin Laden would be leaked so that he would be able to escape.

515 *Oil Platforms (Islamic Republic of Iran v. United States of America)*, paragraph 64. However, Gray points out that it is not clear whether the brief statements of the ICJ on intent were meant as a general requirement for all armed attacks or limited to the particular and unusual case of the involvement of the United States in a conflict between two other states. Gray, *supra* (fn. 27) 146.

sense in domestic criminal law, is hardly practicable in international law.[516] One key question concerns the individuals who are required to have this intention: only the persons at the highest political level who make the decision to launch an armed attack or also all those involved in carrying out the decision? Moreover, governments usually do not state their aggressive plans but prefer to invoke other grounds that are more acceptable to international and their own domestic public opinion and to other states. The 'intent of harming' could therefore be ascertained only in exceptional cases, after the attacking state is defeated and an enquiry into still existing confidential documents produces sufficient evidence. If this prerequisite is retained at all, the burden of proof should be placed on the state that commits an armed attack in accordance with Article 51; it would have to prove that it acted without this intent.

3.9.6 *The Targets of an Armed Attack Permitting Self-Defence*

Sixthly, the targets against which an armed attack entitling a state to self-defence is directed remained to be defined. This is another issue area with two uncontroversial clusters of legality and illegality and a legal 'grey area' in between. On the one hand, that a state may resort to force if its territorial integrity and the population within its borders is assaulted is universally accepted. The same is true in the event of an attack on its armed forces, which may defend themselves and receive military assistance if necessary even outside the territory of their state.

The use of military means to protect public civilian targets like embassy buildings abroad, i.e., on the territory of another state that may demand respect for its territorial integrity, is more problematic.[517]

A related issue again revolves around the scope of the attack, the above-mentioned scale and effect criterion formulated by the ICJ.[518] Is an attack on a single ship or aircraft sufficient to fall under Article 51? The question was answered in the negative with regard to aggression in the definition adopted

516 Zemanek, *supra* (fn. 488) paragraph. 9. According to Dinstein, an armed attack justifying the use of force must be intentional and not be due to an accident or mistake, for which the state concerned may incur responsibility but without bearing the blame for an armed attack. However, a state victim of an accident or mistake can hardly be supposed to sit idly by. Dinstein, *supra* (fn. 27) 231.

517 In its judgment of 1979 in the *Diplomatic and Consular Staff in Tehran* case, the ICJ used the term 'armed attack' for the overrunning of the premises of the U.S. Embassy and seizure of the diplomatic and consular staff as hostages by Iranian militants. *United States Diplomatic and Consular Staff in Tehran (United States of America v. Islamic Republic of Iran)*, paragraphs 57 and 91.

518 See *supra* 123.

by the UN General Assembly in 1974. Article 3(d) of the definition refers to an attack by the armed forces of a state on marine or air *fleets* (italics added) without indicating, however, the number of vessels or planes required for a 'fleet'.[519]

The lawfulness of the use of force by a state in order to save its threatened nationals abroad is even more controversial.[520] No legal problem arises if military action is taken by a state to rescue its nationals with the consent of the state on whose territory they are held hostage. The situation becomes more complicated if the territorial state fails to act against the hostage takers. One reason for inaction may be fear for the lives of those foreigners by trying to free them by force of arms against heavily armed terrorists who threaten to kill them if such an attempt is made. Another may be that the government concerned sympathizes with or even aids and abets the terrorists. Yet another scenario is that of the inability of whatever government there is in place in a failed state to take effective action. It is above all in the latter two situations that a state may feel that a military operation to save its nationals is necessary and justified.

The advocates of the lawfulness of this variant of 'humanitarian intervention' with a view to rescuing a state's own citizens argue that the latter are the most important constitutive element of a state, the equivalent of an individual's body. By protecting them a state protects its highest value, higher than its territorial integrity, namely its own 'life'.[521] Moreover, a rule of customary international law is invoked, since states frequently resorted to armed force for this purpose in the past.[522]

519 See *supra* 64, and Dinstein, *supra* (fn. 27) 217. However, in the *Oil Platforms* case, the United States claimed that the attack on a single vessel, the *Sea Isle City*, allowed it to exercise the right of self-defence against Iran which it accused of the attack. The ICJ rejected the contention, but not because it disagreed with the argument concerning the basis for self-defence but because the United States could not prove its contention that Iran had committed the missile attack on the ship. *Oil Platforms (Islamic Republic of Iran v. United States of America)*, paragraph 61.

520 Ronzitti, *Rescuing Nationals Abroad through Military Coercion and Intervention on Grounds of Humanity* (1985); Neuhold, *supra* (fn. 7) 143.

521 In favour of the legality of use of force for this purpose are Waldock, *supra* (fn. 27) 466, 503; Bowett, *supra* (fn. 27) 87; Franzke, 'Die militärische Gewalt zur Abwehr von Angriffen auf Staatsangehörige im Ausland – insbesondere ihre Zulässigkeit nach der Satzung der Vereinten Nationen', 16 *Österreichische Zeitschrift für öffentliches Recht* (1966) 128; Dinstein adds the condition that the attack is mounted primarily because of the nationality of the persons concerned. Dinstein, *supra* (fn. 27) 218, 255.

522 For instance, according to Offutt the United States used force more than 70 times from 1913 to 1927 in order to protect its nationals in Latin America. Offutt, *The Protection of Citizens Abroad by the Armed Forces of the United States of America* (1928).

Those who hold the opposite view point out that the existence of the state concerned is not at stake in such a situation.[523] Therefore the analogy with the threat to the life of an individual human being is misleading. Moreover, a customary law basis for the alleged right is contested. For, after the entry into force of the prohibition in Article 2(4) of the UN Charter, which turned a new page in the development of international law, only relatively few precedents can be quoted: notably, military action by Belgium in the Congo in 1960; by the United States in the Dominican Republic in 1965, in the hostage crisis in Iran in 1980, in Grenada in 1983 and Panama in 1989; by Israel in Uganda in 1976; by the United Kingdom in Sierra Leone in 2000; and more recently by Russia in the secessionist Georgian territories of South Ossetia and Abkhazia in 2008, as well as in Ukraine in 2014. However, most importantly, these operations met with widespread protests so that the necessary general *opinio juris* cannot be proven. Furthermore, a teleological interpretation of the UN Charter, whose principal object and purpose is the limitation of the use of force, leads to the same conclusion.

Still more problematic is the other type of 'humanitarian intervention', which is undertaken for the protection not of a state's nationals but of foreigners. Since states using force for this purpose are not defending themselves they can hardly justify their action under Article 51. Rather, a separate legal basis has to be established.[524]

The use of military means in order to defend a state's economic interests, the equivalent of an individual's property, has also to be placed at this other end of the above-mentioned cluster of targets which may not be protected by force of arms in the exercise of the right of self-defence. The operation by France and the United Kingdom against Egypt after the nationalization of the Suez Canal by the latter country under President Gamal Abdel Nasser in 1956 was a case in point. The effort of those two states to justify the occupation of the Canal area as self-defence was widely criticized because of the absence of an armed attack. However, if a state is deliberately cut off from vital resources, like food or energy, to such an extent that the survival of its population is threatened, an exception to the above rule might not be completely ruled out.

3.9.7 *Anticipatory Self-Defence*

After dealing with the problems posed by the 'armed attack' required under Article 51, the next word in this provision, 'occurs', has raised another complex

523 Wright, 'United States Intervention in Lebanon', 53 *AJIL* (1959) 112; Brownlie, *supra* (fn. 27) 255, 289; Bothe, 'Das Gewaltverbot im allgemeinen', in: Schaumann (ed.), *supra* (fn. 233) 23; Fawcett, 'Intervention in International Law: A Study of Some Recent Cases', 137 *RCADI* (1972) 419 (535).

524 On the difficulties of developing such a legal basis see *supra* 102.

issue: the legality of self-defence before the actual occurrence of an armed attack. The search for an answer in the UN Charter provides a particularly interesting example of the difficulties of treaty interpretation, because the entire 'toolbox' of the applicable rules and methods can and should be used. The relevant legal rules are laid down, first and foremost, in Articles 31–33 of the VCLT.[525] Several arguments may be advanced in favour as well as against the lawfulness of anticipatory self-defence, with leading experts on the law governing the use of force in international relations reaching opposite conclusions.[526] Both sides argue rationally, but weigh the same arguments differently, also for 'meta-legal' reasons which often are not stated clearly.

525 Although according to its Article 4, the Convention applies only to treaties concluded by states after its entry into force with regard to such states, its provisions on interpretation are generally regarded as codifying customary international law existing in 1969. This view has been confirmed by the ICJ on several occasions, by other international courts and arbitral tribunals, as well as national courts. Articles 31–33 are therefore also applicable to the UN Charter which became binding on its parties on 24 October 1945. Torrres-Bernárdez, 'Interpretation of Treaties by the International Court of Justice following the Adoption of the 1969 Vienna Convention on the Law of Treaties', in: Hafner et alii (eds.), *Liber Amicorum: Professor Ignaz Seidl-Hohenveldern in Honour of his 80th Birthday* (1998) 722; Gardiner, *Treaty Interpretation* (2008) 12; Villiger, *Commentary on the 1969 Vienna Convention on the Law of Treaties* (2009) 421.

526 Among those supporting the lawfulness of anticipatory self-defence *de lege lata* see Waldock, *supra* (fn. 27) 497; Bowett, *Self-Defence in International Law* (1958) 191; Stone, *supra* (fn. 233) 94; Higgins, 'The Legal Limits to the Use of Force by Sovereign States: United Nations Practice', 37 *BYIL* (1961) 269 (299); Schwebel, 'Aggression, Intervention and Self-Defence in Modern International Law', 136 *RCADI* (1972) 419 (463); Franck, *supra* (fn. 225) 50, 97; Sofaer, 'On the Necessity of Pre-emption', 14 *EJIL* (2003) 209; Randelzhofer and Nolte, 'Article 51', in: Simma et alii (eds.), *supra* (fn. 82) 1397 (1423); for the opposite view see Kunz, *supra* (fn. 469) 878; Jessup, *A Modern Law of Nations* (1948) 166; Kelsen, 'Collective Security and Collective Self-Defense Under the Charter of the United Nations', 42 *AJIL* (1948) 783 (791); Tucker, 'The Interpretation of War under Present International Law', 4 *ILQ* (1951) 11 (29); Wehberg, *supra* (fn. 27) 81; Jiménez de Aréchaga, *supra* (fn. 225) 405; Brownlie, 'The Use of Force in Self-Defence', 37 *BYIL* (1961) 183 (266); Brownlie, *supra* (fn. 27) 278; Skubiszewski, 'Use of Force by States. Collective Security. Law of War and Neutrality', in: Sørensen (ed.), *Manual of Public International Law* (1968) 739 (767); Lamberti Zanardi, *La legittima difesa nel diritto internazionale* (1972) 245; Constantinou, *supra* (fn. 488) 111; Cassese, 'Article 51' in: Cot, Pellet et Forteau (eds.), *supra* (fn. 82) 1329 (1335); Corten, *supra* (fn. 27) 165; O'Connell, 'Defending the Law against Preemptive Force', in: Fischer-Lescano et alii (eds.), *supra* (fn. 180) 237; Neuhold, 'Anticipatory Self-Defence : Legal Analysis *versus* Strategic Realities', 14 *Austrian Review of International and European Law* (2009) 61; Dinstein, *supra* (fn. 27) 196.

According to Article 31(1) VCLT, 'A treaty shall be interpreted in good faith in accordance with the ordinary meaning to be given to the terms of the treaty in their context and in the light of its object and purpose.'

The proponents of the legality of anticipatory self-defence can invoke a number of arguments that carry considerable weight.

1) Firstly, the right of self-defence is qualified as 'inherent' in Article 51. This adjective can be understood as a reference to an element of state sovereignty under customary law as it existed at the time of the drafting of the Charter. It may be recalled that the 'classical' definition of the right of self-defence by U.S. Secretary of State Webster on the occasion of the *Caroline* incident in 1837 required an 'instant' necessity, i.e., an imminent but not yet launched attack.[527] Subsequent state practice in the 19th and 20th centuries, including the jurisprudence of the Nuremberg and Tokyo International Military Tribunals, confirmed this view. The third primary source of international law listed in Article 38 of the ICJ Statute, a general principle of law, points in the same direction. Even without a comprehensive analysis it may be assumed that self-defence is also permitted against an imminent attack under the criminal law of the main domestic legal systems of the world.
2) Secondly, as mentioned above, the preparatory work of the Charter indicates that Article 51 was inserted in order to ensure the lawfulness of the collective defence system of the American states, and not to change existing customary law.[528]
3) Thirdly, the advocates of the legality of anticipatory self-defence advance a semantic argument: in accordance with Article 51, self-defence is permitted 'if', and not 'if, and only if', an armed attack occurs. Therefore, states may also exercise this right in other situations, i.e., before an armed attack is actually mounted.
4) Fourthly, according to Article 2 of the 1974 definition of aggression adopted by the UN General Assembly, the first use of armed force by a state in contravention of the Charter shall (only) constitute *prima facie* evidence of an act of aggression.[529] Consequently, the actual aggressor in a given conflict is not necessarily the party that fires or apparently fires the first shot.[530]

527 See *supra* 118.
528 Ibid.
529 See *supra* 64.
530 See *supra* 46.

5) Fifthly, according to the *in dubio mitius* principle, in case of doubt the provisions of a treaty should be construed in favour of state sovereignty. With regard to the issue of anticipatory self-defence, the prohibition of the use of force ought therefore to be interpreted restrictively; consequently, a state may also use military means if it has convincing grounds to believe that an opponent is about to attack it before the forces of the latter cross its borders.

Yet, the supporters of the illegality of anticipatory self-defence are able to rely on a number of counter-arguments that equally merit serious consideration.

1) Firstly, the point of departure of treaty interpretation mentioned in Article 31(1) of the VCLT is the ordinary meaning of the words agreed on by the negotiators. The ordinary meaning of the word 'occurs' is clear: the armed attack must already be underway. The equally authentic French,[531] Chinese and Russian texts[532] lead to the same conclusion. Only the Spanish version is more ambiguous, since it contains no equivalent of 'occurs'.[533] However, according to Article 33(3) of the VCLT, the terms of the treaty are presumed to have the same meaning in each authentic text.
2) Secondly, Article 31(1) requires that a treaty be interpreted in the light of its object and purpose. Article 1(1) of the Charter sets out as the UN's main purpose the maintenance and restoration of international peace and security. A teleological approach to the relevant provisions therefore calls for a restrictive interpretation of self-defence, prohibiting anticipatory military action. This limitation contributes to the preservation of international peace defined as the absence of armed violence.[534]
3) Thirdly, the terms of a treaty must also be construed in their context which, according to Article 31(2) of the VCLT, first and foremost includes the text of the treaty itself. It should be recalled that Article 2(4) of the UN Charter outlaws not only the use but also the threat of force. Moreover, in addition to a breach of the peace and act of aggression, a threat to the peace is also mentioned in Article 39 of the Charter as one of the three

531 '*...dans le cas où un Membre des Nations Unies est l'objet d'une agression armée,...*'.

532 I am indebted to Susanne Weigelin-Schwiedrzik and Gerhard Hafner for information on the Chinese and Russian texts.

533 '*...,en caso de ataque armado contra un Miembro de las Naciones Unidas,...*'

534 Unless it encourages an aggressor to benefit from the strategic advantages of choosing the optimal time and area for an attack against which the victim must not take anticipatory military action. See *infra* 136.

situations that ought to lead to action by the Security Council within the framework of the system of collective security under Chapter VII.[535] In contrast, the reference to the occurrence, but not the threat, of an armed attack in Article 51 as the prerequisite for the exercise of the right of self-defence can hardly be due to an accident or careless drafting.

4) Fourthly, a principle of logic calls for the restrictive interpretation of an exception to a rule. Since Article 51 constitutes the exception to the rule laid down in Article 2(4) of the Charter, the broader construction of the right of self-defence including the resort to force against a merely expected but not actual armed attack ought to be rejected.[536]

5) Fifthly, practice following the entry into force of a treaty is another relevant element of its interpretation according to Article 31(3)(a) and (b) of the VCLT. In this regard, relevant international practice, in particular within the UN, supports the view that anticipatory self-defence is regarded as unlawful. For instance, the Security Council and the General Assembly strongly condemned the Israeli air raid on the Iraqi nuclear reactor *Osirak* in 1981.[537] Moreover, most states, especially the small and weak members of the international community, reject the lawfulness of anticipatory self-defence. In particular, the Non-Aligned Movement which comprises 120 members has repeatedly done so.[538]

6) Sixthly, treaties on collective self-defence, like the 1947 Rio Treaty (Article 3), the 1948 Brussels Treaty (Article V), the 1949 Washington North Atlantic Treaty (Article 5) and the 2007 Lisbon Treaty on European Union (Article 42[7]), define the *casus foederis* as an armed attack and not an imminent armed attack. The conclusion to be drawn is that the contracting parties did not include the obligation to provide mutual assistance if one or

---

535 See *supra* 45.

536 Another rule of logic that may be invoked is that of *expressio unius est exclusio alterius:* the insertion of the right of self-defence against an armed attack that has already commenced implies the exclusion and thereby the illegality of attacks that have not. Moreover, given the risks of abuse, anticipatory self-defence would have required even stricter explicit regulation than the defensive use of force against actually 'occurring' attacks. Dinstein, *supra* (fn. 27) 198.

537 SC Resolution 487 (1981); General Assembly Resolution 36/27, adopted by a vote of 109:2:34. D'Amato, 'Israel's Air Strike upon the Iraqi Nuclear Reactor', 77 *AJIL* (1983) 584.

538 For a survey of the positions taken by member states of the UN, including those belonging to the Non-Aligned Movement, also in recent debates on the issue, in particular in the context of the 2005 high-level meeting of the General Assembly leading to the 'World Summit Outcome', which shows that a small minority pleaded in favour of the legality of anticipatory self-defence, see Corten, *supra* (fn. 27) 644.

> some of them merely felt threatened by an attack. Had they considered anticipatory self-defence lawful they would have inserted an express provision to this effect in their treaties.

On balance, this writer finds the above 'technical' legal arguments against the lawfulness of anticipatory self-defence more persuasive, for the following reasons.

The ordinary meaning of the English word 'occurs' in Article 51 is clear: the armed attack must have started and already be going on. The other authentic texts of the Charter can also be understood in the sense that self-defence is permitted only against an attack that has already been launched.

The teleological interpretation of Article 51 in the light of the object and purpose of the Charter equally carries considerable weight, especially against the backdrop of the destructive power of modern weapons. The objective of the international community as a whole should in principle prevail over the self-preservation of individual states that feel threatened.

In addition, the context of the treaty and subsequent practice are important elements of treaty interpretation which must be duly taken into account.

The contradiction between the actual occurrence of an armed attack required by the wording of Article 51 and the 'inherent' right equally mentioned in this provision can be solved in favour of the former by applying the *lex posterior* and *lex specialis* principles. As a result, the 1945 treaty law of the Charter has primacy over the earlier 'inherent' right under customary law[539] and over the general principle of law permitting anticipatory self-defence.[540]

As regards the *travaux préparatoires* of the Charter, it ought to be borne in mind that the VCLT relegates them to a secondary role. According to Article 32 of the Convention,

---

539 Dinstein argues that a customary right of self-defence could only evolve after the 1928 Briand-Kellogg Pact that interdicted war between states. However, no relevant practice of a state launching a war of anticipatory self-defence can be detected between the entry into force of the Pact of Paris and the UN Charter. The British action against the *Caroline* was not anticipatory but directed against ongoing attacks that had started earlier, since the vessel had already been regularly used for transporting men and materials across the Niagara River. Moreover, at a time when states had the unlimited *jus ad bellum* the dispute concerned the use of force 'short of war'; the issue was whether the United Kingdom could use forcible measures of self-defence within U.S. territory without plunging the two states into war. Dinstein, *supra* (fn. 27) 197.

540 Thouvenin, 'Article 103', in: Cot, Pellet and Forteau (eds.), *supra* (fn. 82) 2133 (2140). Paulus and Leiß, 'Article 103', in: Simma et alii (eds.), *supra* (fn. 82) 2110 (2132).

> 'Recourse may be had to supplementary means of interpretation, including the preparatory work...to determine the meaning when the interpretation according to Article 31:
> (a) leaves the meaning ambiguous or obscure; or
> (b) leads to a result which is manifestly absurd or unreasonable'.[541]

These prerequisites are not met with respect to Article 51 of the UN Charter, because the interpretation of this provision in accordance with the rules laid down in Article 31 of the VCLT produces a clear result that appears to be reasonable, at least at first sight.

The continued validity of the traditional presumption against restrictions on state sovereignty has been increasingly called into question in an age of growing international interdependence and the need for cooperation across state borders, coupled with the 'devaluation' of the state and the attributes of sovereignty.[542]

If the above-mentioned logical and semantic arguments are weighed against each other, preference ought to be given to the rule that exceptions to a rule have to be construed restrictively.

However, if the strategic and military aspects of the issue are included in the debate a different picture emerges. The prohibition of anticipatory self-defence may result in two important, potentially crucial benefits for the aggressor. He can choose the optimal time and the best location for his attack. These two advantages may further tilt the military balance against the victim[543] which is forced to remain a 'sitting duck' and seal its defeat.

In this non-legal context it is the arguments against permitting anticipatory self-defence that are hardly convincing. Those who support a narrow definition of self-defence point out that a state which feels threatened does not have to sit idly by but has more than one option to improve its security: to try to solve the dispute with its adversary by using the methods and mechanisms for the peaceful settlement of international disputes; to prepare and strengthen its own defence; to ask for assistance by the UN and/or regional security organizations of which it is a member; or to request ad hoc help from other states.

---

541 For a second look at Article 32 of the VCLT see *infra* 143.

542 This development is reflected, for example, in the concept of the responsibility to protect. See *supra* 104.

543 As a rule, governments tend to act rationally and therefore opt for an armed attack against another state only if they expect victory because of sufficient military superiority. That they may miscalculate the military balance between their own armed forces and those of the victim of their attack is another matter.

However, as will be pointed out in more detail below, the various means for peacefully resolving international conflicts, from negotiations, good offices and enquiry to mediation and conciliation to arbitration and adjudication, require the consent of all conflicting parties.[544] Different scenarios are possible in this context. The parties may previously have employed one or more of these means without a positive outcome, so that one of them considers the recourse to force in order to achieve its objectives. One party may have proposed to use such pacific procedures but the other rejected the proposal for whatever reasons. Even if an arbitral tribunal or an international court whose jurisdiction the states concerned accepted has handed down an award or judgment, the party which is not satisfied with this decision may nonetheless resort to force. The fact that it would thereby, in addition to violating the prohibition of the threat or use of force, commit another breach of international law by ignoring a legally binding arbitral award or court judgment will hardly dissuade it from mobilizing its armed forces if it expects to prevail over its adversary because of its military superiority.

Moreover, even if the state concerned tries to prepare for the expected attack as best it can, its efforts may not offset the two above-mentioned advantages from which the aggressor benefits. Admittedly, even an anticipatory strike may not avert defeat if the adversary is clearly stronger militarily. Yet, it might tip the scales in favour of the state launching the attack in self-defence if the military balance between the two parties is roughly equal.

So far as help by international organizations is concerned, reliance on the UN does not offer a sufficient security guarantee for the reasons discussed above.[545] Only a state belonging to a military alliance may expect effective assistance from its allies, although it cannot be absolutely sure that the latter will always live up to their collective defence commitments.

A national security doctrine based on eventual ad hoc requests for help by other states in case of future need, especially in a volatile international environment where the use of force must be expected, seems risky, if not irresponsible. Such appeals will more often than not fall on deaf ears because of the costs such assistance is likely to entail without any benefit for the countries offering it. The chances of a state calling for help may be somewhat better if it has close ties to those asked for support or if the latter expect to become the next victims of the presumed aggressor.[546]

---

544 See *infra* 174.

545 See *supra* 51.

546 See *supra* 44.

However, the interdiction of anticipatory self-defence makes strategic sense within the small group of nuclear-weapon states that possess a second-strike capability but not an effective missile-defence system. This means that even if one of these powers launches a first strike against another member of the group with all the arms at its disposal it cannot completely destroy the nuclear arsenal of the victim of the attack. The latter will still be able to use some of its weapons deployed in hardened concrete silos, carried by planes in the air and, above all, under water aboard submarines, and therefore with its retaliatory second strike inflict unacceptable damage on the attacker.[547]

The resulting 'balance of (thermonuclear) terror' averted armed conflict between antagonistic nuclear powers, in particular the United States and the Soviet Union, despite the deep-seated hostility which opposed them to each other, throughout the Cold War.[548] This balance would be upset if a state that possessed nuclear weapons succeeded in developing an effective missile-defence system. It would still be unable to annihilate the entire nuclear arsenal of its adversary with a first strike but would be capable of destroying the latter's remaining counter-strike weapons before they could cause damage on its territory.

Yet, under the 1972 ABM Treaty concluded in the context of the Strategic Arms Limitation Talks (SALT) I and the 1974 Protocol thereto, the United States and the Soviet Union practically renounced this option and thereby stabilized the strategy of deterrence.[549]

547 While the aggressor will logically aim its first strike at the nuclear arsenal of the target state, the latter will direct its second strike against major non-military targets, i.e., industrial centres and big cities instead of empty missile launchers. This prospect ought to enhance the effectiveness of mutual deterrence among nuclear powers governed by rational decision makers. On strategic deterrence see Wohlstetter, 'The Delicate Balance of Terror', 37 *Foreign Affairs* (1958/1959) 211; Brodie, *Strategy in the Missile Age* (1959); Kahn, *On Thermonuclear War* (1961); Schelling, *Arms and Influence* (1966); Jervis, Lebow, and Stein, *The Psychology of Deterrence* (1985); Freedman, *Deterrence* (2004); Paul and Wirtz (eds.), *Complex Deterrence: Strategy in the Global Age* (2009). On strategy in general see Freedman, *Strategy: A History* (2013). On the principles of crisis management between states that possess nuclear second-strike capabilities and the legal relevance of these rules see Neuhold, *supra* (fn. 7) 258.

548 The probability of eventual escalation across the nuclear threshold also prevented conventional military conflicts between members of the two camps led by the two superpowers. See *supra* 27.

549 Article III of the ABM Treaty allowed for two exceptions – one around each party's capital, the other around ICBM (intercontinental ballistic missile) silo launchers –, the Protocol for only one such exception. In 2001, President George W. Bush gave Russia notice that the United States would withdraw from the ABM Treaty in accordance with its Article XV(2).

Regarding the legal issue at hand, anticipatory self-defence is senseless in this strategic constellation. A nuclear-weapon state cannot prevent an expected attack by attempting to completely destroy the presumed aggressor's nuclear arsenal. At the same time, a first strike by an adversary is highly unlikely, since it must reckon with the devastating effects of the victim's second strike which cannot be thwarted. On the one hand, the probability of the feared attack actually occurring is thus very low. On the other hand, anticipatory self-defence would be suicidal for the state resorting to it.

However, successful mutual deterrence depends on the fulfilment of one crucial condition. Irrespective of how deep their enmity may be, all parties concerned must regard the preservation of their own lives as their supreme value. The resulting shared priority of common survival provides the necessary basis for the strategic logic of deterrence and the mutual renunciation of the use of armed force.

This foundation is challenged by two types of actors who are posing a growing threat to international security: terrorists and 'rogue states'. Terrorists risk their lives[550] or, like those responsible for '9/11', deliberately commit suicide when launching their deadly attacks. They value their own lives less than the cause they are fighting for and therefore cannot be deterred by the threat that they may or will die. The regimes of 'rogue states' are supposed to accept the sanctions which major violations of international law may entail for their populations, not only economic hardships but eventually also human casualties.[551]

Termination of the treaty was to set the stage for lawfully installing a U.S. missile-defence system which was also to be deployed in the Czech Republic and Poland. Although the United States stressed that its 'missile shield' was directed against 'rogue states' like North Korea and Iran, the Russian Federation also felt threatened by the project. In 2009, the new administration of President Barack Obama abandoned this project for a sea- and land-based interceptor system that was at least initially more acceptable to Russia. Fitzpatrick, 'A Prudent Decision on Missile Defence', 51 *Survival*, No. 6 (December 2009–January 2010) 5; Thränert, 'NATO Missile Defence and Extended Deterrence', ibid. 63.

550 For 'cyber terrorists', however, this risk is rather low. See *supra* 33.

551 The administration of President George W. Bush included a more elaborate U.S.-oriented definition in the 2002 National Security Strategy of the United States, according to which 'rogue states'

- brutalize their own people and squander their national resources for the personal gain of the rulers;
- display no regard for international law, threaten their neighbours, and callously violate international treaties to which they are a party;
- are determined to acquire weapons of mass destruction, along with other advanced military technology, to be used as threats or offensively to achieve the aggressive designs of these regimes;

On balance, in light of these strategic realities, this writer reluctantly proposes that strictly limited self-defence against an imminent armed attack should be accepted as lawful, although a 'technical' legal interpretation of Article 51 suggests a different conclusion. In this connection, the difference between 'pre-emptive' and 'preventive' defence as defined in the terminology of military strategy becomes relevant. Pre-emptive action is taken against a highly certain attack in the immediate, while preventive defence is directed against a more speculative threat in the distant future.

Lawful pre-emptive self-defence ought to fulfil the following conditions.[552] Imminence, i.e., the time frame within which the attack is expected to occur, should be counted in a few weeks, if not days. The required certainty has to be based on a psychological and a material element: on the one hand, the clear intent of the presumptive aggressor to launch an attack, on the other, concrete measures actually to carry out the threat, in particular the mobilization of a sizeable number of armed forces. Admittedly, the intent to attack may be difficult to ascertain if it is not expressly stated. Whether overwhelming evidence based on conclusive action also suffices will depend on the merits of each case, with the burden of proof on the state claiming lawfully to exercise its right of self-defence. In any event, the scope of military preparations and the type of forces and weapons mobilized by the suspected attacker should, in principle, be sufficient to launch an armed attack as defined above. Denials of aggressive intentions might further complicate the problem.

The state that exercises the right of pre-emptive self-defence must of course comply with the general prerequisites of self-defence, the principles of necessity and proportionality,[553] as well as with international humanitarian law. If possible, the issue should be referred to the Security Council for emergency action, however weak the hopes for effective measures by the Council may be,

---

- sponsor terrorism around the globe; and
- reject basic human values and hate the United States and everything for which it stands.

Furthermore, in his State of the Union Address on 29 January 2002, President George W. Bush placed three 'rogue states' on the 'Axis of Evil': Iraq, Iran and North Korea. On 6 May 2002, Undersecretary of State John R. Bolton added three more names to the list: those of Libya, Syria and Cuba. On 18 January 2005, the then incoming Secretary of State Condoleezza Rice offered another variation on the theme, calling Cuba, Burma (Myanmar), North Korea, Iran, Belarus and Zimbabwe 'outposts of tyranny'.

552 Cassese proposed a similar solution which all states should approve, for example, by unanimously adopted resolutions of the UN General Assembly and the Security Council – a precondition unlikely to be fulfilled in the foreseeable future. Cassese, *supra* (fn. 526) 1342.

553 See *infra* 144.

before force is employed in self-defence; but there may be situations where there is no time for waiting for the activation of the UN system of collective security. It goes without saying that a UN member state resorting to pre-emptive self-defence must also comply with its obligation under Article 51 of the Charter and immediately report the measures taken to the Security Council, including the evidence on which it relies.

In contrast, preventive self-defence ought to remain unlawful. A state fearing an attack in the remote future still has time to attempt a peaceful settlement of its dispute with the adversary suspected of planning an armed attack. Its chances for assistance by international organizations and friendly states may be better if no immediate military response is necessary. A state that perceives a threat on the more distant political horizon may successfully apply for admission to a military alliance and thereby considerably improve its defensive position. The presumptive aggressor should be given time to reconsider its options for achieving his goals. Moreover, the danger that states will abuse preventive self-defence as a more or less plausible pretext for military action ought to be taken into consideration.

The debate on anticipatory self-defence is further complicated by terminological confusion, which may be caused by the lack of conceptual clarity or could also be deliberate. The words 'anticipatory', 'pre-emptive' and 'preventive' are often used interchangeably and/or without precise definition.

According to the above-mentioned National Security Strategy of the United States adopted in 2002 in the wake of the '9/11' terrorist attacks, the concept of imminent attack had to be adapted to the capabilities and objectives of today's adversaries. The United States had therefore to take anticipatory action, even if the time and place of the attack by the enemy remained uncertain.[554] As a result, the line between pre-emptive and preventive force became blurred.[555]

The solution proposed by this author was endorsed by the High-level Panel on Threats, Challenges and Change in its 2004 report on the basis of what its members regarded as long established international law.[556] At the same time, the Panel upheld the illegality of preventive self-defence against a non-imminent attack.[557] Secretary-General Kofi Annan agreed with the Panel in his report to the

554 For critical comments on this doctrine see, for example, Bothe, 'Terrorism and the Legality of Pre-emptive Force', 14 *EJIL* (2003) 227.

555 The essence of the 2002 doctrine was reiterated in the 2006 U.S. National Security Strategy.

556 However, the Panel only referred to three prominent U.S. American lawyers, Oscar Schachter, Wolfgang Friedmann and Louis Henkin. Paragraph 188 and endnote 106 of the report. See *supra* 106.

557 Paragraphs 189–192.

summit General Assembly, considering self-defence against imminent threats fully covered by Article 51 of the UN Charter and long recognized by lawyers, without, however, quoting any names.[558] Moreover, he suggested that the Security Council should deal with latent threats, but did not indicate measures to be taken if the Council failed to act. Unfortunately, the Heads of State or Government at their UN General Assembly meeting in 2005 remained silent on this important issue in their 'World Summit Outcome'.[559]

The problem that remains to be addressed is caused by the divergent conclusions reached by a strictly legal interpretation of Article 51 of the UN Charter, on the one hand, and the assessment of the strategic aspects of the issue, on the other. One solution is to rely in general terms on a 'dynamic' or 'evolutionary' interpretation of Article 51 which has to be adapted to the security needs of states.[560] Another is the attempt to build more specific 'legal bridges' across the gap between law and facts.

Expressly legalizing pre-emptive self-defence by amending Article 51 would offer the most solid solution. However, the adoption and ratification of an amendment to the Charter by a two-thirds majority of member states, including the 'P5', required under Article 108 is unlikely. The reluctance of many UN members is, on the one hand, due to concerns about the precedent effect that could lead to calls for modifying other Charter provisions as well. On the other hand, especially small and medium-sized member states may be expected to oppose an explicit extension of the right of self-defence for fear of its abuse by their more powerful peers. Moreover, even the inclusion of some criteria for the lawfulness of anticipatory self-defence as proposed above would not necessarily prevent disputes over the imminence of an armed attack. A party involved in a crisis would judge the certainty of the attack individually for itself. Disagreement within the Security Council, above all between its permanent members, would often have to be expected, preventing the Council from performing its task of rapidly deciding the issue and taking appropriate action.

Other solutions which would also carry considerable legal and particularly political weight would be resolutions adopted by the UN Security Council or the General Assembly, preferably by consensus or an overwhelming majority

558 Paragraph 124 of his report. See *supra* 106.

559 According to paragraphs 3 and 6 of the 2007 Santiago Resolution of the IDI, the right of self-defence arises in the event of an actual or manifestly imminent armed attack, whereas there is no basis in international law for doctrines of 'preventive' self-defence. See *supra* 124.

560 Böth, *Evolutive Auslegung völkerrechtlicher Verträge. Eine Untersuchung zu Voraussetzungen und Grenzen in Anbetracht der Praxis internationaler Streitbeilegungsinstitutionen* (2013).

including the great powers. However, they appear out of reach for the same reasons at the present time and in the foreseeable future.

For reliance on the second main source of international law, customary law, which evolved after the entry into force of the Charter, sufficient practice and the *opinio juris* not only of great powers would have to be demonstrated. Yet, the existence of neither the factual nor the psychological element of customary law can be proven during the decades after 1945.

However, recourse to the *travaux préparatoires* could help solve the dilemma. As mentioned above, they may be used, under Article 32(b) of the VCLT, if the interpretation according to Article 31 of the Convention produces a manifestly absurd or unreasonable result. This would arguably be the case if the target state of an imminent attack were not allowed to use military means before the forces of the aggressor enter its territory. This requirement could, as pointed out above, penalize the innocent victim by leaving the potentially decisive choice of the time and location of the attack to the aggressor.

At least a thin plank, if not a bridge, might be placed across the gap by a less narrow definition of the point in time at which an armed attack begins to occur. The argument is tenable that the attack already gets underway when ground forces, navy vessels, war planes and missiles start moving in the direction of the target state and not just when they actually cross its borders. However, the time thus gained may not be sufficient to cope effectively with an attack by resorting to 'interceptive self-defence',[561] especially if the attack is carried out with supersonic aircraft and missiles.

With regard to one of the principal contemporary threats to national and international security, terrorism, the application of the 'accumulation-of-events' theory seems plausible. Terrorism may indeed be construed as a process. Terrorist organizations will, if possible, not limit their activities to a single attack but will try to strike again. Attempts to capture or kill them after their most recent criminal act in order to prevent future lethal 'pinpricks' could therefore be regarded as defensive measures against a still ongoing attack. In this context, the recognition of the right of self-defence by the Security Council after '9/11' may be recalled.[562]

Another bridging argument, however tempting it may be, should not be used: a fundamental change of circumstances in accordance with Article 62 of the VCLT. It could be claimed that the consent of UN member states to be bound by the Charter, in particular the restrictive provisions on self-defence in

561 This is the term used by Dinstein for this kind of defensive military action. Dinstein, *supra* (fn. 27) 201.

562 See *supra* 119.

Article 51, was based on the assumption that the system of collective security of the World Organization would function effectively. This may have been true of some decision makers in 1945, although the deadlock within the Security Council due to disagreement between the Western powers and the Soviet Union could be foreseen after the anti-Axis allies had defeated their common enemies.[563] In any event, states admitted during and after the Cold War must have known that the UN was unable to guarantee their security. Another serious objection concerns the precedent effect of invoking a fundamental change of circumstances. It could trigger *rebus sic stantibus* claims concerning other provisions and even erode the entire legal fabric of the Charter. The temptation to open this Pandora's box should therefore be resisted.

In conclusion, this author joins those who support the lawfulness of preemptive self-defence only reluctantly. Its foundation on *lex lata* as formulated in Article 51 of the UN Charter is weak at best. The practical effects of this solution may include abuse; nor can fatal errors in good faith, leading to the conclusion that an armed attack by another state is imminent, be ruled out. The resulting armed conflict may cause death and destruction on both sides.

However, insistence on an absolute prohibition of anticipatory self-defence entails another, equally serious danger. Governments facing what they perceive as an existential threat are likely to use force anyway in order to protect their citizens and territorial integrity as best they can. The prospect of accusations that they thereby violated Article 51 will not impress and dissuade them. To make matters worse, the key provision on the resort to force, Article 2(4) of the UN Charter, and the entire legal regime based on it could eventually be undermined. Therefore, an additional limited exception beyond self-defence against an actual armed attack should be accepted as the lesser evil for the sake of preserving the crucial principle, the prohibition of the threat or use of force.

3.9.8 *Necessity, Proportionality and Immediacy*

In contrast, an issue that caused fewer headaches concerned the principles of necessity and proportionality on which the authors of Article 51 remained silent. There is broad consensus that these two requirements still have to be met in the lawful exercise of the right of self-defence.[564] This contention is supported by the argument that the pre-existing customary law remains in force unless expressly modified by the UN Charter. The ICJ confirmed this view

563 See *supra* 52.

564 Cassesse, *supra* (fn. 82) 1333; Corten, *supra* (fn. 27) 705; Gray, *supra* (fn. 27) 148; Dinstein, *supra* (fn. 27) 231, 262; Randelzhofer and Nolte, *supra* (fn. 526) 1425. However, this view is not shared by Kunz, *supra* (fn. 469) 878.

in the 1986 *Nicaragua*[565] case and reiterated the two principles in its 1996 *Nuclear Weapons* advisory opinion,[566] the 2003 *Oil Platforms* case[567] and the 2005 *Armed Activities in the DRC* case.[568]

As a result, force may be used as a means of last resort only after all available non-violent methods have been exhausted or clearly appear futile, and it must be proportional to the attack.[569] If a state acting in self-defence exceeds the thresholds of necessity and proportionality it violates in turn the prohibition of the use of force under Article 2(4) of the Charter.[570]

However, some questions still remain open. Whether permissible necessary force is limited to repelling the armed attack or also allows for the elimination of the source (for instance, a terrorist camp) of the attack is unclear.

In addition, in accordance with the principle of proportionality, the level of defensive force must not exceed that of the armed attack. Yet, as Greenwood points out, the fulfilment of this condition is not to be assessed by comparing the number of forces or the types of weapons used or even the casualties and damage caused by the initial attack.[571] He gives the example of a surprise attack resulting in control over an area of the victim state with relatively little force. If the attacking state then rapidly reinforces its positions the other state will need a far greater degree of force to reverse the effects of the attack. Therefore proportionality is not to be measured by the relation of force used in self-defence to the force employed by the attacking state but depends upon whether the degree of defensive force is needed to undo the effects of the initial attack.

Moreover, it may be asked whether an attacked state which is on the verge of defeat is allowed to use weapons of mass destruction against the aggressor. In particular, may the victim of a conventional attack employ tactical nuclear or radiological weapons, whose effects are more limited than those of strategic nuclear

---

565 *Military and Paramilitary Activities in and against Nicaragua (Nicaragua v. United States of America)*, Merits, paragraph 194.

566 *Legality of the Threat or Use of Nuclear Weapons*, paragraph 41.

567 *Oil Platforms (Islamic Republic of Iran v. United States of America)*, paragraphs 43 and 74.

568 *Armed Activities on the Territory of the Congo (Democratic Republic of the Congo v. Uganda)*, paragraph 147.

569 The IDI also endorsed this view in paragraphs 2 and 3 of its Santiago Resolution of 2007. See *supra* 124. Gray argues that the two principles are closely related to each other: if the use of force is not necessary, it cannot be proportionate and, if it is not proportionate, it difficult to see how it can be necessary. Gray, *supra* (fn. 27) 150.

570 Moreover, a state defending itself against an unlawful armed attack also has to observe the rules of the law of war and international humanitarian law.

571 Greenwood, *supra* (fn. 463) paragraph 28.

weapons?[572] In its 1996 *Nuclear Weapons* advisory opinion the ICJ did not rule out the lawfulness of the use of nuclear weapons in all circumstances.[573]

Furthermore, lawful self-defence ought to meet a temporal requirement, that of immediacy.[574] This does not mean that the right may not be exercised after the armed attack has been completed. For, in accordance with the principle of necessity, attempts at a peaceful solution of the armed conflict ought to be made by the parties. Moreover, the mobilization of the necessary armed forces and other preparations for the effective use of counter-force may take time.[575] However, there must not be an undue time lag between the attack and the armed response to it.[576]

3.9.9 *Collective Self-Defence*

With respect to collective self-defence also mentioned in Article 51 of the UN Charter, it is generally accepted that states may not just provide military assistance to the victim of an armed attack if they are equally attacked themselves.[577] This narrow view held by Bowett[578] was widely rejected and is contradicted by state practice.[579] Other states that have not (yet) been attacked are equally free to provide military support to the victim of the attack. They

---

572 See *supra* 121.

573 See *supra* fn. 99.

574 As stated by the ICJ in the *Nicaragua* case in the context of necessity. *Military and Paramilitary Activities in and against Nicaragua* (*Nicaragua v. United States of America*), Merits, paragraph 237. For Dinstein, this is a separate requirement. Dinstein, *supra* (fn. 27) 267, whereas Akande and Liefländer argue that this aspect more properly belongs to necessity. Akand and Liefländer, 'Clarifying Necessity, Imminence and Proportionality in the Law of Self-Defense', 107 *AJIL* (2013) 563.

575 Even the only remaining superpower after the Cold War, the United States, with all the troops and weapons at its quick disposal, launched its response to the '9/11' armed attacks, 'Operation Enduring Freedom', not within a few days but four weeks later, on 7 October 2001.

576 Dinstein, *supra* (fn. 27) 233.

577 The term 'collective *self*-defence' makes sense. It is based on the assumption that a state that provides military support to the victim of an armed attack is, as a rule, not only acting out of sympathy and generosity but also concerned about its own security. Above all, it prefers to defend itself at an early stage together with the assisted state(s) on the territory of the latter instead of waiting to be attacked on its soil later on. Moreover, in today's integrated world, security has indeed become indivisible, so that an attack on one state should be perceived as an attack on all. This is all the more so for states that concluded collective self-defence agreements. See *supra* 51, and Dinstein, *supra* (fn. 27) 280.

578 Bowett, *supra* (fn. 526) 200.

579 Cassese, *supra* (fn. 82), 1354; Corten, *supra* (fn. 27) 276, 615; Gray, *supra* (fn. 27) 167; Dinstein, *supra* (fn. 27) 278; Randelzhofer and Nolte, *supra* (fn. 526) 1420.

may either decide to so on an ad hoc basis, especially if they must expect to become the next targets of the aggressor; or they may conclude a bilateral or multilateral treaty on mutual assistance should one/any of them be assaulted by a non-party in the future, agreeing that an attack on one will be regarded as an attack on both/all of them. Yet, if one party to such arrangements becomes the victim of an armed attack the other(s) must not impose its/their assistance on it[580] but may do so only on the basis of a request.

The states parties to such a treaty again have two options. They may limit their obligations to the joint exercise of the right of self-defence whenever the *casus foederis* occurs; or they may go further and establish a genuine military alliance. This means that they also engage in military cooperation already in peacetime, in particular by establishing common command structures, by joint planning, joint training and exercises of their armed forces or the exchange of intelligence, as well as collaboration in the area of procurement and the standardization of equipment, in order to enhance the effectiveness of an eventual joint response to an attack. Moreover, troops of one may be deployed on the territory of another ally in order to enhance the credibility of the resolve of the former to live up to its assistance commitment should the latter be attacked. The 1947 Rio Pact provides an example of the former, NATO of the latter variant of collective self-defence.

A closer look at collective self-defence treaties shows once more that a 'soft-law' obligation is not necessarily less effective in practice than a 'hard' formulation.[581] Under Article V of the 1948 Brussels Treaty that provided the basis for

---

580 A tempting option for great powers in their relations with weaker partners.

581 Neuhold, 'Variations on the Theme of "Soft International Law"', in: Buffard et alii (eds.), *supra* (fn. 27) 343 (350). See also Schachter, 'The Twilight Existence of Nonbinding International Agreements', 71 *AJIL* (1977) 296; Seidl-Hohenveldern, 'International Economic "Soft Law"', 163 *RCADI* (1979) 173; Bothe, 'Legal and Non-Legal Norms – a meaningful distinction in international relations?', 11 *Netherlands Yearbook of International Law* (1980) 65; Frowein, 'The Internal and External Effects of Resolutions by International Organizations', 49 *ZaöRV/HJIL* (1989) 778; P.-M. Dupuy, 'Soft Law and the International Law of the Environment', 12 *Michigan Journal of International Law* (1991) 420; Heusel, *'Weiches' Völkerrecht* (1991); Reisman, 'The Concept and Functions of Soft Law in International Politics', in: Bello and Ajibola (eds.), *Essays in Honour of Judge Taslim Olawale Elias* (vol. I, 1992) 135; Fastenrath, 'Relative Normativity in International Law', 4 *EJIL* (1993) 305; Klabbers, 'The Redundancy of Soft Law', 65 *Nordic Journal of International Law* (1996) 167; Tomuschat, 'The Concluding Documents of World Order Conferences', in: Makarczyk (ed.), *Theory of International Law at the Threshold of the 21st Century: Essays in Honour of Krzysztof Skubiszewski* (1996) 563; Klabbers, 'The Undesirability of Soft Law', 67 *Nordic Journal of International Law* (1998) 381; Zemanek, 'Is the Term "Soft Law" Convenient?', in: Hafner et al. (eds.), *supra* (fn. 525) 843; Hillgenberg, 'A Fresh Look at Soft Law', 10 *EJIL* (1999) 499; Abbott and Snidal, 'Hard and

the WEU, the members of this by now defunct alliance of eventually ten Western European States[582] had to afford an attacked party 'all the military and other aid in their power'.[583] In contrast, under Article 5 of the 1949 North Atlantic Treaty, it is up to each party to 'take such action *as it deems necessary*,[584] including the use of armed force'. The discretion left to each ally to decide how to react to the occurrence of the *casus foederis* was necessary to obtain the approval of the Washington Treaty by the U.S. Senate, given the reluctance of the United States to accept military assistance obligations in advance.

However, the degree of security offered by NATO to its members is much higher than that which the WEU, the 'kid brother' of the Atlantic Alliance, could ever provide. The membership of the United States of the former but not the latter alliance and the scope of integration developed within NATO guarantee a joint military response which ought to make each potential aggressor think twice before launching an armed attack on any NATO member. The success of

---

Soft Law in International Governance', 54 *International Organization* (2000) 421; Thürer, 'Soft Law', in: Bernhard (ed.), *Encyclopedia of Public International Law,* (vol. IV, 2000) 452; Hafner, 'The Effect of Soft Law on International Economic Relations', in: Griller (ed.), *International Economic Governance and Non-Economic Concerns* (2003) 149; Barba, 'Norme narrative, soft law e teoria delle fonti', in: Mansel, Kronke and Pfeiffer (eds.), *Festschrift für Erik Jayme* (vol. 2, 2004) 1027; Boyle, 'Soft Law in International Law-Making', in: Evans (ed.), *International Law* (2nd ed., 2006) 141; Shelton, 'International Law and Relative Normativity', ibid. 159; Thürer, 'Soft Law', MPEPIL.

'Soft law' is usually understood as rules that are not 'fully' legally but at best politically binding, whatever this means. But according to Weil who rejects this definition, because there is only law or no law at all, less stringently worded engagements can be distinguished from clearly formulated obligations. Weil, 'Towards Relative Normativity in International Law', 77 *AJIL* (1983) 413.

582 Western European not in a geographic but in a political sense since it also included, in particular, Greece – just as the North Atlantic Treaty Organization included Greece and Turkey since 1952; moreover, after the end of the Cold War many formerly 'socialist' Eastern European states were admitted to NATO.

583 The WEU was dissolved in 2011 after the EU had taken over its military functions and assets. Article 42(7) of the Lisbon Treaty on European Union similarly provides: 'If a Member State is the victim of armed aggression on its territory, the other Member States shall have towards it *an obligation of aid and assistance by all the means in their power* [italics added], in accordance with Article 51 of the United Nations Charter'. However, this sentence is followed by the so-called Irish clause which was already inserted in the 1992 Maastricht Treaty on European Union at the insistence of Ireland in order to safeguard the country's neutrality: 'This shall not prejudice the specific character of the security and defence policy of certain Member States'.

584 Italics added.

a collective defence treaty depends on the deterrent effect the parties are able to achieve.[585] It is therefore not measured by the number of cases in which military support was provided to an attacked party. On the contrary, a truly effective mutual assistance regime does not have to be activated, because would-be aggressors are deterred from carrying out their plans by the resistance they must expect, so that members do not have to incur the human and material costs of fighting off aggression.

Membership of a military alliance entails both advantages and disadvantages for small and medium-sized countries as well as great powers, which governments are well advised to weigh before choosing this option of their security policy.[586] For the first category of states, the most positive aspect of joining an alliance is the often dramatic increase in their security as a result of protection by powerful allies, as, for example, for Luxembourg within NATO thanks to, above all, the participation of the United States. In addition, they sit at the same table with the more powerful members and have a say on vital security decisions taken by consensus.[587] Their international visibility and prestige are likely to be enhanced, especially if they host important meetings of alliance organs.[588] Furthermore, they benefit from state-of-the-art technology not available to non-members[589] and easier access to the markets of their allies in general. Their military expenditure which is shared with their allies is likely be lower than if they have to take care of their defence individually, provided they take national security seriously.

On the negative side of the balance, a collective defence commitment constitutes a far-reaching sacrifice of sovereignty. The state concerned may be drawn into an armed conflict which it does not consider a direct vital threat to itself and which might have been rashly triggered by an alliance member that counted on the eventual support of its allies. Moreover, the alliance may provide a framework for pressure on the weaker by the more powerful members

---

585 See *supra* 43.

586 See also Liska, *Nations in Alliance: The Limits of Interdependence* (1962); Walt, *The Origins of Alliances* (1987).

587 Which is, for example, the decision-making principle of NATO.

588 For instance, a ministerial meeting of the North Atlantic Council in the Icelandic capital of Reykjavik, which normally does not make headlines, issued the 1968 'Reykjavik signal'. This declaration set the stage for negotiations on Mutual Balanced Force Reductions between the members of NATO and the Warsaw Treaty Organization. However, these talks on conventional disarmament between the blocs that were held in Vienna failed to reach an agreement.

589 Not only military but also 'dual-use' technology which can be used for military and non-military purposes.

not only in security matters. Although consensus gives each ally the possibility to block a decision not to its liking, in practice small and medium-sized member states will have little choice but to toe the line indicated by the leading powers. Alliance membership does not necessarily increase international prestige; on the contrary, less powerful states may be criticized and looked down on as 'satellites' of the dominant member(s) of the group. If a country has previously neglected its military security, it may have to spend more on defence than before if it joins an alliance which insists that it shoulder a fair share of the common burden. Finally, even the most solemn high-level pledges and extensive joint military preparations do not provide an absolute guarantee that if the *casus foederis* really occurs all allies will honour their assistance commitments.

For great powers, especially a superpower, alliance membership may not be vital to their national security but may offer a number of welcome 'fringe benefits'. These gains may include geostrategic assets like bases on the territories of their allies, as well as some useful military 'niche' contributions by the forces and additional intelligence obtained by their partners. As mentioned above, an alliance facilitates influence and control over less powerful member states that can more easily be prevented from going their separate ways and acting contrary to the will and interests of the dominant power(s). Moreover, the latter may use the alliance to enhance the international acceptance and legitimacy of decisions which they initially take unilaterally but which are then endorsed by all the other allies.

The main downside for powerful members is the likelihood that they will have to bear most of the military and financial costs in the event of an armed attack that leads to the activation of collective self-defence because the expected deterrence effect has not been achieved. Smaller and weaker members are more likely to become the victims of attack than the alliance leader(s).[590] Moreover, the latter may be irritated by the need for consensus within the alliance and prefer ad hoc coalitions of the able and willing for joint military action to 'war by committee'.[591]

Alliances are usually formed against an adversary perceived as a common threat by the contracting parties even it is not named in their treaty.[592] Given

590 However, as '9/11' showed, this is not necessarily the case. See *supra* 121.

591 As the United States did when launching 'Operation Enduring Freedom' in light of the experience with 'Operation Allied Force'. See *supra* 120.

592 Thus NATO was founded against the Soviet Union and the other members of the 'socialist' bloc, although the North Atlantic Treaty did not mention them expressly. By contrast, the Brussels Treaty of Economic, Social and Cultural Collaboration and Collective Self-Defence,

the various political and material costs, let alone human casualties members may risk, alliances are likely to be dissolved once the common enemy has been defeated or disappeared. However, NATO still exists more than two decades after the disintegration of the enemy Soviet bloc. The Atlantic Alliance, which is also a value community,[593] decided to 'go out of area and not out of business'.[594] This meant that, while remaining an alliance for the collective self-defence of its members, NATO embarked on additional military action outside the North Atlantic Area. It may be recalled that the alliance helped the UN to enforce Security Council decisions in the Balkan conflicts[595] and Libya;[596] it has also engaged in cooperative security activities, in particular by conducting peace(keeping) operations, in the Balkans[597] but also Afghanistan.[598] 'Operation Allied Force' mounted without Security Council authorization should also be mentioned in this context.[599]

A variation on the theme of collective self-defence is a security guarantee. Such an arrangement establishes a non-reciprocal military support commitment: the guarantor or the guarantors pledge, in the event of an armed attack by a third party, assistance to the beneficiary, while the latter is not obligated to help defend the guarantor(s). For a guarantee to make sense, the latter parties are powerful and the beneficiaries weak states that are unable to defend themselves effectively against most aggressors.

---

which was concluded by Belgium, France, Luxembourg, the Netherlands and the United Kingdom in 1948, did include, in paragraph 6 of its Preamble, as one of its main purposes 'to take such steps as may be held to be necessary in the event of a renewal by Germany of a policy of aggression'. However, when in 1954 the Federal Republic of Germany and Italy were invited to join, this paragraph was deleted in the Paris Protocol which established the WEU. Instead of the deleted paragraph, the parties agreed to 'promote the unity and encourage the progressive integration of Europe'. See *supra* fn. 583.

593 The Preamble to the North Atlantic Treaty mentions the 'freedom, common heritage and civilization of their [the parties' – the author] peoples, founded on the principles of democracy, individual liberty and the rule of law'. Pursuant to Article 2, the parties will strengthen their free institutions by bringing about a better understanding of the principles upon which these institutions are founded. For other reasons why alliances survive without their initial *raison d'être* see Walt, 'Why Alliances Endure or Collapse', 39 *Survival* no. 1 (Spring 1997) 156.

594 This was the formulation of the choice NATO faced after the end of the Cold War by U.S. Senator Richard Lugar. See *supra* fn. 263.

595 See *supra* 69.

596 See *supra* 113.

597 See *supra* 81.

598 See *supra* 84.

599 See *supra* 101.

Such asymmetrical agreements are rather rare in practice. Prospective guarantors may hesitate precisely because the other side accepts no corresponding duties. They unilaterally run the risk of being drawn into an armed conflict by a third party attacking the beneficiary. But small states may equally be reluctant to welcome the protection of their more powerful peers. This may at first sight be surprising, since a guarantee seems to be the ideal solution to the security problems of weak countries. However, the downside is the risk of even more pressure, control and interference by the powerful guarantors, who can argue that the beneficiaries owe them compliance with their wishes in return for their generosity. Moreover, it cannot be taken for granted that a guarantee will be honoured in each and every case of an actual attack.

A 'classical' example of a guarantee was granted by the then European great powers when they recognized the permanent neutrality of Switzerland in 1815.[600] Similar protection by the 'Big Four' (France, the Soviet Union, the United Kingdom and the United States) in Austria's favour was envisaged in the Moscow Memorandum initialled by high-ranking Austrian and Soviet governmental delegations in 1955. This crucial 'soft-law' agreement set the stage for the subsequent conclusion of the Austrian State Treaty. This treaty re-established the sovereignty of the country occupied by Allied troops after World War II, in exchange for the declaration of permanent neutrality similar to that of Switzerland by Austria. However, the Western powers did not agree to such a guarantee in order to avoid a military vacuum in Central Europe; they rather wanted Austria to defend its sovereignty and neutrality on its own.[601]

On closer look, the security relationship between the Soviet Union and Finland under their 1948 Treaty of Friendship, Cooperation and Mutual Assistance,[602] as well as the United States and Japan under their still valid 1960 Treaty on

600 For a comparative analysis of the neutrality of Switzerland, Sweden, Finland and Austria up to the end of the Cold War see Neuhold, 'The Neutral States of Europe: Similarities and Differences', in: Leonhard (ed.), *Neutrality: Changing Concepts and Practices* (1988) 97 (100).

601 Ibid. 113.

602 Article 1 of the Treaty read as follows: 'Should either Finland, *or the Soviet Union through the territory of Finland* [italics added; and not elsewhere – the author], become the object of military aggression on the part of Germany or any Power allied with Germany, Finland will carry out its duty as a sovereign State and will fight to repel aggression. In so doing, Finland will direct all the forces at its disposal towards defending the integrity of its territory..., with the help, if necessary of the Soviet Union or together with the Soviet Union.' After the end of the Cold War, relations between Finland and Russia were placed on a new basis by the 1992 Agreement on the Foundations of Relations between the Republic of Finland and the Russian Federation which no longer contains a guarantee.

Mutual Cooperation and Security[603] constituted/constitutes a guarantee, since the respective superpower pledged assistance to the other party in the event of an armed attack on the latter, while Finland and Japan undertook no corresponding obligation.

Another guarantee regime worth mentioning was established by the 1960 Nicosia Treaty of Guarantee. Its scope is problematic because it goes beyond collective self-defence. Under Article II of the Treaty, Greece, Turkey and the United Kingdom not only guarantee the independence, territorial integrity and security of Cyprus but also the state of affairs established by the Basic Articles of its Constitution. Moreover, pursuant to Article IV, in so far as common or concerted action may not prove possible, each of the three guaranteeing Powers reserves the right to take action with the sole aim of re-establishing the state of affairs created by the Treaty. Turkey invoked this provision as justification for its invasion of Cyprus in response to a coup ousting Cypriot President Archbishop Makarios and supported by the ruling military junta in Greece, in order to protect the Turkish minority on the island.[604]

To return to the legal aspects of collective self-defence, it should be added that the ICJ ruled in the *Nicaragua* case that not only must the attacked state declare itself to have been attacked; it must also request the assistance of other states.[605] The Court reiterated this requirement in its judgment in the *Oil Platforms* case.[606] This means that military assistance, whether ad hoc or on the basis of a collective defence (or guarantee) treaty, may not be imposed on the victim of an armed attack without its consent. Moreover, the ICJ stated in the *Nicaragua* case that the principles of necessity and proportionality must also be observed in the exercise of collective self-defence.[607] The same applies to the obligation to report measures taken to this end to the Security Council.[608]

---

603 Article V of the Treaty provides: 'Each Party recognizes that an armed attack against either party *in the territories under the administration of Japan* (italics added; and not elsewhere – the author) would be dangerous to its own peace and safety and declares that it would act to meet the common danger in accordance with its constitutional provisions and processes.'

604 Dinstein, *supra* (fn. 27) 292.

605 *Military and Paramilitary Activities in and against Nicaragua (Nicaragua v. United States of America)*, Merits, paragraph 199. The latter requirement is equally included in paragraph 8 of the 2007 Santiago Resolution of the IDI. See *supra* 124.

606 *Oil Platforms (Islamic Republic of Iran v. United States of America)*, paragraph 51.

607 Similarly, the condition of immediacy must be met. See *supra* 146.

608 *Military and Paramilitary Activities in and against Nicaragua (Nicaragua v. United States of America)*, Merits, paragraph 235.

3.9.10 *When Does the Exercise of the Right of Self-Defence End?*

Another question concerns the point in time when the lawful use of force in self-defence has to stop. An answer is given in Article 51 of the UN Charter: the right may be exercised 'until the Security Council has taken measures necessary to maintain international peace and security'. This provision, together with the obligation of UN member states immediately to report measures taken in the exercise of the right of self-defence, adds to the customary law laid down in Article 51. While each state initially decides for itself whether the above-mentioned conditions for the use of armed force in self-defence are met, this determination is thus subject to the subsequent assessment by the Security Council.

Article 51 also raises another question: who decides whether the measures taken by the Council are sufficient for the maintenance of international peace and security and for the effective protection of the attacked state? For instance, must the victim of the attack cease military action if the Security Council adopts non-military sanctions which, as pointed out above, usually fail to achieve their purpose, at least in the short run?[609]

Different scenarios have to be distinguished in this context.[610] On the one hand, if the Security Council decides that hostilities must stop the parties have to comply with its decision. On the other, if the Council fails to act, the attacked state may continue to use force, provided it observes the principles of necessity, proportionality and immediacy. If the Security Council merely appeals for a ceasefire or imposes non-military sanctions, the continued use of force by the victim of the armed attack entails a certain risk. The Council may determine that this continuation constitutes (at least) a threat to the peace under Article 39 of the Charter and take action against the initially attacked state. Yet, in practice this response by the UN organ in charge of collective security is rather unlikely. If the state claiming to act in self-defence is not one of the 'P 5', it can in all probability still count on the support of at least one permanent member that would block enforcement measures by the Council.[611] Regrettably, the Council has failed effectively to play the role of the arbiter on the lawful recourse to self-defence in practice, mainly because of the disagreement among the 'P 5'.

---

609 See *supra* 76.

610 Dinstein, *supra* (fn. 27) 236.

611 It is worth recalling in this context that the United States and its partners relied on the right of self-defence until the end of 'Operation Enduring Freedom' against Al Qaeda and the Taliban in Afghanistan, although the Security Council took action by authorizing the use of force by ISAF in 2001 and extended the mandate of the force to the entire territory of Afghanistan in 2003. See *supra* 84.

3.9.11 *'Wars of National Liberation' as Self-Defence?*

Finally, two issues which were very highly controversial during the Cold War but receded into the background afterwards may be addressed. Advocates of the lawfulness of the use of armed force by colonial peoples in the exercise of their right of self-determination justified it, *inter alia*, as self-defence.[612] This contention gave rise to debates between representatives of 'socialist' and Third World states on the one hand and Western members on the other, in the UN General Assembly and the special committees tasked by the General Assembly with drafting the Friendly Relations Declaration and the definition of aggression.[613]

The supporters of the legality of 'wars of national liberation' pointed out that the armed attack required under Article 51 of the UN Charter was committed by the establishment of colonial regimes by force. Although this had happened in the past, colonialism had never been accepted by the oppressed peoples and constituted permanent aggression. Now that these peoples finally had the necessary weapons and other means to get rid of the colonial yoke they had the right to use them. Moreover, peoples were also subjects of international law and protected by the prohibition in Article 2(4) of the Charter. This provision outlawed the threat or use of force not only in inter-state but in international relations in which peoples also participated. Furthermore, they were equally entitled to collective self-defence, which meant that other states were allowed (and, according to one view, even obligated) to assist them, also by military means. The widespread practice of 'wars of national liberation' in the era of decolonization, backed by the *opinio juris* of a majority within the international community, reflected, above all, in resolutions of the UN General Assembly,[614] had given rise to a rule of customary law on the lawfulness of the use of force by colonial peoples in self-defence.

Those who rejected these arguments emphasized that Article 51 granted the right of self-defence only to members of the UN, i.e., states. A teleological interpretation of the Charter in the light of its principal purpose, the maintenance of international peace and security, led to the same restrictive conclusion. Furthermore, Article 2(4) of the Charter only prohibited the threat or use of force against the territorial integrity or political independence of any *state*.[615]

---

612 Dugard, 'The Organisation of African Unity and Colonialism: An Inquiry into the Plea of Self-Defence as a Justification for the Use of Force in the Eradication of Colonialism', 16 *ICLQ* (1967) 157.

613 Neuhold, *supra* (fn. 7) 191; Cassesse, *supra* (fn. 82) 1356.

614 For example General Assembly Resolutions 1514 (XV), 2105 (XX) and 2160 (XXI).

615 Italics added.

In addition, the UN Charter itself provided for colonial regimes with its Declaration regarding Non-Self-Governing Territories and the Trusteeship system in its Chapters XI–XIII. Finally, because of the objections of Western states, no customary rule on self-defence by colonial peoples could come into existence.

It was finally agreed to include in the texts of the first principle of the Friendly Relations Declaration, the prohibition of the threat or use of force, and of the fifth principle, that of equal rights and self-determination of peoples, the duty of every state to refrain from any forcible action which deprives peoples of their right to self-determination and freedom and independence. Moreover, the latter principle adds, without referring to self-defence, that in their struggle against, and resistance to, such forcible action peoples are entitled to seek and to receive support in accordance with the purposes and principles of the Charter. Whether such support includes military assistance has remained controversial.

A similar provision was inserted into Article 7 of the 1974 definition of aggression adopted by the UN General Assembly.[616] In addition, Article 6 provides that the definition does not in any way enlarge or diminish the scope of the Charter, including the provisions concerning cases in which the use of force is lawful.[617]

With the completion of decolonization in the Third World, the issue has lost some of its practical relevance. However, the principle of self-determination is far from being a matter of the past, as the examples of Kosovo, Abkhazia, South Ossetia and Crimea, as well as secessionist movements in other parts of the world, have shown.

3.9.12 *Self-Defence by Hegemonic Powers in their 'Zones of Influence'?*

During the Cold War, the two superpowers, the Soviet Union and the United States, resorted to force in order to prevent states within their blocs from deviating from the prevalent political, economic and social system. They also invoked the right of self-defence as the legal basis for the use of force to this end within the 'socialist' camp in Eastern Europe and the Western hemisphere, respectively.[618]

---

616 See *supra* fn. 249.

617 Dinstein is among those who insist that since the Charter allows for the use of force only in the exercise of the right of self-defence and as a measure based on a Security Council decision in the framework of collective security, resort to armed force in support of 'wars of national liberation' is unlawful. Dinstein, *supra* (fn. 27) 70.

618 Franck,' Who Killed Article 2(4)? or: Changing Norms Governing the Use of Force by States', 64 *AJIL* (1970) 809 (822); Bothe, *supra* (fn. 523) 26; Firmage, 'Summary and

The Soviet Union crushed the Hungarian uprising in 1956 and, together with other members of the Warsaw Treaty Organization, the 'Prague Spring' in 1968. Both popular movements aimed at political and economic reforms, notably the introduction of multiparty democracy. Hungary under the government of Prime Minister Imre Nagy also withdrew from the Warsaw Pact and opted for permanent neutrality. According to the so-called Brezhnev Doctrine named after the then Secretary-General of the Communist Party of the Soviet Union, the members of the 'socialist' camp had opted for a superior political and economic system once and for all and given up the right to choose a different model.[619] The same principle applied to their joint foreign and security policy.

If one of them nevertheless strayed from the correct path, the other states had the right and even the duty to bring the deviant member back into the 'socialist' fold. Such lawful 'fraternal assistance' also included the recourse to armed force. It was considered as part of the 'international law of socialism' which was given primacy over the 'international law of peaceful coexistence' that governed relations between 'socialist' and 'non-socialist' states. The essence of this doctrine was included in a number of bilateral treaties which the Soviet Union concluded with its 'socialist' allies after the invasion of Czechoslovakia.[620]

The Western equivalent of the 'Brezhnev Doctrine', the exact opposite of the latter, was, on the contrary, designed to prevent the further spread of communism in the Americas. Its legal basis was sought in Article 6 of the 1947 Rio Treaty.[621] This provision includes collective defence measures against aggression which is not an armed attack or by an extra-continental or intra-continental conflict, or by any other fact or situation which might endanger the peace of America. At the Tenth Inter-American Conference in Caracas in 1954, those challenges below the threshold of an armed attack were defined. In the Caracas Declaration

---

Interpretation', in: Falk (ed.), *supra* (fn. 135) 405 (418); Schweitzer, 'Erleidet das Gewaltverbot Modifikationen im Bereich von Einflußzonen?', in: Schaumann (ed.), *supra* (fn. 523) 219; Wildhaber, 'Gewaltverbot und Selbstverteidigung', ibid. 147 (158).

619 Meissner, *The Brezhnev Doctrine* (1970); Grant, *supra* (fn. 74) paragraphs 22–27. Under President Mikhail Gorbachev, the Soviet Union rejected the doctrine, and, together with the four other former 'socialist' states that had invaded Czechoslovakia, condemned the invasion as unlawful. The illegality of the invasion of Hungary was also admitted. Gray, *supra* (fn. 27) 93.

620 Hafner, 'Der sozialistische Begriff der kollektiven Sicherheit und die Probleme seiner Realisierung in Europa', 13 *Österreichische Zeitschrift für Außenpolitik* (1973) 131 (145). Since the prohibition of the threat or use of force is part of *jus cogens*, the respective treaty provisions ought to be considered void in accordance with Article 53 of the 1969 VCLT. See *supra* 25.

621 See *supra* 4.

of Solidarity, the aggressive character of the international communist movement was denounced as a special and immediate threat to the national institutions and the peace and security of the American states and its activities condemned as constituting intervention in American affairs. This interpretation was put into practice still in 1954 when the government of Jacobo Árbenz Guzmán, accused of communist leanings, was ousted by a coup assisted by the CIA in Guatemala, in 1961 when the United States supported Cuban emigrants in their failed attempt to overthrow the Castro regime in Cuba, and in 1965 in the crisis in the Dominican Republic. The Johnson administration initially justified the dispatch of some 30,000 U.S. troops to the island by invoking a request by the governing junta and the protection of endangered American citizens, but finally relied on the need to prevent an alleged communist takeover – 'One Cuba is enough', as the so-called Johnson Doctrine may be put in nutshell.[622]

However, neither doctrine had any foundation in international law. They were incompatible with the right of each sovereign state and its population freely to choose and change its political, economic, social system. Their implementation constituted a violation of the *jus cogens* prohibition in Article 2(4) of the UN Charter. Because of the absence of an armed attack required for the exercise of this right, it could not be based on the right of self-defence.

622 R.-J. Dupuy, 'Les États-Unis, l'O.E.A. et l'O.N.U. à Saint-Domingue', 11 *AFDI* (1965) 71; Bohan, 'The Dominican Crisis: Unilateral Intervention', 60 *AJIL* (1966) 809; Fenwick, 'The Dominican Republic: Intervention or Collecitve Self-Defense', ibid. 64; McLaren, 'The Dominican Crisis: An Interamerican Dilemma', 4 *The Canadian Yearbook of International Law* (1966) 178; Akehurst, 'Enforcement Action by Regional Agencies, with Special Reference to the Organization of American States', 42 *BYIL* (1967) 175.

CHAPTER 4

Non-Intervention in the Internal Affairs of States

4.1 Introduction: Conceptual Problems

When Talleyrand served as Ambassador in London, he replied to a lady who asked him about the meaning of the word 'non-intervention': '*Madame, non-intervention est un mot diplomatique et énigmatique qui signifie à peu près la même chose qu'intervention*'.[623] The prohibition of intervention in the internal affairs of a state remains one of the most complex and controversial principles of international law to this day.[624]

The problems begin with the manifold and contradictory meanings of the term 'intervention' which refer to both lawful and illegal action. They range from an oral statement at a conference to the illegal use of armed force. A discussant is called '*intervenant*' in French. Even in diplomatic and legal parlance no generally accepted definition exists. 'It is not too much to say that there are as many textbook definitions of intervention as there are of war.'[625]

The basic legal issue is caused by the difficulty of drawing a line between unlawful coercion and interference, on the one hand, and the exercise of permissible, even desirable, influence, for which the word '*Interzession*' is used in German legal terminology,[626] on the other hand. What is at stake once more is the conflict between two key rules on which the international legal order is based, both of which therefore deserve special protection. On the one

---

623 Stowell, 'La théorie et la pratique de l'intervention', 40 *RCADI* (1932) 91 (92).

624 Potter, 'L'intervention en droit international moderne', 32 *RCADI* (1930) 611; Stowell, *supra* (fn. 623); Mosler, *Die Intervention im Völkerrecht* (1937); T. Komarnicki, 'L'intervention en droit international moderne', 60 *RGDIP* (1956) 521; Thomas and Thomas, *Non-intervention: The Law and Its Import in the Americas* (1956); Fabela, *Intervention* (1961); Fawcett, 'Intervention in International Law: A Study of Some Recent Cases', 103 *RCADI* (1961) 347 ; Stanger (ed.), *Essays on Intervention* (1964); Gerlach, *Die Intervention: Versuch einer Definition* (1967); Jaquet (ed.), *Intervention in International Politics* (1971); Neuhold, *supra* (fn. 7), 269; Jäckel (ed.), *Ist das Prinzip der Nichteinmischung überholt?* (1995); Fisler Damrosch, 'Politics across Borders: Nonintervention and Nonforcible Influence over Domestic Affairs', 83 *AJIL* (1989) 1; Sapienza, *Il principio di non intervento negli affari interni* (1990); Kunig, 'Intervention, Prohibition of', MPEPIL; Jamnejad and Wood, 'The Principle of Non-intervention', 22 *Leiden Journal of International Law* (2009) 345.

625 Grob, *The Relativity of War and Peace* (1949) 227.

626 Verdross and Simma, *supra* (fn. 2) 304.

 | DOI 10.1163/9789004299931_005

hand, the sovereignty especially of small and weak states ought to be preserved; on the other, the collective promotion and enforcement of a growing number of values and interests of the international community, such as the respect for human rights or the protection of the environment, are more important than ever in an increasingly interdependent and globalized world.

The difficulties of distinguishing illegal from lawful attempts to influence the behaviour of other international actors are reflected in the writings of legal scholars.[627] They propose different criteria which in their opinion characterize prohibited interference: the means used by, the intention of and the objective pursued by the intervening state; the targets against which the measures taken are directed; or the 'adequate' relation, i.e., the proportionality between the objective and the means used.[628] Yet, the illegality of certain means and forms of pressure may be contested; the intention of a state trying to influence another state is often difficult to establish;[629] the internal affairs of states in which others must not interfere are in flux; the proportionality between means and ends is problematic because of the lack of precise criteria. As in the case of other complex issues of international law, no simple and perfect solution can therefore be offered.

What is feasible once more is the identification of areas of clear legality and illegality, with a rather large 'grey area' between them. Thus, on the one hand, coercion by military means, which is usually included in definitions of intervention, is clearly unlawful and already prohibited under Article 2(4) of the UN Charter.[630] Moreover, as early as 1936 the parties to the International Convention

---

627 Neuhold, *supra* (fn. 7), 290.

628 This is the criterion ('*Sozialadäquanz*' – 'social adequacy') emphasized by Gerlach. As an example, he mentions the refusal of the United States to grant Argentina economic assistance during World War II in order to force the latter state to break off diplomatic relations with Nazi Germany and close its territory to German nationals. In order to achieve goals of minor importance, the United States threatened the existence of the target state. Gerlach, *supra* (fn. 624) 203. A similar view is held by Fisher, 'Intervention: Three Problems of Policy and Law', in: Stanger (ed.), *supra* (fn. 624) 3.

629 See *supra* 127.

630 In addition to the treaties and 'soft law' quoted below, the ICJ formulated the principle of non-intervention in its judgment in the *Nicaragua* case as follows: '…the principle forbids all States of groups of States to intervene directly or indirectly in the internal or external affairs of other States. A prohibited intervention must accordingly be one bearing on matters in which each State is permitted, by the principle of State sovereignty, to decide freely. One of these is the choice of a political, economic, social and cultural system, and the formulation of foreign policy.… The element of coercion, which defines, and indeed forms the very essence of, prohibited intervention, is particularly obvious in the case of intervention which uses force, either in the direct form of military action, or in the indirect

concerning the Use of Broadcasting in the Cause of Peace outlawed, *inter alia*, transmissions inciting the population of any territory to acts incompatible with the internal order or security of the territory of a contracting party (Article 1) and obligated the parties to ensure that transmissions do not incite war against another contracting party or acts likely to lead to war (Article 2).[631]

On the other hand, according to other treaty law, the offer of good offices and mediation by a third party must not be regarded as an unfriendly act (and consequently as unlawful intervention) by the parties to an international conflict.[632] Furthermore, acts that would normally be regarded as intervention are justified as countermeasures[633] and sanctions adopted by the UN Security Council. Moreover, forcible attempts to change the political, economic and social system of a state are, in principle, illegal; however, political and economic pressure in order to prevent or oust a political regime based on apartheid and calls for the respect of human rights in general do not constitute illegal interference.

It is submitted that, contrary to the usual understanding of the term, the debate on intervention should focus on acts below the threshold of armed force.[634] As recalled above, the latter type of coercion is already proscribed by the prohibition of the threat or use of force, as enshrined, in particular, in the UN Charter, and has become part of universal international law and *jus cogens*. 'Humanitarian intervention' should therefore be discussed in the context of this principle.[635] As a separate rule, the principle of non-intervention should be limited to pressure short of the use of weapons.

The legal problem becomes even more complex if insights from the social sciences are taken into account. One actor may act in accordance with the demands or wishes of another actor for several reasons. Successful intervention means, according to the definition proposed above, compliance with the demands of another actor as a result of the effective threat or actual use of illegal non-military coercion by the latter. In the case of a successful threat, a

---

form of support for subversive or terrorist activities within another State'. *Military and Paramilitary Activities in and against Nicaragua (Nicaragua v. United States of America)*, Merits, paragraph 205. See *infra* 168.

631 32 *AJIL* (1938), Suppl. 113; Goldberg, 'Transnational Communication and Defamatory Speech: A Case for Establishing Norms for the Twenty-First Century', 50 *New York Law School Review* (2005–2006) 145.

632 Article 3(3) of the 1899 and 1907 Hague Conventions for the Pacific Settlement of International Disputes.

633 See *supra* fn. 358.

634 This view was also shared, for example, by Wengler, *Völkerrecht* (vol. 2, 1964) 1038.

635 See *supra* 102, 129.

power relationship exists between the two actors.[636] The less powerful party gives in because it concludes that if the threat were carried out, the consequences for it would be more negative than if it behaved in accordance with the demands of its more powerful adversary. If the threat has to be executed, (non-military) force is used between the actors concerned. But compliance can also be obtained on the basis of an authority relationship: one actor regards the demands of another actor as reasonable and well-founded in terms of his/her own value system. This type of relation may exist in a hegemonic system where the ruling elites of the 'satellites' follow the orders of the hegemon, also because they want to maintain their dominant positions and material benefits within their own states. Finally, the addressee may fulfil the wishes of another actor of his/her own free will because of positive feelings like affection and friendship towards the latter.

Given these manifold possibilities, the correct assessment of the reason for the compliance of one state with the wishes and demands of another is important for ascertaining whether intervention has occurred or not in a given situation. If the victim openly complains about unlawful pressure and is able to prove it, the question is easy to answer. However, threats are not always explicitly stated, and governments whose states become the targets of intervention may prefer to remain silent for fear of further negative consequences.

A look at the current political and economic situation in international relations shows that the need for adequate legal rules on coercion short of the use of military means has increased in recent decades. States tend to avoid resort to armed force for a number of reasons.[637] As a rule, governments do not wish to face the odium of violating Article 2(4) of the UN Charter, all the more so because other tools are equally effective. With the extension and intensification of international interaction more and more areas lend themselves to exerting non-military pressure. Another aspect makes intervention particularly 'attractive': the costs of this type of coercion are lower for a state than those caused by the use of its armed forces. Even if it attacks a much weaker state which it can expect to defeat easily and quickly, some human casualties and material damage cannot be excluded should the victim of the attack resist, in addition to the financial costs and the political opprobrium of at least part of the international community. The existence of a large number of small and weak countries

636 Bachrach and Baratz, 'Decisions and Non-decisions: An Analytical Framework', 57 *The American Political Science Review* (1963) 632. For a more recent conceptualization of the complex notion of power see Barnett and Duvall, 'Power in global governance', in: Barnett and Duvall (eds.), *Power in Global Governance* (2005) 1.

637 See *supra* 27.

that are also vulnerable to coercion below the threshold of armed force further exacerbates the problems of intervention.

4.2 The Evolution of the Principle of Non-Intervention

The development of the prohibition of intervention took a long time. This delay was due the fact that reciprocity did not work as a 'normative engine' as in other areas of international law, for instance, diplomatic and consular relations. There states found themselves at both ends of the relationship, both as receiving and sending states with the resulting divergent interests. In the former capacity, they wanted to curtail and control the activities of foreign representatives; but as sending states, they were interested in the protection and freedom of action of their own diplomats and consuls. In contrast, powerful states only interfered with the affairs of weaker countries but did not themselves become victims of intervention.[638] In this sector of international law the legal principle of sovereign equality between all states irrespective of their power was 'overruled' by political reality for a long time.

Interestingly, the United States, the hegemon in the Western hemisphere, was one of the countries leading the way. Quite typically, the young and relatively weak United States initially insisted on the principle of non-intervention. In accordance with the Monroe Doctrine named after President James Monroe, who proclaimed it in his annual address to Congress in 1823, the government in Washington, D.C. opposed attempts by European powers to extend their system to any part of the western hemisphere as 'dangerous to our peace and safety' and opposed interposition for the purposes of oppression or control in any other way 'as a manifestation of an unfriendly disposition toward the United States'.[639] The concrete reason for this statement of principle was U.S. opposition to efforts of European powers to regain control over former Spanish and Portuguese colonies in Latin America, which had benefited from the weakening of their colonial masters during the Napoleonic Wars to declare their independence.

Towards the end of the 19th century the United States joined the ranks of great powers, especially after defeating Spain in the 1898 War. Following the sober logic of power politics, it intervened itself in Latin American states, also

---

638 Although less powerful states occasionally even tried to influence politics in the United States. For examples see Fisler Damrosch, *supra* (fn. 624) 14, 22.

639 Root, 'The Real Monroe Doctrine', 8 *AJIL* (1914) 427; Hughes, 'Observations on the Monroe Doctrine', 17 *AJIL* (1923) 611; Grant, *supra* (fn. 74) paragraphs 3–7.

resorting to armed force. Under President Theodore Roosevelt, in 1904, the Monroe Doctrine was reinterpreted as the political basis for U.S. hegemonic aspirations in its hemisphere.

Some 40 years later, the administration of President Franklin D. Roosevelt switched from the previous 'Big Stick' to the new 'Good Neighbor Policy' towards Latin America. This new orientation was reflected in the 1933 Montevideo Convention on the Rights and Duties of States[640] and in more detail in the 1936 Protocol of Buenos Aires on Non-intervention and confirmed in the 1938 Lima Declaration on the Principles of Solidarity in America. The prohibition of direct or indirect intervention in the internal or external affairs of any other state was reiterated after World War II in Articles 15 and 16 of the 1948 Bogotá Charter of the OAS and Articles 19 and 20 under the 1993 Managua Protocol of Amendment to the Charter of American States. In addition to armed force, these treaties outlawed, in a somewhat repetitive fashion, any other form of interference or attempted threat against the personality of the state or against its political, economic and cultural elements, as well as the use or the encouragement of the use of coercive measures of an economic or political character.

The 'socialist' countries led by the Soviet Union also contributed to the development of the non-intervention principle in international law. After the 1917 October Revolution, the young Soviet state found itself in an ambiguous position. On the one hand, it proclaimed an expansionist ideology aimed at the worldwide triumph of communism. On the other, since the expected transition of other countries to communism failed to materialize, the Soviet Union was isolated and on the defensive. The result was a double standard concerning intervention. It was deemed illegal if practiced by the capitalist-imperialist powers against the Soviet Union. This principle constituted one of the cornerstones of the 'international law of peaceful coexistence' governing the relations between 'socialist' and 'non-socialist' states. However, the prohibition did not apply on the non-state level, that of political parties, trade unions and grass-root movements in their fight against the class enemy. Moreover, what was regarded as lawful ideological struggle on one's own side was denounced as hostile propaganda if used by the adversary.

Furthermore, there was no room for the principle of non-intervention in the relations between 'socialist' states which were bound by the higher law of 'socialist internationalism'. As pointed out above, the 'Brezhnev Doctrine' even included the right to use force in order to prevent a member of the bloc from

640 Article 8: 'No state has the right to intervene in the internal or external affairs of another.' The United States made a reservation to this provision. 28 *AJIL* (1934), Suppl. 78.

opting for a different political and economic system or leaving the Warsaw Treaty Organization.[641]

Like the League of Nations Covenant, the UN Charter does not contain the non-intervention principle in relations between member states. At the 1945 San Francisco Conference Mexico proposed to include the essence of the prohibition in the Buenos Aires Protocol in Article 2(4) of the Charter. However, this amendment was not adopted. On the other hand, Article 2(7) obligates the UN to respect the principle in its relations with states.[642] According to this provision, nothing in the Charter shall authorize the organization to intervene in matters which are essentially within the domestic jurisdiction of any state.[643]

On the basis of an *argumentum a maiore ad minus*, the conclusion may be drawn that if the UN itself is bound by this prohibition, the principle must all the more be observed by the member states in their relations with each other. In addition, the illegality of intervention in the internal affairs of states may be deduced from the sovereign equality of states, the very foundation of the international legal order and the first principle listed in Article 2 of the UN Charter.[644] In the meantime, the principle of non-intervention which was included in numerous treaties and in important 'soft law' documents, some of which will be mentioned below, has also become part of universal customary international law.[645]

Not surprisingly, after the entry into force of the UN Charter the states of the Third World became another driving force behind the further development and strengthening of the principle of non-intervention. Most of them had only recently become independent in the process of decolonization and were militarily weak countries with underdeveloped economies. Therefore they felt threatened as potential targets of intervention by the more powerful members

---

641 Although the principle of respect for the independence and sovereignty of the contracting parties and non-interference in their internal affairs was enshrined in Article 8 of the 1955 Warsaw Treaty of Friendship, Co-operation and Mutual Assistance. See *supra* 157.

642 Without prejudice to the application of enforcement measures under Chapter VII. See *supra* 46.

643 Similarly, under Article 15(8) of the League of Nations Covenant, the League Council was precluded from making a recommendation for the settlement of a dispute which it found to arise out of a matter which by international law was solely within the domestic jurisdiction of the party that claimed this to be the case.

644 Other indirectly relevant provisions are Article 2(4) with its reference to political independence against which force must not be threatened or used, as well as Articles 1(2) and 55 which affirm the principle of equal rights and self-determination of peoples that can also become the victims of by non-forcible pressure. Fisler Damrosch, *supra* (fn. 624) 8.

645 As confirmed by the ICJ in the *Nicaragua* case. See *supra* fn. 630, and *infra* 168.

of the two Cold War blocs competing for influence in Africa, Asia and Latin America.

The obligation to abstain from any action aimed at regime change was already laid down in Article 8 of the 1945 Pact of the League of Arab States.[646] Mutual non-interference in each other's internal affairs was equally included in the '*Pancha Shila*', the five principles of peaceful coexistence in the preamble to the agreement between the People's Republic of China and the Republic of India on trade and intercourse which was signed in Peking in 1954.

The broadest political formation of the Third World countries, the Non-Aligned Movement, also consistently condemned intervention in all its forms, in particular in the concluding documents adopted at the summit meetings of the group. Thus two of the ten principles proclaimed at the 1955 Bandung Conference referred to abstention from intervention and interference in the internal affairs of another country and from exerting pressure on other countries. The Bandung meeting set the stage for the first summit conference of the non-aligned states in Belgrade in 1961. In their final Declaration, the heads of state and government again emphasized in the Yugoslav capital their opposition to intimidation, interference or intervention, more specifically in the exercise of the right of self-determination of peoples.

The developing and 'socialist' member states also used their majority in the UN General Assembly for the adoption of resolutions on the illegality of intervention.[647] Against the background of U.S. military action in Vietnam and in the Dominican Republic, the Soviet Union took an initiative which resulted in the almost unanimous adoption of Resolution 2131 (XX), the Declaration on the Inadmissibility of Intervention in the Domestic Affairs of States and the Protection of Their Independence and Sovereignty.[648] 109 States voted in favour, none against, and only the United Kingdom abstained. The Declaration reiterated the above-mentioned provisions in the Bogotá Charter, thus again

646 'Every member State of the League shall respect the form of government obtaining in the other States of the League, and shall recognize the form of government obtaining as one of the rights of those States, and shall pledge itself not to take any action tending to change that form.'

647 However, the plenary organ of the UN had already taken a stand against intervention at a time when Western member states held a majority in the Assembly. In 1949, in Resolution 290 (IV) 'Essentials of peace', it called not only upon every nation 'To refrain from threatening or using force contrary to the Charter' (paragraph 2), but also 'To refrain from any threats or acts, direct or indirect, aimed at impairing the freedom, independence or integrity of any State, or at fomenting civil strife and subverting the will of the people in any State' (paragraph 3).

648 Neuhold, *supra* (fn. 7) 304.

introducing a broad definition of intervention which comprised the use of armed force. It added a specific prohibition concerning subversive, terrorist or armed activities directed towards the violent overthrow of the regime of another state or interference in civil strife in another state.[649] The Declaration also stressed the link to self-determination and independence of peoples and nations and the inalienable right of every state to choose its political, economic, social and cultural systems, without interference in any form by another state.[650]

A group of Third World states led by Guyana obtained the adoption by the General Assembly of a lengthy and, in the eyes of the 22 Western member states[651] that voted against it, radical resolution on the principle in 1981.[652] For instance, this Declaration on the Inadmissibility of Intervention and Interference in the Internal Affairs of States also contained the duty of a state to refrain from the exploitation and the distortion of human rights issues as a means of interference in the internal affairs of states.[653]

The prohibition of interference in the internal affairs of states was further reaffirmed on the regional level. It was one of the principles enshrined in Article 3 of the 1963 Charter of the OAU and Article 4 of the 2000 Constitutive Act of the AU.

Non-intervention was equally emphasized by the Association of South East Asian Nations (ASEAN). In the preamble to the 1967 Bangkok Declaration establishing the Association, the five founding members[654] expressed their

---

649 Paragraph 2. See *supra* 39.

650 Paragraph 5. The 1987 Declaration on the Enhancement of the Effectiveness of the Principle of Refraining from the Threat of Use of Force in International Relations, which included non-military coercion as unlawful force, restated the prohibition of armed intervention and all other forms of interference or attempted threats against the personality of the state or against its political, economic and cultural elements (Article 7). It may also be pointed out that Article 8 of the Declaration prohibited the use or the encouragement of the use of economic, political or any type of measures to coerce another state in order to obtain from it the subordination of the exercise of its sovereign rights and to secure from it advantages of any kind. See *supra* 28.

651 Including Venezuela. Six states abstained.

652 General Assembly Resolution 36/103.

653 Part II, paragraph (1). The Declaration also included, in Part III(b), the right and duty of states fully to support the right to self-determination, freedom and independence of peoples under colonial domination, foreign occupation or racist régimes, as well as the right of these peoples to wage both political and armed struggle to that end, in accordance with the purposes and principles of the Charter.

654 Indonesia, Malaysia, the Philippines, Singapore and Thailand. Subsequently, Brunei Darussalam (in 1984), Vietnam (in 1995), Laos and Myanmar (in 1997), and Cambodia (in 1999) also became members of ASEAN.

determination to ensure their stability and security from external interference in any form or manifestation in order to preserve their national identities in accordance with the ideals and aspirations of their peoples. The right of every state, large or small, to lead its national existence free from outside interference was reiterated in the preamble to the Kuala Lumpur Declaration of 1971 on transforming South East Asia into a Zone of Peace, Freedom and Neutrality. The principles in Article 2 of the 1976 Bali Treaty of Amity and Cooperation of ASEAN include the right of every state to lead its national existence free from external interference, subversion or coercion and non-interference in the internal affairs of one another.

Similarly, the 'Decalogue' in the CSCE Final Act of 1975[655] contained as its 'Sixth Commandment' non-intervention in internal affairs and thus clarified that the principle also applied to Europe. The addition that the participating states will refrain from any intervention, regardless of their mutual relations, can be read as an implicit rejection of the above-mentioned 'Brezhnev Doctrine', since as a result, the principle must also be respected in the 'special' relations between 'socialist' states.[656]

Given all these legal developments, it could come as no surprise that the ICJ concluded in the *Nicaragua* case in 1986 that the principle of non-intervention was part and parcel of customary international law. According to the Court, the existence in the *opinio juris* of states was backed by established and substantial practice.[657]

4.3 Non-Intervention Today: Still a Controversial Issue

The main differences of opinion in international practice continue to revolve around the question whether a state may reject as unlawful intervention demands by other states or international organizations that it respect human rights.[658] On the one hand, it may be pointed out that as a result of the conclusion

---

655 See *supra* 1.

656 See *supra* 157.

657 *Military and Paramilitary Activities in and against Nicaragua* (*Nicaragua v. United States of America*), Merits, paragraph 202.

658 During the Cold War this issue overshadowed the CSCE and its follow-up meetings from the beginning, with the Western states on the political offensive against the 'socialist' participants. On the one hand, as mentioned above, the Declaration on Principles in the 1975 Helsinki Final Act of the CSCE contained non-intervention in internal affairs as Principle VI. On the other, respect for human rights and fundamental freedoms, including freedom of thought, conscience, religion or belief, followed as Principle VII. However, the Declaration

of treaties providing for the respect for these rights they cease to be an internal matter for the contracting states. Many states are bound not only by the general principle in the UN Charter but also by other treaties containing more specific provisions, like the two UN Covenants and other UN human rights conventions or regional treaty regimes. As in the case of any other treaty, the parties may call on each other for compliance with the obligations under the treaty. The world-wide recognition of the universality of human rights, in particular at the 1993 UN Human Rights Conference in Vienna, strengthens the contention that, by now, respect for human rights has also become a principle of universal customary law. According to the ILC, fundamental human rights even belong to the realm of *jus cogens*.[659]

On the other hand, it is objected that even if respect for human rights is a universal principle, its concrete implementation is still left to the discretion of each state in accordance with its cultural tradition, political system and the level of its economic and social development. Some governments also argue that the granting of human rights is a long-term project which can only be realized gradually over a long period of time.

Therefore the problem of intervention in the internal affairs of states has lost nothing of its relevance. Western states and organizations, above all the United States and the EU, continue their human rights campaigns. However, their demands for the respect of these rights by powerful states sometimes conflict with their economic and political interests, be they energy supplies or strategic considerations. In these cases, quiet diplomacy behind the scenes is preferred, even if the results are limited and only concern certain individuals or specific measures.

Another issue which has already been touched upon is raised by action of the UN Security Council against human rights violations. Even though the barrier of matters falling essentially within the domestic jurisdiction of any state cannot be opposed to the application Chapter VII, and despite the commitment to the secondary responsibility to protect, the members of the Security Council, in particular those holding a permanent seat, find it difficult to agree on enforcement measures against governments accused of massive human rights abuses.

failed to indicate which of the two ought to have primacy in case of conflict. See *supra* 5. Eventually, the controversy receded into the background within the CSCE/OSCE when the members of the Eastern bloc also opted for the individual-oriented Western concept of human rights after the end of the East–West conflict.

659 See *supra* 25, 102.

To recall recent examples, on the one hand, the Council adopted sanctions against the Gaddafi regime in Libya in 2011.[660] On the other, at the same time, the demands not only of Western but also Arab states for measures against the government of Basher al-Assed in Syria, which also suppressed mass demonstrations calling for political reforms and committed large-scale atrocities against its own civilian population, fell on the deaf ears of non-Western states, above all Russia and China. They opposed interference with what they considered as internal affairs of Syria, although the UN Commissioner for Human Rights, Navi Pillay, had presented to the Security Council a report on the brutal repression of the democratic reform movement in Syria and proposed that the Council refer the situation in the country to the ICC.[661] Moreover, in 2012 the UN General Assembly adopted, by an overwhelming majority of 137:12:17, Resolution 66/253, in which it condemned the use of force against civilians, the killing and persecution of protesters and journalists, and sexual violence and ill-treatment, including against children, by the Syrian government and pro-government militias.[662]

---

660 See *supra* 111.

661 See *supra* 95.

662 The votes against the draft resolution included those of China and Russia.

CHAPTER 5

The Peaceful Settlement of International Disputes

5.1 The Principle

The obligation of the subjects of international law to settle their disputes by peaceful means is the logical corollary of the prohibitions of the threat or use of force and the interdiction of intervention.[663] These principles may be seen as the inscriptions on the two sides of the same coin. States resorted to coercion in order to prevail over their adversaries in conflicts. The gradual ban on force and other forms of pressure has not, however, eliminated international disputes caused mainly by the scarcity of goods or contradictory values. Therefore, conflicting parties must be obligated to seek a non-violent solution to their controversies.

The terms 'settlement' or 'solution' are usually employed interchangeably. Their meaning is usually taken for granted without further discussion. However, two definitions that vary in scope seem possible. They can either refer to the elimination of the root causes of a dispute; or they may at least signify the agreement of the parties not to pursue their claims anymore, even if their differences of opinion have not completely disappeared.

The slow development of the principle of the peaceful settlement of international disputes followed the above logic and went in parallel with that of the non-use of force. Thus Article 1 of the Hague Conventions for the Pacific Settlement of International Disputes of 1899 and 1907 set out: 'With a view to obviating as far as possible recourse to force in the relations between States, the

663 Northedge and Donelan, *International Disputes: The Political Aspects* (1971); Randolph, *Third Party Settlement in Theory and Practice* (1973); Neuhold, *supra* (fn. 7) 357; Bowett, 'Contemporary Developments in Legal Techniques in the Settlement of Disputes', 180 *RCADI* (1983) 177; Collier and Lowe, *The Settlement of Disputes in International Law: Institutions and Procedures* (1999); Caflish, 'Cent ans de règlement pacifique des différends interétatiques', 288 *RCADI* (2001) 257; Neuhold, 'The United Nations System for the Peaceful Settlement of International Disputes' in: Cede and Sucharipa-Behrmann (eds.), *supra* (fn. 205) 59; Peters, 'International Dispute Settlement: A Network of Cooperational Duties', 14 *EJIL* (2003) 1; O'Connell (ed.), *International Dispute Settlement* (2003); Charpentier and Sierpinski, 'Article 2 Paragraphe 3', in: Cot, Pellet and Forteau (eds.), *supra* (fn. 82) 435; Merrills, *International Dispute Settlement* (5th ed., 2011); Pellet, 'Peaceful Settlement of International Disputes', MPEPIL; Tomuschat, 'Article 2(3)', in: Simma et alii (eds.), *supra* (fn. 82) 181.

 | DOI 10.1163/9789004299931_006

Contracting Powers agree to use their best efforts to insure the pacific settlement of international differences.' The cautious wording short of a firm commitment should be noted: even the use of their best efforts by the contracting parties may fail.[664]

The member states of the League of Nations were bound to choose between three procedures – arbitration, adjudication by the PCIJ or enquiry by the Council[665] – for settling disputes likely to lead to a rupture and not to go to war against members which complied with an arbitral award, a judgment of the PCIJ or the recommendations in a unanimously adopted report of the Council.[666]

A general duty (merely) to seek to settle disputes opposing them to each other by pacific means was accepted by the parties to the 1928 Briand-Kellogg Pact.[667]

This obligation was also enshrined and further specified in the UN Charter. Thus one of the purposes of the new World Organization in Article 1(1) of its constituent treaty is to bring about by peaceful means, and in conformity with the principles of justice and international law, adjustment[668] or settlement of international disputes or situations which might lead to a breach of the peace. Moreover, the third principle included in Article 2 imposes on all members the obligation to settle their international disputes in such a manner that international peace and security, and justice, are not endangered.

The wording of these two provisions refers to a crucial problem which may arise in a conflict where the more powerful party renounces the use of force in favour of a non-violent solution. Quite significantly, the draft of the Charter drawn up by the great powers at Dumbarton Oaks in 1944 did not mention the duty of dispute settlement in conformity with justice and international law or not endangering international peace and security, and justice. It was the small and medium-sized countries that insisted on the insertion of these additional requirements at the founding conference of the UN in San Francisco in 1945. These states also agreed that the main task of the new organization ought to be the maintenance and restoration of international peace and security, but not at the price of imposing a non-violent but inequitable solution on the less

664 The same is true of the avoidance of the recourse to force 'as far as possible'.

665 The term 'enquiry' was a misnomer, since the Council actually engaged in conciliation by also making recommendations for a solution. See *infra* 184.

666 See *supra* 19.

667 See *supra* 21.

668 Another undefined term that adds to the terminological confusion.

powerful parties. The memory of the Western 'appeasement' policy vis-à-vis Nazi Germany, in particular the 1938 Munich Agreement on the annexation of the *Sudetenland* by the 'Third *Reich*' as the most dramatic example of such an unjust deal, where the weakest side had to foot the bill for avoiding an armed confrontation, was still fresh in the minds of the sponsors of those amendments at the end of World War II.[669]

The UN Charter is thus based on two concepts of peace. While 'negative peace' denotes the absence of armed force, 'positive peace' means the achievement of social justice by the gradual elimination of the main causes of international as well as intrastate conflicts on a worldwide scale.[670] Measures to this effect range from the reduction of the prosperity gap between rich and poor nations to the respect for human rights, democracy and the rule of law, as well as the protection of the environment. According to the philosophy underlying the Charter, genuine peace requires that both types of peace be established. At the same time, the constituent treaty of the World Organization puts more emphasis on 'negative' than on 'positive peace', as a comparison between Chapters VII and IX in general and the powers of the Security Council and the Economic and Social Council (ECOSOC) in particular clearly shows. This preference is again understandable in its historic context, as the main preoccupation in 1945 was to avert another major war.

The authors of the Charter not only laid down the principle of the peaceful settlement of disputes in general terms; they also inserted a special Chapter (Chapter VI) entitled 'Pacific Settlement of Disputes' which contains more detailed rules. In addition, numerous other provisions of the constituent treaty of the UN – especially on the Security Council, the General Assembly, the ICJ, the Secretary-General, as well as regional arrangements or agencies – are relevant to the principle.

It was further elaborated, for example, in resolutions of the UN General Assembly, above all the 1970 Friendly Relations Declaration,[671] the 1982 Manila Declaration on the Peaceful Settlement of International Disputes[672] and the 1988 Declaration on the Prevention and Removal of Disputes and Situations Which May Threaten International Peace and Security and on the Role of the

669 Goodrich, Hambro and Simons, *Charter of the United Nations: Commentary and Documents* (3rd ed. 1969) 28.

670 In the terminology of 'critical peace research'. Galtung, Gewalt, Frieden und Friedensforschung', in: Senghaas (ed.), *Kritische Friedensforschung* (1971) 55.

671 See *supra* 1.

672 Annex to General Assembly Resolution 37/10.

United Nations in this Field.[673] However, all these documents added only few substantive innovations that went beyond the provisions of the UN Charter.

As a rule of universal international law the principle laid down in Article 2(3) of the UN Charter, as further defined, in particular, by the Friendly Relations and Manila Declarations, imposes on all states the obligation actively to attempt a pacific settlement of their international disputes.[674] These disputes still are, above all, conflicts with other states, but also include controversies with other subjects of international law, notably international organizations and peoples entitled to self-determination.

However, the duty includes neither the application of a particular method of dispute solution, nor the order in which these means are to be used, nor the achievement of a specific result. This would be contrary to the principle of free consent, which still underlies this principle and is one of the main facets of sovereignty, still the cornerstone of the international legal order. The settlement of international conflicts therefore belongs to the realm of cooperative security.[675] This means that all conflicting parties must agree both on the settlement method and, except if they choose arbitration or adjudication on the substance of the solution – a consent they may also refuse to give. The principle thus imposes an obligation only of conduct or behaviour, not of result.[676] States must merely refrain from the threat or use of force and solely seek, but need not achieve, a pacific outcome of their conflicts. Arguably, only a state that consistently obstructs all efforts to peacefully resolve a dispute to which it is a party violates the principle.[677] Another weakness of the peaceful settlement regime is due to the absence of mechanisms for effectively enforcing the terms of a settlement in the event of non-compliance by a party.

5.2 The Main Methods of Dispute Settlement: General Remarks

The first article in Chapter VI of the UN Charter, Article 33, contains a list of the traditional means for the peaceful resolution of international conflicts: 'The parties to any dispute, the continuance of which is likely to endanger the maintenance of international peace and security, shall, therefore, first of all, seek a

---

673 Annex to General Assembly Resolution 43/51.

674 The ICJ stated in 1986 in the *Nicaragua* case that the principle also had the status of customary law. *Military and Paramilitary Activities in and against Nicaragua* (*Nicaragua v. United States of America*), Merits, paragraph 290.

675 See *supra* 56.

676 Pellet, *supra* (fn. 663) paragraph 16; Tomuschat, *supra* (fn. 663) 190.

677 Tomuschat, *supra* (fn. 663) 191.

solution by negotiation, enquiry, mediation, conciliation, arbitration, judicial settlement, resort to regional agencies or arrangements, or any peaceful means of their own choice.'

However, this list is incomplete, since it does not mention, in particular, good offices, a method that has proved its worth in practice. The criterion that underlies the order in which these means are listed is the degree to which the conflicting parties keep or relinquish control over the outcome of their dispute in favour of a third party;[678] it will also be applied below.

Although these methods can be clearly defined and differ from each other in theory, some of them are frequently applied together in practice without a clear distinction[679] and terminological precision.[680]

It should also be stressed that each of the methods of peaceful dispute settlement has its advantages and shortcomings. Therefore, in the opinion of this author,[681] none of them is inherently superior to and *a priori* 'better' than the others, so that parties should be urged to apply it to all their conflicts. The words 'first of all' in Article 33 do not establish a hierarchy among the procedures according to the order in which they are listed; they mean that the conflicting parties should first try to solve their dispute by using one or more of these methods before turning to the Security Council.[682]

A line is sometimes drawn between adjudication and arbitration as the 'legal' and the other as the 'diplomatic' methods. However, this distinction is problematic, since it may lead to the erroneous conclusion that the latter are the opposite of 'legal' methods and consequently 'illegal', although they are of course equally lawful. Furthermore, proceedings before international courts and arbitral tribunals are also accompanied by diplomatic activities.[683]

678 Since only two parties are involved in most conflicts and for the sake of simplicity, the following remarks will focus on bilateral disputes and refer to other actors that try to help with a settlement as third parties. However, the number of the conflicting parties may occasionally be more than two, so that the non-party involved in the settlement process is not the 'third' actor.

679 This is particularly true of good offices, enquiry, and mediation. See *infra* 177, 179, 180.

680 See *supra* 19 – enquiry by League Council – and *infra* 178 – good offices.

681 Although some governments and writers favour one or the other method (in particular, negotiations on the one and adjudication on the other hand). See *infra* 202.

682 See *infra* 207.

683 Like between 'hard' and 'soft law', one might distinguish between 'hard' and 'soft' dispute settlement methods. The former leave the solution to the agreement of the parties; the latter (arbitration and adjudication) lead to the binding decision of a third party. Once again, this does not necessarily mean that the 'hard' variant is more effective, since the enforcement of an arbitral award or the judgment of an international court in the event of non-compliance must not be taken for granted. Neuhold, *supra* (fn. 581) 353. See also *infra* 199, 202.

5.3 Negotiation

Direct negotiations between the conflicting parties without the involvement of a non-party are simple, confidential, flexible and usually the least expensive, as well as the most frequently used method.[684] Skilful negotiators may find a genuine solution through balanced mutual concessions leading to an agreement that both parties accept of their own free will and prefer to a continuation of their conflict.[685] Basically, they can aim at the lowest common denominator or a package deal between the common and divergent positions of the parties.

Negotiations are often the first step in a dispute settlement process, either because they lead to an agreement to use other methods or because they are provided for in an existing treaty.[686]

The main drawback of face-to-face talks without the participation of a third actor is the unmitigated negative impact of the power relationship between the parties on the outcome, especially if the stakes of the dispute are high. On the one hand, if this relationship is symmetrical, negotiations are likely soon to result in deadlock, because neither party will be ready to move towards a compromise. On the other hand, where one side is clearly more powerful than the other, the weaker party may have to accept an inequitable solution favouring its stronger opponent.

The possibility of invoking the invalidity of such an agreement under the international law of treaties on the ground that is was concluded under coercion[687] is not really helpful in this context. Not only are opinions divided over whether, in addition to the threat or use of armed force, the exertion of political or economic pressure should also have this far-reaching effect on the validity of an international treaty.[688] Furthermore, to invoke coercion may be counterproductive in political reality for the less powerful side. For, irrespective of the legal situation, this step may result in further negative measures by the stronger against the weaker party.[689]

---

684 Hakapää, 'Negotiation', MPEPIL; Merrills, *supra* (fn. 663) 1.

685 In 1998, in its Resolution 53/101, the UN General Assembly adopted rather general principles and guidelines for international negotiations.

686 For instance, in Article 41 of the 1978 Vienna Convention on Succession of States in respect of Treaties and Article 42 of the 1983 Vienna Convention on Succession of States in respect of State Property, Archives and Debts.

687 In accordance with Article 52 of the 1969 VCLT.

688 See *supra* 129.

689 See *supra* 162.

Legal analysis focuses on the formal aspects of negotiations. They can be held bilaterally or in a multilateral framework, ad hoc or within existing institutions, such as mixed commissions or international organizations, as well as on different levels. The latter may range from that of diplomats and officials from other ministries to that of ministers and 'summit meetings' of heads of state or government. Talks may be kept secret until an agreement is reached or be announced to the public, in which case modifications of known positions towards compromise solutions may become difficult because they tend to be seen as signs of weakness.

Quite typically, the 1969 VCLT regulates the question of the organs which may represent states in the process leading to the conclusion of a treaty (Articles 7 and 8) and the formal end of negotiations through the adoption of the text of a treaty (Article 9). It remains silent on the crucial negotiating process itself, although lawyers subsequently try to establish the intentions of the parties by interpreting the text of the treaty. Social sciences can contribute useful insights into the politics, tactics and psychology of negotiations.[690]

5.4 Good Offices

A third party – a state, international organization, or an individual – that offers its good offices (as pointed out above, not mentioned in Article 33 of the UN Charter[691]) tries to bring the conflicting parties together and to facilitate negotiations between them, especially by placing communication channels or conference facilities at their disposal.[692] However, the third party does not take part in the negotiations.[693]

---

690 Iklé, *How Nations Negotiate* (1964); Lall, *Modern International Negotiation: Principles and Practice* (1966); Nicolson, *Diplomacy* (3rd ed. 1969); Schelling, *The Strategy of Conflict* (1980); Fisher and Ury, *Getting To Yes: Negotiating Agreement Without Giving In* (1981); Zartmann and Berman, *The Practical Negotiator* (1982); Fisher, Kopelman and Kupfer-Schneider, *Beyond Machiavelli: Tools for Coping with Conflict* (1994); Zartmann and Rubin, *Power and Negotiation* (2002); Fisher and Shapiro, *Beyond Reason: Using Emotions as You Negotiate* (2005); Starkey, Boyer and Wilkenfield, *International Negotiation in a Complex World* (2010).

691 But already included, for example, in Article 3 of the 1899 and 1907 Hague Conventions for the Pacific Settlement of International Disputes.

692 Lapidoth, 'Good Offices', MPEPIL.

693 Thus Article IX of the 1948 American Treaty on Pacific Settlement (Pact of Bogotá) provides: 'The procedure of good offices consists in the attempt by one or more American Governments not parties to the controversy, or by one or more eminent citizens of any

The usefulness of good offices is therefore sometimes downplayed. Yet, they may help to achieve a decisive breakthrough towards the peaceful solution of a dispute. Both conflicting parties may want to overcome a standoff and be ready for talks; however, disagreement on what might seem a merely technical and formal problem may still prevent the opening of negotiations: the place where these talks should be held. Each side will prefer its own territory or that of a friendly country as the venue for negotiations. However, each party is likely to refuse to give in to the wishes of the adversary in order not to appear weak and undercut its own position by making the first concession.

One way out of this impasse may be to agree to hold talks alternately in the territories of the conflicting parties. Another could be to send their representatives to a state which both regard as neutral in their controversy, in particular a permanently neutral country. Neutrals may only provide the second-best but a mutually acceptable option to both sides. States like Switzerland and Austria that have opted for permanent neutrality, i.e., remaining neutral in all future international armed conflicts, are in turn well advised to make themselves useful to other countries, especially those involved in conflicts. In addition to fulfilling their legal obligations, permanently neutral states ought to practice an active neutrality policy in order to counter accusations of an egoistic, cowardly and immoral position instead of supporting what each conflicting party and its supporters consider the just cause.[694]

Good offices are one of the generally appreciated third-party functions for which permanent neutrals are particularly qualified. Their mere existence is a standing offer of good offices which they may more or less explicitly emphasize in a given conflict. In any event, it cannot be a coincidence that so many international talks and conferences have been held in Geneva and Vienna, cities in permanently neutral states.

In this context, international organizations may also be seen as providing 'institutionalized good offices', since they constitute permanent forums for negotiations between their member states. Permanently neutral states are again attractive as host countries, because no member state of an organization feels that it is sending its representatives to a hostile country. The numbers of international organizations that established their headquarters in Switzerland

American State which is not a party to the controversy, to bring the parties together, so as to make it possible for them to reach an adequate solution between themselves.' Article x adds: 'Once the parties have been brought together and have resumed direct negotiations, no further action is to be taken by the states or citizens that have offered their good offices or have accepted an invitation to offer them;...'

694 Neuhold, *supra* (fn. 600) 99.

and Austria are disproportionately high, although these two states do not hold an oligopoly in this area.

In practice, the term 'good offices' is also used in a broader sense. It includes an active role by the third party as investigator establishing controversial facts and mediator offering comments and proposals for a peaceful settlement. The rather frequent good offices missions of the UN Secretary-General and his Special Representatives may be mentioned as examples, *inter alia* in Cyprus, Cambodia and Namibia.[695]

5.5 Early Warning

Another third-party activity not included in Article 33 is the issue of an early warning which, for example, is one of the tasks of the High Commissioner on National Minorities of the CSCE/OSCE whose post was created at the CSCE Follow-Up Meeting in Helsinki 1992. Such a diplomatic 'wake-up call', an instrument of preventive diplomacy, may only be a modest contribution to avoiding or peacefully settling a domestic or international conflict. It may nevertheless be useful, since the attention of political decision makers, like that of all human beings, is limited and focuses on the most acute problems and challenges. However, if an emerging dispute is addressed at an early stage the costs of settling it will be lower than after it enters its 'hot' phase, in particular if the threshold to the recourse to armed violence is crossed.

5.6 Enquiry

The purpose of an enquiry/inquiry (or fact-finding or investigation) in a narrow sense is to clarify controversial facts without passing judgment on the legal aspects of the dispute.[696] However, the parties to a conflict may also charge a fact-finding body with addressing the question of responsibility and making

---

695 Franck, 'The Secretary General's Role in Conflict Resolution: Past, Present and Pure Conjecture', 6 *EJIL* (1995) 360; Lapidoth, *supra* (fn. 692) paragraph 6. An example of good offices in the technical, narrow sense was provided in 1993 by Norway which hosted secret meetings between Israel and the PLO.

696 Under Article 9 of the 1899 and 1907 Conventions for the Pacific Settlement of International Disputes, the purpose of an International Commission of Inquiry is to facilitate a solution by elucidating the facts by means of an impartial and conscientious investigation. Article 14 of the 1899 Convention and Article 25 of the 1907 Convention provide that the Report of the Commission is limited to a statement of the facts. For commissions of inquiry that

recommendations for a solution of the dispute.[697] In any event, the decision on the consequences they wish to draw from the results of an enquiry rests with the conflicting parties.

Even an enquiry *stricto sensu* may contribute to the peaceful settlement of a dispute. However, most international conflicts are not caused just by differences of opinion on verifiable facts but are more complex, so that fact-finding tends to be just a step on the road to a pacific solution.[698] Moreover, conflicting parties often insist on their version of controversial facts and may not be willing to be proven wrong by an investigation. Yet, in recent years, this method has proven its worth, especially in the field of human rights.[699]

5.7 Mediation

Mediation consists in the active participation of a third party in the negotiation process between the parties to the dispute.[700] A mediator not only comments

conducted investigations in accordance with the provisions of the Hague Conventions see Merrills, *supra* (fn. 663) 44.

697 The mandate of a five-member commission, which was set up by Russia and the United Kingdom pursuant to the provisions of the above-mentioned 1899 Hague Convention, to inquire into and report on the circumstances of the Dogger Bank incident included the establishment of responsibility for the incident. The incident was caused by the Russian Baltic Sea Fleet which opened fire on British trawlers because it (wrongly) suspected an attack by Japanese torpedo boats hiding among the British fishing vessels during the night of 21 to 22 October 1904. The report of the commission was accepted by both parties, and Russia paid £65,000 in compensation to the United Kingdom. Irmscher, 'Dogger Bank Incident (1904)', MPEPIL.

698 In 1967, in its Resolution 2329 (XXII), the UN General Assembly urged Member States to make more effective use of the existing methods of fact-finding and invited them to take into consideration, in choosing means for the peaceful settlement of disputes, the possibility of entrusting the ascertainment of facts to competent international organizations and bodies established by agreement between the parties concerned. In 1991, in the Annex to its Resolution 46/59, the UN General Assembly adopted the more detailed Declaration on Fact-Finding by the United Nations in the Field of the Maintenance of International Peace and Security.

699 Jacheć-Neale, 'Fact-Finding', MPEPIL, paragraph 2.

700 Touval and Zartmann (eds.), *International Mediation in Theory and Practice* (1985); Bercovitch (ed.), *Resolving International Conflicts: The Theory and Practice of Mediation* (1996); Kleiboer, *The Multiple Realities of International Mediation* (1998); Orrego Vicuña, 'Mediation', MPEPIL; Merrills, *supra* (fn. 663) 26.

on the positions of the parties but also offers his/her own proposals for a solution.

From a legal perspective, the formal aspects of this method are emphasized. According to Article 3(3) of the 1899 and 1907 Hague Conventions for the Pacific Settlement of International Disputes, the exercise of the right of Powers strangers to the dispute to offer their good offices or mediation can never be regarded by either of the parties in dispute as an unfriendly act.[701] Moreover, there neither is an obligation to offer nor to accept good offices and mediation. Mediation may be performed by organs of states or international organizations, by NGOs or private individuals.[702]

Some international lawyers consider two essential characteristics of this method as critical weaknesses. Firstly, the conflicting parties are not legally bound by the proposal submitted by a mediator but are free to reject it; secondly, the suggested solution need not be based on existing international law by which the parties are bound.

Mediation may nonetheless make major contributions to a peaceful settlement in six different areas.[703]

1) Like a third party offering its good offices, a mediator may help the parties to a dispute to save face. It is easier for each of them to accept a proposal submitted by a mediator than the same proposal made by its opponent. Agreement to the latter will again be regarded as a sign of weakness, by both the other party and other states.
2) There is a second reason why the proposal presented by a mediator stands a better chance of acceptance than exactly the same solution proposed by the other conflicting party. Any initiative taken by the latter is likely to be received with distrust by the other side, even if a settlement plan appears balanced and fair at first sight; but if it comes from the adversary,

701 And therefore does not constitute illegal intervention. See *supra* 161. Article 4 of the two Conventions defines the part of the mediator as 'reconciling the opposing claims and appeasing the feelings of resentment which may have arisen between the States at variance'.

702 Mediation by states or IGOs is referred to as 'track-one', mediation by NGOs or private individuals as 'track-two mediation'. The lower profile and possible experience of the latter may increase its attractiveness in the eyes of the parties.

703 In 2012 the UN General Assembly adopted Resolution 66/291 on strengthening the role of mediation in the peaceful settlement of disputes, conflict prevention and resolution. In particular, it encouraged the use of the Guidance for Effective Mediation submitted by the Secretary-General in UN Doc. A/66/811 in accordance with General Assembly Resolution 65/291.

a hidden ploy will probably be suspected. In contrast, a mediator tries to project an image of impartiality and has one basic ambition, namely to succeed in his/her role and lead the parties to an agreement each of them approves of. His/her proposals will therefore meet with a more favourable response.

3) Thirdly, a mediator may add an important intellectual input to the efforts of the parties to find a mutually acceptable way out of their conflict, beyond helping to dispel misunderstandings between them. The findings of psychology are helpful in this respect and shed some light on this type of contribution. Decision makers and negotiators of the parties may suffer from misperceptions that are particularly marked and frequent in situations of stress, above all in conflict and crisis situations.[704] For instance, 'tunnel vision', understood in psychological/intellectual terms, may rivet their attention on only one solution. The mediator may come up with other options which the parties have overlooked in the 'heat' of their controversy. He or she ought to help the parties better to understand each other's positions and find common ground between them.
4) A fourth contribution of mediation may be material in nature and combine 'carrots' and 'sticks'. In other words, a mediator could promise the parties incentives like financial assistance or military guarantees if they accept his/her proposal; should one of them or both refuse to do so, negative consequences, for example the non-renewal of a favourable cooperation agreement, may be threatened.
5) The agreement of parties on mediation may defuse their conflict in situations where the dispute in which they are involved could escalate, even across the threshold of the resort to armed force. Turning to the assistance of a mutually acceptable third party but retaining the final say over the eventual solution may 'depoliticize' a controversy and help to reduce tensions, also by buying time.
6) The mediation process ought to be confidential. The lack of publicity should facilitate mutual concessions without the loss of face until, with the help of the mediator, a solution to the conflict is reached that is acceptable to both parties.

Several conditions must be met for mediation to get underway. The conflicting parties are likely to give their necessary consent if neither of them expects to prevail, in particular by the use of armed force or other forms of coercion. Moreover, they must be ready to seek a way out of their conflict and to make at least minor concessions to each other. Last, but not least, they have to agree on

704 Jervis, *Perception and Misperception in International Politics* (1976).

the identity of the mediator. In addition, a third party will accept the role of mediator only if it sees a reasonable chance of leading the conflicting parties to a peaceful settlement. For failure to achieve an agreement means a blow to the prestige and power of the mediator. Conversely, success will enhance his/her international standing and influence. Readiness to offer mediation may be increased by additional interests of the third party in a pacific solution, for instance stability in a neighbouring region.

Mediators ought to possess a number of special qualifications: diplomatic and psychological skills and experience, patience and perseverance, creativity and flexibility. The parties to the conflict must trust them and believe in their impartiality. A mediator has to be ready to make his/her contributions to a pacific solution appear less important than they actually are and give most of the credit for an agreement to the parties. He or she needs a thorough knowledge of the details of the dispute which he or she is trying to help settle.

The above-mentioned deficiencies of mediation could prove less serious than sometimes claimed, and even turn out to be advantages. Although even a proposal made by a powerful mediator is not legally binding, the positive and negative pressure exerted by him/her may be more effective in practice than a binding decision of an international court or arbitral tribunal that cannot be enforced. Moreover, mediation may result in a solution that is attractive to both conflicting parties, precisely because it is not constrained by existing law but goes beyond it. This is particularly true if is 'enriched' by the 'carrots' offered by the mediator. The relations between the former adversaries will then be placed on a new, more satisfactory legal basis.

Recent successful mediation initiatives include those of the United States between Egypt and Israel in 1978,[705] Algeria between Iran and the United States in 1980, the United States between the parties involved in the conflict in Bosnia and Herzegovina in 1995,[706] and Pope John Paul II between Argentina and Chile in the dispute over the Beagle Channel that led to the 1984 Treaty of Peace and Friendship between the two states.[707] The mediatory assistance by EU representatives, above all Catherine Ashton, to the normalization of relations between Serbia and Kosovo may also be recalled in this context.[708] Mediation by an international organization was also successfully performed by the World Bank in the Indus basin dispute between India and Pakistan,

705 President Jimmy Carter acted as mediator between Egyptian President Anwar El Sadat and Israeli Prime Minister Menachem Begin at Camp David, setting the stage for the 1979 Peace Treaty.

706 See *supra* 80.

707 Moncayo, 'La mediation pontificale dans l'affaire du Canal Beagle', 242 *RCADI* (1993) 207.

708 See *supra* 92.

paving the way to the Indus Waters Treaty in 1960.[709] Successful mediation by an NGO was achieved in 2005 by former Finnish President Martii Ahtisaari and his Crisis Management Initiative in the armed conflict between the Free Aceh Movement and the Indonesian government.[710]

At first sight, (permanently) neutral states also seem specially qualified as mediators. Their scores on the first two assets of mediation are high indeed, and they may also be ingenious in developing solutions the conflicting parties have not envisaged. However, their potential of incentives and threats is limited, since they are relatively small and weak by definition.[711] Practice also shows that previous support for one party against the other does not exclude successful mediatory efforts. Mediation by the Soviet Union, which was known for its sympathies for India, between the latter country and Pakistan resulting in the 1966 Tashkent Declaration,[712] as well as the traditionally pro-Israel United States in the conflict between Egypt and Israel, may be mentioned in this context.

As these examples suggest, it may even be a good idea for a state to accept a mediation offer from a third party that up to now has sided with its adversary. As pointed out above, a mediator who invests considerable efforts in his/her function is primarily motivated by the desire to succeed in brokering a solution to the conflict to which both parties agree and thereby to increase his/her own prestige and power. This may mean suggesting a settlement that is more beneficial to the party with which the mediator has less amicable relations and exert pressure on the traditional friend to accept such a deal, in order to avoid being accused of bias in favour of the latter. Moreover, there remains the option of rejecting a proposal regarded as unsatisfactory and blaming the mediator for failing to offer a truly fair solution.

5.8 Conciliation

Conciliation may be defined as a combination of enquiry and (weak) mediation, either ad hoc or institutionalized.[713] This method emerged rather late, with the intensification of international relations in the early 20th century, and

709 Subedi, 'Indus River', MPEPIL.

710 See also *supra* 90.

711 A great power may be defined as a state with global interests and the will and the means to defend, promote and enforce those interests. Therefore, a great power is bound to become involved in any major conflict sooner or later and cannot remain neutral.

712 Soviet Prime Minister Alexei Kosygin acted as mediator between Indian Prime Minister Lal Bahadur Shastri and Pakistani President Muhammad Ayub Khan after the 1965 armed conflict between the two countries over Kashmir.

713 Cot, *La conciliation internationale* (1968); idem, 'Conciliation', MPEPIL.

was given a more prominent place in the repertory of dispute settlement methods in recent years. Conciliation commissions are, as a rule, composed of experts with little political clout whose recommendations will hopefully be accepted by the conflicting parties on the strength of convincing arguments and their readiness to end their dispute.

An early example of conciliation was agreed on by the parties to the Bryan Treaties of 1913/1914.[714] Conciliation procedures are also included, for instance, in the 1969 and 1986 VCLTs,[715] the 1982 UN Convention on the Law of the Sea;[716] they were also agreed on in the framework CSCE/OSCE.[717] Furthermore, in 1995 the UN General Assembly adopted detailed Model Rules for the Conciliation of Disputes between States.[718]

Conciliation has indeed been included in numerous bi- or multilateral treaties, also together with or as an alternative to other dispute settlement methods, notably arbitration or adjudication. However, this increase has not been reflected in the actual resort to this method in practice.

5.9 Arbitration and Adjudication

5.9.1 *Similarities and Differences*

Arbitration and adjudication share two characteristics which distinguish them from the other, the 'diplomatic' dispute settlement methods and are regarded as decisive advantages by their advocates.[719]

---

714 See *supra* 18.

715 Article 66(b) of the 1969 Convention and Article 66(4) of the 1986 Convention.

716 Annex V.

717 In the 1992 Convention on Conciliation and Arbitration providing for subsidiary but compulsory conciliation, as well as by the 'directed-conciliation' mechanism adopted at the 1992 Stockholm meeting of the CSCE Council. According to this procedure, the Ministerial Council or the Senior Council of the CSCE/OSCE may direct any two participating states to resort to conciliation if they fail to settle a dispute within a reasonable period of time. Contrary to the consensus principle which governs CSCE/OSCE decision making, the consent of the conflicting parties is not required for this decision. However, they are not bound by the 'soft law' recommendations of the conciliation commission.

718 In Resolution 50/50 (2011).

719 Jenks, *The Prospects of International Adjudication* (1964); Mosler and Bernhardt (eds.), *Judicial Settlement of International Disputes: International Court of Justice – Other Courts and Tribunals – Arbitration and Conciliation* (1974); Virally, 'Le champ opératoire du règlement judiciaire international', 87 *RGDIP* (1983) 281; Janis (ed.), *International Courts for the Twenty-First Century* (1992); Pellet, 'Judicial Settlement of International Disputes', MPEPIL.

1) Both the judgment of an international court and the award of an arbitral tribunal are legally binding on the litigants.
2) The decisions of the court and tribunal are based on international law as it exists between the conflicting parties. To this end, the latter have to present their differences of opinion as a 'legal' dispute, i.e., disagree on whose position prevails on the basis of the rules of international law governing their relations.[720]

However, like the other methods, arbitration and judicial settlement also require the consent of the parties to the dispute – a crucial difference between domestic and international courts of law, of which non-lawyers are often not aware. The extent to which the jurisdiction of an international court or tribunal is accepted and, as a result, the scope of what the parties know about essential elements of the proceedings before an arbitral or judicial body, vary. Four questions appear particularly relevant in this context: they concern the stakes of a concrete case; the chances of winning or losing; the identity of the opponent; and whether the party concerned will appear as plaintiff or defendant before the court or tribunal.

1) The parties may agree to submit an already existing specific dispute that opposes them to each other to an international court or tribunal. If they conclude a so-called compromise to this effect, each of them knows the answers to these four questions. They know what is at stake, will be advised by their legal experts about the likelihood of a favourable or unfavourable decision, know who the other party is, as well as their role in the proceedings.

What is puzzling is the fact that a party which must expect to lose the case nevertheless agrees to judicial or arbitral proceedings. Various reasons may explain this decision. Almost certain defeat could be accepted in order to remove an obstacle to beneficial future cooperation with the other party. Another explanation could be the hope of triggering a practice of adjudication

720 Again, this does not mean that 'legal' disputes have no political implications. On the contrary, many conflicts decided by arbitration or adjudication have been highly political, beginning with the *Alabama* case. See *infra* 189. As the ICJ stated in the *Diplomatic and Consular Staff in Tehran* case: '...legal disputes between sovereign States by their very nature are likely to occur in political contexts, and often form only one element in a wider and long-standing political dispute between the States concerned'. *United States Diplomatic and Consular Staff in Tehran* (*United States of America v. Islamic Republic of Iran*), paragraph 37. For further details of the distinction see *infra* fn. 748.

or arbitration as the preferred method of dispute settlement between the parties in the future. Moreover, a government might accept a negative judgment or award in order to prove to a restive pressure group within the country that all means to support the claims of the latter against another state have been exhausted. Finally, legal advisers might inform the decision makers that the chances of winning or losing a case with limited stakes are unclear, so that skillful reasoning before the judges or arbitrators may tip the scales in favour of their state.

2) If the contracting parties include a compromissory clause in their treaty they agree that all future disputes concerning the application and interpretation of the treaty will be decided by a specific international court or tribunal. In this scenario, the parties roughly know the stakes which are determined by the contents of the treaty. For instance, a border treaty will not give rise to a dispute over the payment of debts. Unless the clause is inserted in a bilateral treaty, the parties ignore the exact identity of their adversary in a specific dispute, but can be sure that it will be one of the other contracting parties. What they ignore is whether they will be plaintiffs of defendants and what their chances of success in future proceedings will be.
3) The most far-reaching recognition of jurisdiction is based on a treaty under which the parties agree to submit all future legal disputes to a court or tribunal or a declaration under the so-called optional clause in Article 36(2) of the ICJ Statute.[721] As a result, the parties can predict neither the stakes of future conflicts, nor the likelihood of a positive or negative outcome of the proceedings, nor whether they will act as plaintiff or defendant. In the case of a bilateral treaty conferring such sweeping jurisdiction they know the identity of the other party. If the treaty is multilateral, then the opponent will come from among the other contracting states. In the case of the ICJ, the circle of possible adversaries is rather large with currently 71 states.

Small wonder that states tend to exclude from such a 'blank cheque' certain sensitive categories of disputes, especially if they must expect to be sued by another party and lose the case.[722]

The similarities between adjudication and arbitration outweigh the differences. In addition, the lines between these two methods are blurred in practice.

---

721 See *infra* 193.

722 Ibid.

1) International courts are permanent judicial institutions, while arbitral tribunals are usually established for a certain period of time. However, on the one hand, conflicting parties are free to create tribunals without limiting the duration of their existence. On the other hand, international courts also cease to exist, even after a relatively short period of time.[723]
2) The composition of the bench of a court is established in advance, while conflicting parties appoint at least some of the arbitrators.[724] Yet, on the one hand, as in the case of the ICJ,[725] a party to a dispute may have the right to nominate a judge of its own choice if no member of the bench has its nationality. On the other hand, one or several arbitrators may be appointed by a third party, especially if the conflicting parties or the arbitrators selected by them fail to agree.
3) It is sometimes also pointed out that if the parties opt for arbitration they may agree on specific legal rules to be applied by the tribunal, as they did in the famous *Alabama* case,[726] or authorize arbitrators to decide the case *ex aequo et bono*. However, nothing prevents parties from also doing so if they opt for adjudication.[727]
4) Another difference that is occasionally mentioned concerns the smaller size of an arbitral tribunal compared with the larger number of judges. Yet courts may also include smaller chambers or may have the option of appointing them, as, for instance, the ICJ,[728] the European Court of Human Rights and the ICC.
5) Finally, resort to a court is said to be more expensive than arbitration. Although this aspect may be true in general, it is not necessarily the case but depends on the number of counsel hired by a party and the fees paid to them, as well as the duration of the proceedings. Moreover, litigants involved in adjudication may be offered financial assistance by third parties.[729]

---

723 Such as the Central American Court of Justice after ten years, as well as the PCIJ. See *infra* 191.

724 Conflicting parties may agree on a single arbitrator or appoint a tribunal composed of several persons. Examples of the former option include the eminent Swiss lawyer Max Huber for the *Palmas* and the King of Italy for the *Clipperton* disputes in 1928 and 1931, respectively.

725 On the *judex ad hoc* see *infra* 195.

726 See *infra* 189.

727 Thus, according to Article 38(2) of the Statute of the ICJ, the Court has the power to decide a case *ex aequo et bono*, if the parties agree thereto.

728 Articles 26 and 29 of the Statute. See *infra* fn. 757.

729 See *infra* fn. 794. It should also be borne in mind that the establishment of an arbitral tribunal may not only take time but also entail expenses which the parties can avoid if they submit their dispute to an already existing court. Merrills, *supra* (fn. 663) 165.

What counts, however, is the general perception of conflicting parties that they have more influence on arbitral proceedings that are also regarded as more flexible and less cumbersome.

5.9.2 *The History of Arbitration and Adjudication*

Another, real difference emerges from a look at the history of these two methods. Arbitration is much older than adjudication in international relations. It can be traced back to Antiquity, where it was resorted to by the Greek city states, and also played a role in medieval Europe, with the Pope as the supreme authority to decide disputes. When the Reformation challenged this position of the head of the Catholic Church, and with the emergence of the modern system of territorial states jealous of their sovereignty in the wake of the Thirty Years' War, arbitration receded into the background.

Towards the end of the 18th century, the so-called Jay Treaty of 1794 between Great Britain and the young United States[730] marked a turning point towards a revival of this method of conflict settlement. The two parties agreed, *inter alia*, on the establishment of three mixed claims commissions. These arbitral bodies were charged with deciding an open border issue between the two states, as well as claims of British nationals against the United States and claims of Americans against the former colonial power.

Another milestone in the history of arbitration was the *Alabama* case.[731] The dispute was caused by a ship initially called *Enrica* which was built during the War of Secession (1861–1865) in a British shipyard, officially for private owners but destined to become a Confederate warship. After leaving Liverpool without arms and a small crew for what was presented as a trial trip, the vessel was manned and armed by British ships off the Azores and changed its name to *Alabama*. The *Alabama* then wrought havoc on commercial ships of the Union, burning or sinking more than 60 of them, until she was finally destroyed by the Union warship *Kearsarge* off the coast of the French port city of Cherbourg.

The resulting serious conflict between the United Kingdom and the United States, leading the two countries again to the brink of war, was eventually settled by the 1871 Treaty of Washington between these two powers. The parties agreed

---

730 The treaty was named for the U.S. chief negotiator, John Jay, the first Chief Justice and former Secretary of Foreign Affairs. He negotiated with his British counterpart, Lord Grenville, the Treaty of Amity, Commerce and Navigation on several issues that had brought the two states to the brink of war. Newcomb, 'New Light on Jay's Treaty', 28 *AJIL* (1934) 685; Ziegler, 'Jay Treaty', MPEPIL.

731 Bingham, 'The *Alabama* Claims Arbitration', 54 *ICLQ* (2005) 1; idem, 'Alabama Arbitration', MPEPIL.

to submit the dispute to arbitration. The five arbitrators were to apply the three rules on neutrality in sea warfare laid down in the Treaty. These rules focused on the principle of due diligence. According to this principle, a state is also responsible for unlawful acts committed by persons who are not its organs if it fails to prevent them from committing such acts, in accordance with the international standard observed by other states in similar situations. The arbitrators unanimously ruled that the United Kingdom had not complied with its due diligence obligations in the case of the *Alabama* and therefore had to pay compensation.[732]

The *Alabama* case was an important step because it proved that a state's national honour was no longer an obstacle to arbitration.[733] At the political level, it paved the way for the 'special relationship' between Great Britain and the United States, those close ties between the two Atlantic powers that still exist today.

Many conflicts have also been decided by arbitration in modern times; an attempt to draw up a list even of the most important cases would be beyond the scope of this chapter.

Moreover, it should be noted that the value of a dispute settlement method agreed upon in advance ought to be measured not just by the frequency of its use. Its acceptance has a certain 'deterrent' or rather dissuasive effect, since the prospect of another party resorting to the method tends to induce a state to comply with its legal obligations towards that party.

The Permanent Court of Arbitration (PCA) housed in the Peace Palace in The Hague should also be included in this historic survey, although it is neither a court, nor does it arbitrate international disputes.[734] It was established under Articles 20–29 of the 1899 Hague Convention for the Pacific Settlement of International Disputes.[735] These provisions were revised by Articles 41–50 of the 1907 Hague Convention for the Pacific Settlement of International Disputes. The PCA mainly acts as a facilitator of arbitration, in the meantime not only

---

732 By a majority of four to one, the British member Lord Chief Justice Cockburn dissenting, they also decided against the United Kingdom in the similar case of the vessel *Oreto* which later changed her name to *Florida*. The sum of U.S.$15,500 in gold Great Britain had to pay to the United States under the award was enormous by the then budgetary standards.

733 In 1865, British Foreign Secretary Earl Russell still opposed arbitration, arguing that 'Her Majesty's Government are the sole guardians of their honour'.

734 François, 'La Cour permanente d'arbitrage. Son origine, sa jurisprudence, son avenir', 87 *RCADI* (1955) 457; Ando, 'Permanent Court of Arbitration', MPEPIL.

735 The attempt to establish a genuine permanent court at the 1907 Hague Conference failed because of differences of opinion on the composition of such a court.

between states but also in disputes involving international organizations and private parties.[736] It offers them a list of qualified arbitrators appointed by the parties to the two Hague Conventions, the services of its Bureau, as well as rules of procedure.

Prior to World War I, contracting states brought 17 cases before the Court, on which it handed down awards,[737] except one which the parties settled by agreement. In the inter-war period and the first decades after World War II, the PCA was overshadowed, above all, first by the PCIJ and then the ICJ. Between 1918 and 1980 only eight cases were submitted. They included the first dispute between a state and a private party, the Radio Corporation of America and China, decided in 1935. In recent decades, the PCA has been playing a much more active role, in particular in numerous investment disputes. This revival has been due to its above-mentioned availability for disputes in which non-state parties are involved, as well as extending its functions to conciliation and inquiry. Moreover, in 1994 a fund designed to help developing countries meet the costs of arbitration or other means of settlement offered by the Court was established.[738]

The first intra-state arbitration under the auspices of the PCA dealt with the politically explosive and economically important dispute between the government of Sudan and the Sudan People's Liberation Movement/Army, the representative of the future state of South Sudan that celebrated its independence in 2011. The five arbitrators were requested to delimit the border between the two parties in the Abyei border area.[739] Unfortunately, their award could not prevent subsequent armed hostilities between the two states in their continuing dispute over this oil-rich region.

The Central American Court of Justice deserves to be included in this survey because it was the first genuine permanent international court. It was created for ten years under a treaty concluded by the five Central American states – Costa Rica, El Salvador, Guatemala, Honduras and Nicaragua – after two wars

736 Several Optional Rules were adopted, beginning with the Optional Rules for Arbitrating Disputes between Two States (1992) and including such rules for Arbitrating Disputes between Two Parties of Which Only One Is a State (1993), Involving International Organizations and States (1996) and between International Organizations and Private Parties (1996), as well as Disputes Relating to Natural Resources and/or the Environment (2001). Moreover, Optional Rules also regulate Conciliation (1996), Fact-Finding Commissions of Inquiry (1997) and Conciliation Relating to Natural Resources and/or the Environment (2002) and Outer Space Activities (2011).

737 Beginning with the *Pious Fund Arbitration* between the United States and Mexico in 1902.

738 See *supra* 188.

739 Daly and Schofield, 'Abyei Arbitration', MPEPIL.

between some of these countries. The text of the treaty was adopted at a peace conference proposed the United States and Mexico in Washington, D.C., in 1907. The jurisdiction of the Court comprised all legal disputes between the contracting parties. Moreover, access to it was also open to nationals of the five states except for claims against their own state. However, during the decade of its existence, from 1908 to 1918, only ten cases were brought before the Central American Court. Negotiations to extend the validity of the 1907 convention failed.[740]

The PCIJ is mentioned here only briefly as the *de facto* predecessor of the ICJ which will be discussed in some detail below. The establishment of the PCIJ was provided for in Article 14 of the Covenant of the League of Nations. After its Statute had been drafted by a committee of jurists, the Court held its first session at the Hague Peace Palace in 1922. During its existence from 1922 to 1939, the Court dealt with 29 contentious cases and gave 27 advisory opinions.

5.9.3 *The International Court of Justice*

Since a comprehensive and detailed presentation of the ICJ cannot be attempted in the present context, the emphasis of the following selective remarks will be put on the differences between the Court of the UN and domestic courts of law.[741] These differences are due to the reluctance of states to abandon their control over the dispute settlement process and its outcome. As a rule, they want to limit the sacrifices of their cherished sovereignty which distinguishes them from the subjects of the 'vertical' legal order of the internal law of states.

Unlike the PCIJ, which was a separate institution, the ICJ is the principal judicial organ of the UN.[742] Its Statute, which essentially reproduces that of the Permanent Court, is an integral part of the UN Charter.[743] Consequently, a state

740 However, in 1962, the Court was refounded in the framework of the OAS for an indefinite period of time but remained inactive for some 30 years. In 1991, a new legal basis was provided by the Protocol of Tegucigalpa in the context of the Central American Integration System, with the Court deciding its first case in 1994.

741 Damrosch (ed.), *The International Court of Justice at a Crossroads* (1976); Lowe and M. Fitzmaurice (eds.), *Fifty Years of the International Courts of Justice* (1996); Amr, *The Role of the International Court of Justice as the Principal Judicial Organ of the United Nations* (2003); Rosenne, *The Law and Practice of the International Court 1920–2005* (4th ed. 2006); Zimmermann, Tomuschat and Oellers-Frahm (eds.), *The Statute of the International Court of Justice* (2006).

742 Article 92 of the Charter.

743 The Charter itself also contains a few provisions on the ICJ (Chapter XIV, Articles 92–96).

that is admitted to the UN and ratifies the constituent treaty of the World Organization becomes *ipso facto* a party to the annexed Statute.[744] Contrary to a widespread error among non-lawyers, this does not mean, however, that the ratification of the Charter also includes the acceptance of the Court's compulsory jurisdiction.[745] This requires a separate act of recognition in one of the above-mentioned variants.[746]

The most far-reaching submission to the jurisdiction of the ICJ is a declaration in accordance with the optional clause in Article 36(2) of the Statute.[747] A state party to the Statute thereby recognizes as compulsory *ipso facto* and without special agreement, in relation to any other state accepting the same obligation, the jurisdiction of the Court in all legal disputes.[748] Article 36(3) permits only two restrictions on this act of recognition, namely the condition of reciprocity on the part of several or certain states or a time limit. In practice, however, states have further limited their submission to the Court's jurisdiction, which both the ICJ and already the PCIJ accepted. In particular, the sweeping

---

744 Article 93(1) of the Charter. The Statute comprises Chapters on the Organization and Competence of the Court, on Procedure, Advisory Opinions and Amendment.

745 Non-member states of the UN may also become parties to the Statute on conditions to be determined in each case by the General Assembly upon the recommendation of the Security Council in accordance with Article 93(2) of the Charter and Article 35(2) and (3) of the Statute. Given the quasi-universality of UN membership, this option is of little practical relevance today.

746 See *supra* 186.

747 Merrills, 'The Optional Clause Today', 50 *BYIL* (1979) 87; idem, 'The Optional Clause Revisited', 64 *BYIL* (1993) 197. As mentioned above, at this writing in 2014, only 71 of the 193 UN member states – among the 'P 5', only the United Kingdom – have made such a declaration.

748 According to this provision, these legal disputes concern a. the interpretation of a treaty; b. any question of international law; c. the existence of any fact which, if established, would constitute a breach of an international obligation; d. the nature or extent of the reparation to be made for the breach of an international obligation.

As mentioned above, a distinction is often made between legal and political disputes. Legal disputes concern the application or interpretation of international law by which the conflicting parties are bound. In contrast, parties to a political dispute or 'conflict of interests' demand a change in the existing or the creation of new law, or do not raise legal issues at all. This distinction is criticized for the discretion it leaves to the parties; whether or not one and the same conflict is dealt with as a legal or political dispute depends on how the disputants formulate their claims. Moreover, on the one hand, a legal dispute also includes political aspects and involves interests; on the other, non-legal disputes can also be decided on the basis of international law, if only by stating that a given behaviour is not prohibited by international law. See *supra* fn. 720.

so-called Connally reservation made by the United States[749] in 1946 excluded 'disputes with regard to matters which are essentially within the domestic jurisdiction of the United States of America as determined by the United States of America'.[750]

The 15 judges of the ICJ must not only possess moral and professional qualifications as practitioners or scholars.[751] Together, they also ought to represent the main forms of civilization and the principal legal systems of the world.[752] They are elected by an absolute majority of votes in the General Assembly and in the Security Council independently of each other, without any distinction

---

749 Named for the influential U.S. Representative and Senator Thomas Connally from Texas, the driving force behind this 'self-judging' or 'auto-interpretative' amendment. Other states followed the example of the United States, but some of them later repealed or amended their declarations of acceptance. For the reservation proved in practice to work to the disadvantage of the state that had made it, because respondents successfully invoked it on the basis of reciprocity. In 1985, in the course of its dispute with Nicaragua on U.S. activities against the leftist Sandinista government in that country, the United States terminated its acceptance of the ICJ's compulsory jurisdiction altogether. Jennings, 'Recent Cases on "Automatic" Reservations to the Optional Clause', 7 *ICLQ* (1958) 349; Rogers, 'The United States' "Automatic" Reservation to the Optional Clause Jurisdiction of the I.C.J.', ibid. 758; Henkin, 'The Connally Reservation Revisited and, Hopefully, Contained', 65 *AJIL* (1971) 374; Crawford, 'The Legal Effect of Automatic Reservations to the Jurisdiction of the International Court', 50 *BYIL* (1979) 63; Tomuschat, 'Article 36', in: Zimmermann, Tomuschat and Oellers-Frahm (eds.), *supra* (fn. 741) 589 (637); Stahn, 'Connally Reservation', MPEPIL.

750 The right claimed by the United States to determine the internal matters falling within its domestic jurisdiction conflicts with Article 36(6) of the ICJ Statute under which the Court settles disputes as to whether it has jurisdiction. It may also be considered incompatible with the object and purpose of compulsory jurisdiction under Article 36(2) of the Statute, since it empties the recognition of the Court's jurisdiction of its essential substance and is therefore unlawful under Article 19(c) of the 1969 VCLT. However, it may also be argued that there is a difference between disturbing, by a reservation, the carefully established balance between mutual concessions in other multilateral treaties and the special case of the recognition of the jurisdiction of the ICJ where states are free to choose the scope of their acceptance. Tomuschat, *supra* (fn. 749) 639.

751 They must qualify in their respective countries for appointment to the highest judicial offices or have to be jurisconsults of recognized competence in international law (Article 2 of the Statute).

752 Article 9 of the Statute. The five permanent members of the Security Council are considered entitled to have a judge of their nationality on the bench. The regional distribution of the other ten judges follows that of the non-permanent Security Council seats agreed on in 1965. Merrills, *supra* (fn. 663) 135. For the first time, the present Court comprises three women: Joan E. Donoghue (United States), Xue Hangin (China) and Julia Sebutinde (Uganda).

between permanent and non-permanent members of the Council, meaning that the 'P 5' do not have a veto.[753]

An interesting option reminiscent of arbitral tribunals[754] that does not exist in domestic law is the right to nominate an additional *judex ad hoc*.[755] If the bench does not include a judge of the nationality of a party before the ICJ, that party may choose a person to sit as judge, according to the terms of Article 31(2) and (3) of the Statute.[756] However, some of the reasons given for this provision are not convincing. The ad hoc judge should explain the position of the party that appoints him/her to the other judges on the bench in their deliberations so that it is fully appreciated by them. Yet these persons are highly qualified jurists and, if they have any questions, they can ask the agents of the parties for explanations. They can also be expected to give due weight to the arguments which the litigants present. The *judex ad hoc* is also supposed to see to it that if the Court rules against the party that appointed him/her, the wording of the judgment should not be too harsh. The real reason seems to be the hope to increase the readiness of states to accept the ICJ's jurisdiction because they have 'their own judge' on the bench, although the *judex ad hoc*, like the other judges, does not represent the party appointing him/her but is independent and ought to be objective.[757] However, whether these expectations have materialized is open to doubt.

753 Article 10(1) and (2) of the Statute.

754 See *supra* 188.

755 Schwebel, 'National judges and judges ad hoc of the International Court of Justice', 48 ICLQ (1999) 889.The examples of the PCIJ and ICJ were followed by the Inter-American Court of Human Rights and the International Tribunal for the Law of the Sea. See Jesus, 'Judges *ad hoc* in the International Tribunal for the Law of the Sea', in: Hestermeyer et alii (eds.), (fn. 251) 1661.

756 Kooijmans, 'Article 31', in: Zimmermann, Tomuschat and Oellers-Frahm (eds.), *supra* (fn. 741) 495. Since the ad hoc judge is not required to have the nationality of the party appointing him/her, the term 'national judge' that is sometimes used is not correct. It is also worth noting that, not surprisingly, ad hoc judges tend to vote in favour of the state appointing them, but this is not always the case.

757 In addition to the plenary Court, the ICJ may also set up smaller chambers. Thus Article 26(1) of the Statute provides for the possibility of the formation of one or more chambers, composed of three or more judges as the Court may determine, for dealing with particular cases, for example, labour cases and cases relating to transit and communication. Pursuant to Article 26(2), the Court may at any time form a chamber for dealing with a particular case. Moreover, with a view to the speedy dispatch of business, in accordance with Article 29, the ICJ shall form annually a chamber of five judges to decide cases by summary procedure at the request of the parties. Ad hoc chambers have been used in practice since the 1980s. Although it is for the ICJ to select the judges, the parties *de facto* have a say on the

The Statute provides for the 'dual-track' jurisdiction of the principal judicial organ of the UN. Under its Article 34, only states may be parties before the Court. International organizations may only present information relevant to contentious cases dealt with by the ICJ.

In addition, the Court may also give an advisory opinion on any legal question which is addressed to it by the UN General Assembly and the Security Council, as well as by other UN organs and specialized agencies authorized by the General Assembly on legal questions arising within the scope of their activities.[758] The Assembly granted this authorization to the ECOSOC and the Trusteeship Council, but not to the Secretary-General,[759] and also generously to the specialized agencies. In advisory proceedings, it is the rights of states that are limited. They may not request an advisory opinion but merely present written or oral statements.[760]

A 'back door' permits at least those international organizations which are authorized to ask for advisory opinions to obtain a binding decision from the Court. They may conclude an agreement with a state under which the contracting parties accept an advisory opinion requested by the organization as legally binding on them.[761]

---

composition of the chambers. They can therefore opt for judges with a particular expertise and/or background as a result of their nationality. Such chambers thus combine some of the advantages of arbitration with those of adjudication. Merrills, *supra* (fn. 663) 137.

758 Article 96 of the UN Charter and Article 65(1) of the Statute. Oellers-Frahm, 'Article 96', in: Simma et alii (ed.), *supra* (fn. 82) 1975; Frowein and Oellers-Frahm, 'Article 65', in: Zimmermann, Tomuschat and Oellers-Frahm (eds.), *supra* (fn. 741) 1401. Advisory opinions may also be requested from the European Court of Human Rights, the Inter-American Court of Human Rights and the Law of the Sea Tribunal. The right to request advisory opinions from the African Court of Justice and Human Rights is even granted to African NGOs recognized by the OAU/AU, provided the state concerned has recognized the competence of the Court to this effect.

759 There seem to be good reasons for also authorizing the chief administrative officer of the organization. He would be less influenced by power politics than the General Assembly and the Security Council when asking for an advisory opinion; moreover, the competence to submit legal questions to the ICJ would complement his 'alarm bell' competence under Article 99 of the Charter to bring to the attention of the Security Council any matter which in his opinion may threaten the maintenance of international peace and security. See *infra* 212. However, states are obviously reluctant to increase the political weight of the Secretary-General. Oellers-Frahm, *supra* (fn. 758) 1981.

760 Article 66 of the Statute.

761 Section 30 of the 1946 Convention on the Privileges and Immunities of the United Nations and Article 66 of the 1986 VCLT between States and International Organizations or between International Organizations provide examples. Under Article 63 of the 1969 American Convention on Human Rights, not only organs of the OAS but also member

The ICJ, whose foundations were laid after World War I with the creation of the PCIJ and were not substantially changed after World War II, remains a 'conservative' court in another respect. Individuals, who have also become subjects of international law as bearers of human rights and have access to human rights and other courts,[762] do not have *locus standi* before the judicial organ of the UN.

The Court decides all questions by a majority of the judges present, with the President or the judge acting in his place having a casting vote in the event of an equality of votes.[763] Judges who do not agree with the majority may formulate their disagreement in writing which is also published.[764] If a judge comes to the same results as the majority of his/her colleagues but disagrees with their reasoning, he/she may write a separate opinion. A judge expressing a dissenting opinion also reaches operative conclusions that differ from those of the majority.[765] This possibility has the advantage of making the discussions among the judges more transparent. Its critics argue that it undermines the authority of the Court by revealing the lack of unanimity among the judges.

According to Article 59 of the Statute, the decision of the Court has no binding force except between the parties and in respect of that particular case. In other words, the foundation of common law, the *stare decisis* principle, does not apply to the decisions of the ICJ and to international law in general.[766] Therefore, the Court could overrule its own judgments in a new case. However, practice points in a different direction. The judgments of the ICJ are widely quoted, first and foremost by the Court itself, in order to prove the existence of a rule of international law. Moreover, the Court and other judicial and arbitral bodies not only state but also create law by clarifying the meaning of ambiguous norms through interpretation and specifying the contents of general rules.[767]

---

states of the organization may turn to the Inter-American Court of Human Rights for an advisory opinion.

762 Such as the Court of Justice of the EU.

763 Article 55.

764 Article 57.

765 However, this distinction is not made in Article 57 of the Statute. Hambro, 'Dissenting and Individual Opinions in the International Court of Justice', 17 *ZaöRV* (1956/1957) 229; Sereni, 'Les opinions individuelles et dissidentes des juges des tribunaux internationaux', 68 *RGDIP* (1964) 819. The judges of the European Court of Human Rights, the Inter-American Court of Human Rights and the Law of the Sea Tribunal also have the option of expressing their disagreement with the majority.

766 Brant, *L'autorité de la chose jugée en droit international public* (2003); Bernhardt, 'Article 59', in: Zimmermann, Tomuschat and Oellers-Frahm (eds.), *supra* (fn. 741) 1231.

767 McWhinney, *The World Court and the Contemporary International Law-Making Process* (1979).

While a judgment of the ICJ in a contentious case is legally binding, advisory opinions, as their name indicates, are not.[768] This does not mean, however, that they are legally and politically irrelevant. States and international organizations complying with an advisory opinion are presumed to act in accordance with international law; those who ignore them may have to pay a political price in terms of widespread criticisms and isolation. The authority of advisory opinions as pronouncements on questions of international law by the most prestigious international judicial body is considerable in practice. In legal argument, they are quoted on an equal footing with binding judgments. Moreover, they not only concern secondary problems but, on the contrary, often deal with central issues of international law.[769]

The political and legal weight of advisory opinions varies. It is determined by the same variables as non-binding resolutions of international organizations, in particular the UN General Assembly: the more or less categorical wording; the frequency with which the ICJ itself and other courts and arbitral tribunals quote the opinion later on; references to it by states, international organizations and scholarly literature; the actual application of and compliance with the legal rule stated in the opinion in international practice; and its subsequent inclusion in a legally binding treaty.[770]

Practice thus 'upgrades' the pronouncements of the judicial body of the UN, as well as those of other international courts and tribunals, beyond the role of judicial decisions as subsidiary means for the determination of rules of law, which themselves do not constitute sources of international law, under Article 38(1)(d) of the ICJ Statute.[771]

This understandable trend may be problematic especially with regard to customary international law. For the Court frequently states the existence of a customary rule but does not really prove it. It does not present an exhaustive overview of relevant practice and demonstrate the necessary but elusive *opinio juris*.

768 Hambro, 'The Authority of Advisory Opinions of the International Court of Justice', 3 *ICLQ* (1954) 2; Pratap, *The Advisory Jurisdiction of the International Court* (1972).

769 See *infra* 200.

770 Another aspect which could make a difference, the support for an advisory opinion by all, an overwhelming or just a narrow majority of the judges of the ICJ reflected in dissenting and separate opinions, is usually not added in references to it and therefore plays a less important role in practice. The same is usually true of UN General Assembly resolutions, but sometimes the outcome of the vote on them is mentioned.

771 This provision contains the 'classical' list of the sources of international law, treaties, customary law, and general principles of law. The subsidiary means also include the teachings of the most highly qualified publicists. See also *supra* fn. 8.

Moreover, the price for the majority view that eventually prevails may be the lowest common denominator of the opinions of the judges subscribing to it. As a result, dissenting and separate opinions are sometimes more detailed and also more stringent and convincing.

Furthermore, the ICJ tends to be conservative when dealing with new aspects of a legal issue and to hesitate to deviate from its previous jurisprudence. This attitude may also be dictated by considerations of consistency and predictability which ought to encourage states to submit their disputes to the Court.[772]

Whereas enforcement of a court judgment by central state organs is more or less taken for granted in domestic law, compliance with obligations under international law, including decisions of judicial organs, poses a major problem. Yet, at least in the case of the ICJ, Article 94(2) of the Charter seems to provide an effective remedy. If a party to a case fails to perform the obligations incumbent upon it under a judgment handed down by the Court, the other party may have recourse to the Security Council. The latter may, if it deems necessary, make recommendations or decide upon measures to be taken to give effect to the judgment.[773]

However, this mechanism, which looks impressive on paper, has remained a dead letter up to now. Article 94(2) has been resorted to only once, by Nicaragua against the United States. Yet the objection of this permanent member prevented the adoption of a draft resolution calling for full and immediate compliance with the judgment of the Court in the *Nicaragua* case.[774] Nicaragua then turned to the General Assembly which adopted several resolutions to that effect.[775]

Some of the by now numerous judgments of the ICJ[776] made important contributions to the development of international law, such as the principle of

---

772 In the 2004 *Legality of Use of Force* case (*Serbia and Montenegro v. eight NATO member states*) seven judges emphasized in a joint declaration: '(The Court) must ensure consistency with its own past case law in order to provide predictability. Consistency is the essence of legal reasoning.' Joint declaration by Vice-President Ranjeva, Judges Guillaume, Higgins, Kooijmans, Al Khasawneh, Buergenthal and Elaraby, paragraph 3.

773 This provision is redundant to the extent that the Council could qualify non-compliance with an ICJ judgment as a threat to the peace and take enforcement action anyway.

774 Pillepich, 'Article 94', in: Cot, Pellet and Forteau (eds.), *supra* (fn. 82) 1987; Oellers-Frahm, 'Article 94', in: Simma et alii (eds.) *supra* (fn. 82) 1957 (1970); see also Paulson, 'Compliance with Final Judgments of the International Court of Justice since 1987', 98 *AJIL* (2004) 434.

775 Beginning with Resolution 41/31.

776 The frequency of resort to the World Court has increased in recent years.

straight base lines for delimiting the territorial sea of a state in the *Fisheries* case.[777] The same was true of advisory opinions, for example the international legal personality of international organizations, as well as the interpretation of the competences of an international organization under its constituent treaty, according to the implied powers in the *Reparation* opinion[778] or the introduction of the compatibility with object and purpose of a treaty as the criterion for the admissibility of reservations in the *Genocide* opinion.[779] Moreover, especially some of the Court's advisory opinions also dealt with politically explosive issues such as those on *Namibia*,[780] *Nuclear Weapons*,[781] *the Israeli Wall*[782] and *Kosovo*.[783]

5.9.4 *The Multiplication of International Courts and Arbitral Tribunals and the 'Fragmentation' of International Law*[784]

The numbers of international judicial and arbitral bodies have increased considerably over the years.[785] They differ with regard to the

1) geographic scope of the parties subject to their jurisdiction (universal, regional, bilateral)
2) *ratione materiae* (comprehensive v. jurisdiction over specific matters)
3) duration of their existence (permanent v. ad hoc)
4) *locus standi*, i.e., the subjects having access (only states v. also other subjects, IGOs and private persons).

---

777 *Fisheries Case* (*United Kingdom v. Norway*).

778 See *supra* 57.

779 *Reservations to the Convention on the Prevention and Punishment of the Crime of Genocide.*

780 The ICJ also handed down a judgment on this issue.

781 See *supra* 146.

782 See *supra* 125. On the rather far-reaching legal consequences of the *Namibia* and *Wall* opinions see Frowein and Oellers-Frahm, *supra* (fn. 758) 1416.

783 See *supra* 91.

784 The term 'multiplication' is preferred here to the frequently used 'proliferation' because the latter has a negative ring to it, in particular with regard to the spread of weapons of mass destruction.

785 Charney, 'Is International Law Threatened by Multiple International Tribunals?', 271 *RCADI* (1998) 115; Buergenthal, 'Proliferation of International Courts and Tribunals: Is It Good or Bad?' 14 *Leiden Journal of International Law* (2000) 267; Oellers-Frahm, 'Multiplication of International Courts and Tribunals and Conflicting Jurisdiction – Problems and Possible Solutions', 5 *Max Planck YBUNL* (2001) 67; Shany, *The Competing Jurisdictions of International Courts and Tribunals* (2003); Hafner, 'Pros and Cons Ensuing from Fragmentation of International Law', 25 *Michigan Journal of International Law* (2004) 849.

To give just a few examples, globally designed 'legal' settlement institutions today comprise the ICJ with its comprehensive jurisdiction, as well as those dealing with disputes in major areas of international law, such as the International Tribunal for the Law of the Sea, the ICC and the World Trade Organization (WTO) dispute settlement regime. On the regional level, human rights courts and tribunals, for example the European Court of Human Rights, the Inter-American Court of Human Rights and the African Court of Justice and Human Rights, as well as the international criminal tribunals discussed above,[786] may be mentioned. Furthermore, bilateral tribunals like the Iran-U.S. Claims Tribunal deal with specific issues opposing only two states to each other.

With regard to *locus standi*, human rights courts are open to individuals. Similarly, the International Centre for Settlement of Investment Disputes (ICSID) is in charge of investment disputes between contracting states and nationals of other contracting states. In addition, numerous administrative tribunals, within the UN and specialized agencies, as well as regional organizations, have been created for employment and other disputes between international organizations and their staffs.

The Court of Justice of the EU as an essential element of the supranational character of the Union deserves to be singled out in this context. Its jurisdiction does not need a separate act of recognition but is established automatically as part of a state's membership obligations; it covers the broad range of subject matters and policies which members have entrusted to the Union, unlike the rather specific material competences of the other above-mentioned judicial and arbitral institutions; and access to the EU Court is also open to individuals and legal persons.

This multiplication of international courts and tribunals ought to be welcomed. It helps to develop international law and its application and thus the rule of law in international relations. States get used to accepting adjudication and arbitration for the settlement of their disputes.

The possible drawback may be the 'fragmentation' of international law as a result of conflicting decisions of some of these courts and tribunals. Differing decisions on similar issues should not come as a surprise in the light of different priorities. For instance, the International Law of the Sea Tribunal will attach more importance to ecological considerations like sustainability, while the WTO bodies will emphasize free trade.

The above-mentioned judgments of the ICJ in the *Nicaragua* case in 1986, upheld by the Court in two subsequent decisions, on the one hand and the

786 See *supra* 94.

Appeals Chamber of the ICTY in the *Tadić* case in 1999 on the other hand provide an example of such divergent rulings.[787]

The problem of contradictory judgments and arbitral awards could theoretically be solved by introducing a hierarchy among international courts and tribunals, conferring the final decision on a superior instance as in domestic law. Although the ICJ may seem to be the leading candidate for this function, states are unlikely to accept this and similar proposals in the foreseeable future.

The possible 'fragmentation' of international law may be alleviated if international courts and tribunals take each other's decisions into account and explain why they come to different conclusions.

5.9.5 *Arbitration and Adjudication: A Superior Dispute Settlement Method?*

The pros and cons of the various dispute settlement methods gave rise to major debates in the past, especially within the Special Committee that drafted the Friendly Relations Declaration.[788] In particular, in the eyes of many Western governments and scholars arbitration and adjudication were to be given priority because of their unique advantages. It is therefore suggested to take a closer look at the main arguments in their favour.

To begin with, the two above-mentioned characteristics of arbitration and adjudication are regarded by their advocates as particularly relevant. However, upon closer analysis these advantages appear less decisive than at first sight.

1) It is of course true that the judgments of international courts and the awards of arbitral tribunals are legally binding, while the proposals of a mediator or the recommendations of a conciliation commission are not. Yet, as was already pointed out,[789] the legally binding nature of a third-party decision does not mean that it will be effectively enforced. This is particularly true in the case of non-compliance by the more powerful party that is unlikely to change its mind as a result of the prospect of countermeasures/reprisals or retorsions to which the weaker side could resort. On the contrary, such self-help measures are likely to make matters worse for the less powerful litigant that applies them.[790] Moreover, the practice of the ICJ shows that even small and weak states like Albania or Iceland got away with ignoring judgments of the UN court. That the UN Security

787 See *supra* 124.

788 Neuhold, *supra* (fn. 7) 444.

789 See *supra* 199.

790 See *supra* fn. 22.

Council may qualify the refusal to comply with a judgment or award as a threat to the peace and take enforcement action under Chapter VII of the Charter[791] remains a theoretical option without any deterrent effect. In contrast, the 'soft', non-binding proposal submitted by a mediator may be backed up by strong incentives and effective threats.[792]

2) One may also question the claim that adjudication and arbitration are superior methods for conflict resolution since judgments and arbitral awards have to be based on the rules of international law by which the parties are bound. International law is said to be the best foundation for dispute settlement because it provides a just solution and because states are equal before it. This implies equality in its creation, irrespective of the differences in power between great powers and 'micro-states'. However, as pointed out in the introductory chapter, law is not 'power-neutral' but tends to reflect the distribution of power among its subjects.[793]

3) Another inequality could result from the financial means available to parties involved in arbitration or adjudication. The wealthier side may afford the most competent and prominent and therefore also most expensive legal counsel whose experience and extensive preparation might tip the scales in its favour.[794]

4) The objectivity and impartiality of international judges and arbitrators should not be doubted. However, like all human beings, they are shaped by their political, ideological and religious, as well as social, cultural and professional backgrounds. These variables explain why international arbitrators or judges sitting on the same bench come to opposite conclusions on the basis of undisputed facts and the same arguments advanced by the litigants before them. Also as a result of these factors, the answer of a person to a question, including a legal issue, is sometimes predictable. Consequently, the composition of a court or tribunal may have an impact on the judgments or awards handed down by it. Moreover, if mediators and other third parties wish to perform their functions successfully, they must also act impartially.[795]

---

791 Or, in case of non-compliance with a judgment of the ICJ, take action pursuant to Article 94 of the Charter. See *supra* 199.

792 See *supra* 182.

793 See *supra* 6.

794 A UN Trust Fund established in 1989 and the above-mentioned Financial Assistance Fund created by the Administrative Council of the PCA, both financed by voluntary contributions, are designed to reduce the costs of litigation for poor countries. See *supra* 191.

795 See *supra* 183.

5) Another advantage of arbitration and adjudication underlined by their supporters consists in the possibility of not only clarifying but also further developing and filling gaps in existing international law. Critics object that courts and arbitral tribunals should not exercise legislative functions. Gaps in the law may not be caused by oversight but by the opposition of sovereign states to legal rules in a certain area.
6) The advocates of the 'legal' methods of dispute settlement are also of the opinion that the acceptance of the jurisdiction of judicial and arbitral institutions reflects the higher degree of integration within today's international community. Sceptics still regard the contemporary global system as heterogeneous, although progress towards integration cannot be denied on the regional level, especially in Europe. They argue that in principle sovereign states should choose the most appropriate settlement method on the merits of each dispute.
7) It may be added that the typical 'winner-takes-it-all' approach of judicial and arbitral bodies may not produce a solution which is satisfactory for and accepted as just and fair by all conflicting parties. If two litigants claim sovereignty over a piece of land, a court or tribunal has to decide to which of the parties the entire territory belongs, unless the judges or arbitrators have been authorized to render an *ex aequo et bono* decision. Some disputes are too complex and their stakes too high for the parties to run the risk of proceedings at the end of which their hands may be completely empty. They will therefore prefer a negotiated settlement or the services of a mediator.
8) It can also be argued that submitting a dispute to arbitration or adjudication 'depoliticizes' the conflict by entrusting the decision to independent and impartial legal experts. Moreover, since the resulting proceedings usually take a rather long time, the parties may benefit from the cooling-off period to reach a consensual solution. However, the initiation of proceedings by one party on the basis of a previous agreement may be regarded as an unfriendly act by the other and, on the contrary, exacerbate the conflict.
9) Furthermore, the support of many Western lawyers and their governments for judicial or arbitral dispute settlement, at least when it comes to statements of principle, is not shared to the same extent by other cultures and civilizations in Asia and Africa. They are based on different philosophies and religions such as Buddhism, Hinduism, Taoism and Confucianism. These basic orientations are in turn reflected in the respective legal systems of the states concerned, although the latter may also include adjudication and arbitration.

However, general and abstract rules regulating the future behaviour of an indefinite number of persons in an unknown number of situations which are applied by courts and arbitral tribunals are often viewed with scepticism in non-Western societies.[796] Instead, the unique aspects of each situation and therefore also of each dispute are emphasized. A synthesis of the positions of the parties is sought on a higher level and in a broader context, which takes account of these specific aspects, instead of determining which party is right because it has the law on its side and which is wrong because it does not. Flexibility and creativity in finding a solution which all parties accept as just and fair are considered more important than the foreseeability of a binding decision in the light of the applicable legal norms. The informal quest for consensus is preferred to 'legal technicalities'[797] and following rigorous and formal rules of procedure.

Disagreements should be discussed in private behind closed doors but not aired in public. Importance is attached to solutions that allow all parties to save face as equals instead of the more powerful side imposing its will. If a settlement favours one party, it should be presented in a way that the other party does not appear as the loser.

A climate of social harmony and trust is the overarching aim of the settlement process. Reconciliation on the basis of mutual concessions is more highly valued than insistence on individual interests, even if the enforcement of the claims of a party could be legally justified. Given this approach to dispute settlement, negotiations between the parties and mediation are therefore preferred to judicial methods.[798]

This approach is not limited to the settlement of internal disputes but also applies to international conflicts. Thus traditional Indonesian village culture, with its emphasis on '*musjawarah*' (consultations) and '*mufakat*' (consensus), was also included in the diplomacy of ASEAN under the presidency of Blitar Sukarno, the President of Indonesia.[799]

---

796 Northrop, *The Taming of Nations: A Study of the Cultural Bases of International Policy* (1952) 80.

797 Syatauw, *Some Newly Established Asian States and the Development of International Law* (1961) 22, 229. For a different view on India where courts play an important role see Freeman, 'Hindu Jurisprudence', 8 *Indian Year Book of International Affairs* (1959) 196; Anand, 'Rôle of the "New" Asian-African Countries in the Present Legal Order', 56 *AJIL* (1962) 383 (393).

798 This approach also underlies the concept of restorative justice reflected in truth and reconciliation commissions as opposed to retributive justice pursued through trials before criminal courts. See *supra* 96.

799 Acharya, *Constructing a Security Community in Southeast Asia: ASEAN and the Problem of Regional Order* (2nd ed. 2009).

These different attitudes, coupled with an emphasis on sovereignty and the resulting reluctance to submit to the decision of a third party, explain why African and Asian states hesitate to accept adjudication and arbitration for the settlement of their international disputes.

This is not to say that these countries unanimously and categorically reject these methods. This is proven by a look at the states that have accepted the compulsory jurisdiction of the ICJ in accordance with the optional clause in Article 36(2) of the Court's Statute.[800]

The traditional approach subsequently adopted by ASEAN did not prevent a state that became a member of the Association, Cambodia, from initiating contentious proceedings against Thailand, another member state, before the ICJ in the *Temple of Preah Vihear* case. To make matters worse, the area around the temple is still contested after the Court ruled in favour of Cambodia in 1962.[801]

5.10 The UN System for the Peaceful Settlement of Disputes

The rather complex system for the pacific settlement of disputes under Chapter VI of the UN Charter is characterized by flexibility.[802] In the first place, it is up to the parties to solve their international conflicts themselves. It may be recalled that, according to Article 33(1), the parties to any dispute, the continuance of which is likely to endanger the maintenance of international peace and security, shall, first of all, seek a solution by the above-mentioned methods listed in this provision or other peaceful means of their own choice.[803]

The limitation of the Charter regime to disputes endangering international peace and security is meant not to burden UN organs, in particular the Security Council, with conflicts of secondary political importance. However, this

---

800 At this writing in 2014 the list includes, in addition to numerous African states, the two ASEAN members Cambodia and the Philippines, as well as the observer Timor-Leste, in addition to three other Asian states, India, Japan and Pakistan.

801 *The Temple of Preah Vihear* (*Cambodia v. Thailand*), Merits. The judgment of the ICJ did not prevent the two neighbouring countries from resorting to armed force. Military hostilities culminated in major clashes in 2011 that caused fatalities. Also in 2011, Cambodia asked the ICJ for an interpretation of its 1962 judgment and the indication of provisional measures. In 2013, at another request of Cambodia for interpretation, the Court declared that Cambodia had sovereignty over the entire promontory of Preah Vihear. It remains to be seen whether this clarification has settled the dispute which has whipped up nationalist feelings on both sides.

802 Neuhold, *supra* (fn. 663) 62.

803 See *supra* 174.

restriction could be detrimental to a weaker state against which a more powerful adversary commits a breach of international law. Since the former lacks the necessary means to exert effective pressure on the latter, the illegal situation will continue without either side resorting to the use of force or otherwise escalating the conflict. Such a state of affairs may therefore not be considered a danger to international peace and security leading to the application of Chapter VI. However, the UN also became involved in this type of conflict, so that the distinction between major and minor disputes has had little practical relevance.[804]

As already mentioned, Article 33 does not establish an order in which the means it lists have to be used.[805] None of these settlement methods has priority, despite the preference of some, in particular Western states, for arbitration and adjudication and other countries for other means, above all negotiations.[806] Nor are conflicting parties obligated to apply all the means listed in Article 33. All they have to do is to make a serious attempt in good faith to reach a solution before their dispute is dealt with at the UN level.

The Security Council plays the central role among the UN organs not only in the framework of the system of collective security under Chapter VII, but also in the second phase of the pacific settlement regime of the Charter.[807] However, its powers are limited to conducting enquiries and making recommendations that are not legally binding on the parties in the context of Chapter VI. The Council may act on its own initiative, *ex officio*, or at the request not only of the parties to but also of UN members not directly involved in the conflict.

Under Article 35(1), any member of the UN may indeed bring any dispute, or situation of the nature referred to in Article 34, to the attention of the Security Council or the General Assembly. Thus the 'private-law structure' of traditional international law, which limits action to the parties directly affected, is replaced with a different approach. According to it, international disputes not only concern the parties involved but also the other members of the World Organization, even below the threshold of the activation of the system of collective security under the Charter. This community perspective played a significant role in

804 For instance, the Security Council dealt with the abduction of Adolf Eichmann by Israeli agents from Argentina, although this violation of the territorial sovereignty of the latter state did not endanger international peace and security. Tomuschat, 'Article 33', in: Simma et alii (eds.), *supra* (fn. 82) 1069 (1083).

805 See *supra* 175.

806 See *supra* 202.

807 Jiménez de Aréchaga, Le traitement des différends internationaux par le Conseil de Securité', 85 *RCADI* (1954) 5; Sohn, 'The Security Council's Role in the Settlement of International Disputes', 78 *AJIL* (1984) 402.

practice, since UN members frequently made use of this *actio popularis* and brought conflicts to which they were not parties before the Council and the Assembly.[808]

In Article 34 a distinction is made, with regard to an investigation by the Security Council, between a dispute and a situation which might lead to international friction or give rise to a dispute. In a dispute the parties have already formulated their positions. A situation in the context of Article 34 constitutes an early phase, a potential international conflict *in statu nascendi*, where the actors involved have not yet taken a clear-cut stance and precisely articulated their claims.[809]

Under Article 35(2), a treaty provision in favour of third states, even a non-member may bring a dispute to the attention of the Security Council or the General Assembly, provided two conditions are met. The non-member state has to be a party to the dispute and to accept, in advance, for the purposes of the dispute, the obligations of pacific settlement in the Charter. Since the UN reached the goal of (almost) universal membership relatively soon, this provision acquired little practical relevance.

Within the framework of Chapter VI the Security Council has at its disposal what could be called an escalation ladder consisting of several rungs. It enables the Council to exert different degrees of pressure below the threshold of a binding decision in order to move the parties to a peaceful settlement of their dispute.

Even the mere fact that the Security Council places a conflict on its agenda conveys a message which the parties concerned should not ignore: that their dispute has attracted the attention of the World Organization and will receive increased attention and publicity. Governments may wish to avoid negative coverage of their behaviour in a conflict by the media.

On the next rung of the ladder the parties are offered the opportunity to present their arguments to the Security Council. They can thereby ascertain whether and to what extent their positions are supported or opposed not only

808 In practice, states often turn to the Security Council which, unlike the General Assembly, is permanently available and may take binding decisions concerning a dispute if necessary. Schweisfurth, 'Article 35', in: Simma et alii (eds.), *supra* (fn. 82) 1109 (1111).

809 The initial situation may also be of an internal character. For instance, already in its Resolution 4 (1946), the Security Council 'resolved to make further studies in order to determine whether the situation in Spain (the Franco regime; the author) has led to international friction and does endanger international peace and security, and if it so finds, then to determine what practical measures the United Nations may take'. At the same time, the barrier erected by Article 2(7) of the Charter must not be lost sight of. See *supra* 46; Schweisfurth, 'Article 34', in: Simma et alii (eds.) *supra* (fn. 82) 1086 (1098).

by the 15 Council members. For, under Article 31 of the Charter, any UN member state which is not a member of the Security Council may also participate, without vote, in the discussion of any question brought before the Council whenever the latter considers that the interests of that member are specially affected.[810]

However, public debates in the Security Council may make subsequent concessions by a conflicting party more difficult, even if its position has encountered widespread opposition. It may regard giving up even only some of its claims as an unacceptable loss of face. Therefore Security Council meetings are frequently adjourned after initial statements by the disputants. This move should allow the President and other members of the Council, in particular the 'P 5', to enter into informal contacts with the parties in order to sound out the possibilities for a mutually acceptable solution to the conflict.

Another instrument available to the Security Council is an investigation under Article 34 of the Charter in order to determine whether the continuance of a dispute or situation is likely to endanger the maintenance of international peace and security.[811] As a result, the Council may clarify relevant facts on its own initiative and at any stage of a conflict.[812] Moreover, the principle of the free choice of the means of dispute settlement by the parties themselves which pervades Chapter VI does not apply to Article 34. Therefore the Security Council does not need the consent of the disputants to the conduct of an enquiry. What is more, the parties are obligated to cooperate with the investigators appointed by the Council, since the latter must be able to decide whether the continuance of a dispute is likely to endanger the maintenance of international peace and security before exercising its powers under Article 37(2).

However, in practice the Security Council has conducted only a few investigations under Article 34. A decision under this provision may be blocked by a permanent member in accordance with the 'chain-of-events' approach in the context of the 'double veto'.[813] Therefore, the Council preferred to order enquiries without reference to Article 34.[814] The establishment by the Security

810 In accordance with Article 32 of the Charter, any UN Member which is not a member of the Security Council or any non-member state of the UN shall be invited by the Council to participate, without vote, in the discussion relating to a dispute to which it is a party.

811 Kerley, 'The Powers of Investigation of the United Nations Security Council', 55 *AJIL* (1961) 892.

812 It is therefore not necessary for the conflicting parties to have failed in their efforts to settle the dispute by means of their own choice before the Security Council may launch an investigation.

813 See *supra* fn. 191.

814 For examples see Schweisfurth, *supra* (fn. 809) 1092.

Council of a subsidiary organ under Article 29 that may be charged with investigative tasks is a procedural matter not subject to the veto of the 'P 5'.[815] Moreover, the Council also requested the UN Secretary-General to undertake investigations.

Finally, the Security Council may express its views on the settlement of a dispute in resolutions in which it can again put various degrees of pressure on the parties to reach a solution.

The Council may limit itself to stating its concern about and its interest in the pacific settlement of a conflict and call on the parties to keep it informed about their efforts to this end. This is a signal to the disputants that they will have to explain and justify their action or inaction concerning their dispute before the Security Council. This message should, in particular, prevent the more powerful from imposing an inequitable solution on the weaker side. The decision of the Council to remain seized of the matter serves the same purpose. It is up to the Security Council and not to the conflicting parties to decide to remove an issue from its agenda. A joint request by the parties pointing to an agreement which they have reached is not sufficient for this purpose.

Under Article 33(2) of the Charter, the Security Council shall, when it deems necessary, call upon the parties to settle their dispute by the above-mentioned means listed in Article 33(1). It may merely issue a general appeal without specifying in its resolution the method which it regards as most conducive to a pacific settlement. However, pursuant to Article 36(1), the Council may also, at any stage of a dispute referred to in Article 33 or of a situation of like nature, recommend appropriate procedures or methods of adjustment.[816] Such a recommendation does not require a request by the parties or other UN members but may be adopted by the Security Council *ex officio*. The Security Council may adopt more than one recommendation on the same dispute or situation and does so in practice.

When adopting such recommendations the Council should also take into consideration that legal disputes should as a general rule be referred by the parties to the ICJ in accordance with the provisions of the Court's Statute.[817]

815 However, the procedural nature of the decision to create such an organ was contested by the Soviet Union during the early years of the Cold War on the grounds that it constituted a substantive decision under Article 34 which provided the only legal basis for the investigative competence of the Security Council. Consequently, the 'double veto' of the 'P 5' came into play. Schweisfurth, *supra* (fn. 809) 1101.

816 Procedures are applied to disputes, methods to situations. Giegerich, 'Article 36', in: Simma et alii (eds.), *supra* (fn. 82) 1119 (1133).

817 Article 36(3) of the Charter. On the definition of legal disputes see *supra* fn. 748.

However, the Security Council has so far only twice recommended recourse to the World Court to the conflicting parties: to Albania and the United Kingdom in the *Corfu Channel* case in 1947[818] and, less clearly because of the different wording of its resolution, to Greece and Turkey in the *Aegean Sea Continental Shelf* case in 1976.[819] This is therefore another provision which has acquired little relevance in practice.

If the parties fail in their search for a settlement by the means indicated in Article 33, they are obligated ('shall'), pursuant to Article 37(1), to submit their dispute to the Council. On the one hand, the conflicting parties may decide, although one or several methods have been applied in vain, to continue their attempts to reach a solution. On the other hand, no agreement between the parties is needed for the referral of the dispute to the Security Council; this step may be taken by each party individually, even if the other party or parties contest that the search for a settlement has failed.[820]

Under Article 37(2) of the Charter, the Security Council not only has the power but is under an obligation ('shall decide') to recommend not only adjustment procedures or methods in accordance with Article 36 but also such terms of settlement as it may consider appropriate, i.e., the substance of the solution,[821] of a major dispute as defined in Article 33, provided it concludes that the continuance of the dispute is in fact likely to endanger the maintenance of international peace and security.[822]

Finally, under Article 38, the Security Council may, if all the parties to any dispute so request, make recommendations (both procedural and substantive) to them with a view to a pacific settlement of the dispute and thus act, as under Article 37(2), as a mediator. The Council is, however, not obligated to meet

---

818 SC Resolution 22 (1947).

819 SC Resolution 395 (1976). The Security Council 'invited' the governments of the two states 'to take into account the contribution that appropriate judicial means, in particular the International Court of Justice, are qualified to make to the settlement of any remaining legal differences…'. Momtaz, 'Article 36', in: Cot, Pellet et Forteau (eds.), *supra* (fn. 82) 1091 (1105).

820 Giegerich, 'Article 37', in: Simma et alii (eds.), *supra* (fn. 82) 1146 (1151).

821 The Council may include procedural and substantive recommendations in a single resolution.

822 However, since such a recommendation is subject to the veto of the 'P 5', the Security Council has fulfilled its obligation under Article 37(2) if the adoption of a resolution to this effect is prevented by a permanent member. Giegerich, *supra* (fn. 820) 1155.

such a request according to this provision. In practice, conflicting parties have not yet resorted to this option.[823]

It stands to reason that a recommendation in which the Security Council not only proposes a certain settlement method but concrete terms for a solution exerts the strongest pressure on the parties. At the same time, even the most powerful organ of the UN may fail to have such a non-binding recommendation accepted by all the parties if the stakes of their conflict are high and/or concessions are opposed as an unacceptable loss of face.

In practice, the Security Council seldom refers explicitly to a specific provision in Chapter VI. Hence it remains unclear on the basis of which Article it takes action. Moreover, the various terms are used rather loosely. Furthermore, several elements of the rather elaborate peaceful settlement system of the UN Charter have been employed in only a few cases, if at all.

In addition to the Security Council, the UN General Assembly also plays a significant role in the area of conflict resolution. Its powers are based on Articles 10–14 and 35 of the Charter. However, as in the framework of collective security, the Council is also given priority in this field. Article 12(1) provides that while the Security Council is exercising in respect of any dispute or situation the functions assigned to it in the Charter, the General Assembly shall not make any recommendation with regard to that dispute or situation unless the Council so requests.[824] In its efforts to achieve a pacific solution to a conflict, the Assembly uses the same methods as the Security Council. In particular, recommendations adopted by the plenary organ of the UN may also range from general statements to specific proposals for the terms of a settlement.[825]

From the point of view of the parties, bringing their conflict before the General Assembly offers several advantages over approaching the Security Council. The plenary body provides a much larger forum and thereby a wider audience that can be reached. Furthermore, the Assembly does not act under the Damocles' sword of the veto of the 'P 5' and may therefore adopt resolutions that would not pass the Security Council. On the other hand, the attractiveness of the Security Council as an institution for the peaceful settlement of disputes lies in its permanent availability and its broader powers.

The Secretary-General of the World Organization may not only contribute to conflict resolution by ringing the 'alarm bell' placed in his hands by virtue of

---

823 Labouz, 'Article 38', in: Cot, Pellet et Forteau (eds.), *supra* (fn. 82) 1125 (1125).

824 See *supra* 59.

825 A case in point was the detailed 1947 General Assembly Resolution 181 (II) on the future government of Palestine.

Article 99 of the Charter,[826] a tool that he formally used only exceptionally in practice, as Dag Hammarskjöld did in the Congo crisis in 1960.[827] Under this provision, he may bring to the attention of the Security Council any matter[828] which in his opinion may threaten the maintenance of international peace and security. In addition, the persons holding this office, on their own initiative, reported their own findings and also made recommendations to the Security Council informally more frequently. The Secretary-General is thus not only the chief administrative officer of the UN but may also play a political role of his/her own in the context of the maintenance and restoration of international peace and security.

The extent to which this part has been performed has varied and depended on the personality of each Secretary-General and the political situation during his term of office. Dag Hammarskjöld, in particular, took action in the area of dispute settlement without any mandate from another UN organ in line with the 'vacuum theory'. According to this concept, the Secretary-General would step in if other UN organs failed to act. Other Secretaries-General also applied this principle in their practice of preventive diplomacy and peacebuilding.[829]

Moreover, the chief administrative officers of the UN have carried out important functions conferred on them by the Security Council and the General Assembly, for which they in turn often appointed special representatives. These tasks were not limited to good offices, investigations and mediation but also included the conduct of peacekeeping operations.

The UN system also leaves room for the pacific solution of conflicts within regional frameworks. Article 52(2) of the Charter obligates UN members belonging to regional arrangements or regional agencies to make every effort to achieve pacific settlement of local disputes through such regional arrangements or by such regional agencies before referring them to the Security Council. The Council shall, under Article 52(3), encourage such regional endeavours, although this Article in no way impairs the application of Articles 34 and 35.[830]

---

826 See *supra* fn. 759.

827 Cardona Llorens and Aznar Gómez, 'Article 99', in: Cot, Pellet and Forteau (eds.), *supra* (fn. 82) 2051; Chesterman, 'Article 99', in Simma et alii (eds.), *supra* (fn. 82) 2009 (2014). See also Schwebel, *The Secretary-General of the United Nations: His Political Powers and Practice* (1952); Chesterman (ed.), *Secretary or General? The UN Secretary-General in World Politics* (2007); Conrady, *Wandel der Funktionen des UN-Generalsekretärs* (2009).

828 And not only, as is stated in Article 35 of the Charter, any dispute or situation which might lead to international friction or give rise to a dispute. See *supra* 207.

829 Cardona Llorens and Aznar Gómez, *supra* (fn. 827) 2068.

830 Article 52(4).

Regional dispute settlement regimes have in fact been established on several continents. Their record is mixed. On the one hand, the higher degree of homogeneity and integration among the states concerned as compared with the global membership of the UN ought to facilitate the peaceful solution of conflicts within a regional framework. On the other hand, traditional enmities and hegemonic aspirations of powerful states in the region may require the involvement of parties from outside and the search for a settlement at the global level.

The performance of the UN in the area of peaceful dispute settlement under Chapter VI, the 'neglected stepchild of the Charter',[831] can hardly be called satisfactory. Too many international conflicts remained unresolved for a long time. To make matters worse, the World Organization was unable to prevent parties from resorting to armed force.

This disappointing record is not due to the flexibility of the Charter regime which entrusts the principal responsibility for settling a dispute to the parties; nor is it caused by the fact that the Security Council may only address non-binding recommendations to the disputants under Chapter VI. The Council members, above all the 'P 5', could put strong political pressure behind such resolutions.

What is more, the Security Council may – although this option is somewhat controversial – consider at least a flat rejection of its recommendation for a pacific solution as a threat to the peace under Article 39 and consequently take enforcement action within the framework of Chapter VII.[832] However, the crossing of the threshold from cooperative to collective security is rather unlikely in practice. It may be one thing for a Security Council member, especially a permanent one, not to oppose a resolution in which a party (with which that Council member is, in general, on friendly terms) is urged to accept a peaceful settlement. It is another thing for the same member of the Security Council to agree that its traditional friend has committed a threat to the peace and that sanctions should therefore be imposed on that state. This readiness might even be low among those Council members whose relations with the

831 Ratner, 'Image and Reality in the UN's Peaceful Settlement of Disputes', 6 *EJIL* (1995) 426 (428).

832 Stein argues that this possibility would make a recommendation binding and would all the more be unacceptable because it would endow the Security Council with legislative powers. Stein, 'Article 37', in: Simma (ed.), *supra* (fn. 190), 629 (643). However, a resolution under Article 37(2) requires that the Council deems that the continuance of the dispute is in fact likely to endanger the maintenance of international peace and security, so that the line between this provision and a threat to the peace under Article 39 is blurred.

target state against which enforcement action is envisaged are strained. For such measures could lead to an escalation of the conflict and also entail costs and disadvantages for those who apply the sanctions.[833]

In this context, it may also be mentioned that the contributions of the ICJ and the General Assembly to the pacific settlement of international disputes have on balance been rather modest.

The genuine reason for this sobering record is the lack of political will to use the various means available for conflict resolution for which the consent of all parties involved is required. However, this is not only true of the conflicting parties. This criticism also applies to the states members of the Security Council and, to a slightly lesser extent, the General Assembly.

833 See *supra* 44, 74.

Conclusion

The entry into force of the UN Charter at the end World War II undoubtedly marked a milestone in the development of international law. Almost seven decades later and a quarter of a century after the Cold War, some progress has certainly been accomplished with regard to the three principles discussed above.

Article 2(4) of the Charter outlawed the use of force, closing possible back doors left open by the previous ban on war, and, in addition, prohibited the threat of force. This cornerstone of the international legal system was subsequently included among the rules of *jus cogens*. It was further strengthened, in particular, by extending the prohibition beyond the use of conventional armed force in inter-state conflicts.

The UN system of collective security proved more effective than that of its predecessor, the League of Nations, especially after the East–West conflict, that had previously paralyzed the Security Council by the veto of its permanent members, had come to an end. Various types of peace operations not provided for in the Charter were developed and made useful contributions to military stability and the peaceful settlement of the conflict at hand.

Although the Security Council still cannot take military action itself due to the lack of Article 43 agreements under which member states would make military resources available to it, it has authorized states, acting as ad hoc coalitions of the able and willing or within the framework of existing organizations, in particular NATO and ECOWAS, to use force in order to stop the unlawful use of force or other major violations of the UN Charter.

Non-military enforcement measures were imposed more frequently after than during the Cold War. The switch to targeted sanctions showed the willingness of the Security Council to address human rights concerns.

An important step was also taken with the recognition of the responsibility to protect on the global level. The new understanding of sovereignty not only marked a conceptual milestone but was also put into practice by the Security Council a few years after its adoption by the World Summit in the Libyan crisis of 2011.

Moreover, the Council played a key role in introducing new forms of international administration in order to help states and territories on their way to political stability and economic recovery after major conflicts and in order to prevent state failure.

It was also in the framework of Chapter VII that the breakthrough to individual criminal responsibility for major violations of international humanitarian

 | DOI 10.1163/9789004299931_007

law was achieved with the creation of the ICTY, which was followed by the establishment of similar ad hoc tribunals and the ICC.

The right of self-defence was inserted into Article 51 of the Charter as the second main exception to the prohibition in Article 2(4) only in general terms. Many of its often controversial modalities were subsequently clarified by international practice against the background of technological and strategic changes as well as new threats.

The principle of non-intervention in inter-state relations, albeit not expressly included in the constituent treaty of the UN, has been firmly established in customary international law. Unlawful coercion below the threshold of armed force is today equally condemned by the international community.

Progress can also be noted in the area of the peaceful settlement of international disputes. The various methods used to this end have been frequently employed and thereby refined. The multiplication, both at the global and regional levels, of international courts and tribunals, whose jurisdiction covers a broad range of major issue areas, is to be welcomed for strengthening the rule of law in international relations.

Nevertheless, the above positive record cannot conceal the glaring serious deficiencies that still remain. Most importantly, despite general lip service to the interdiction in Article 2(4) of the Charter, armed force, which also leads to large-scale human rights abuses and violations of international humanitarian law, continues to be used frequently and with relative impunity.[834] While armed conflict between states has not disappeared but somewhat receded into the background, the use of force within states, which equally entails heavy

834 However, Glennon goes too far with his contention that, as a result of its frequent and flagrant violations by numerous states over a prolonged period of time, in particular by 'Operation Allied Force' and 'Operation Iraqi Freedom' (both of which the U.S. American writer, unlike many of his colleagues, considers illegal), the prohibition in the Charter has fallen into desuetude, has become obsolete and has been replaced with a new customary rule allowing states to resort to force. Moreover, contrary practice has resulted in a *non liquet* so that the applicable rules are no longer clear. Yet even if the practice of using force illegally is deemed sufficient, which is questionable, the necessary *opinio juris* which is equally required for the emergence of customary law cannot be proven, since the violations of Article 2(4) usually met with widespread protests beyond those of the victims. And while it is true that some modalities of the prohibition are controversial, its essential hard core is still clear. Moreover, the political background against which Glennon develops his arguments, a unipolar international system dominated by the United States, has changed in the meantime towards a more multipolar structure. This means that the risks of using force without a sufficient legal basis and political support by other major international actors have increased. Glennon, *supra* (fn. 462) 16; idem, 'How International Rules Die', 93 *The Georgetown Law Journal*, No. 3 (March 2005) 939 (958). See also Franck, *supra* (fn. 453) 610.

human casualties and massive material damage, has become more widespread, with no adequate clear rules governing the involvement of other states in civil war/non-international armed conflict. Non-state actors, notably terrorists, hackers and private military and security companies not only pose new strategic and tactical challenges but also raise legal issues, both with regard to the principle of the non-use of force, as well as difficult preliminary questions of attribution and responsibility. Further complications are caused by new weapons, such as the misuse of the Internet[835] and drones,[836] with lethal autonomous robots looming on the horizon.[837]

Hopes that the UN system of collective security would function as the guarantor of worldwide peace and security after the fall of the Berlin Wall were short-lived. Effective enforcement action taken by the Security Council still constitutes the exception and not the rule, as the 'P 5' remain divided over many issues. Some key aspects of self-defence are still contested so that it may continue to provide a convenient justification for the recourse to force. The line between laudable pressure to protect and promote common values, on the one hand, and reprehensible intervention, on the other hand, remains to be drawn. With regard to the peaceful settlement of international disputes, the need for consent by the parties to all methods means that many conflicts have not been solved by pacific means.

Consequently – and this is both good and bad news – many difficult but also, in the event of success, rewarding tasks are left, while new challenges will arise in an ever more rapidly changing world. They will have to be tackled by the next generation of international lawyers, some of whom attended the courses offered by the Xiamen Academy of International Law in 2012.

---

835 See *supra* 31.

836 Byman, 'Why Drones Work: The Case for Washington's Weapon of Choice', 92 *Foreign Affairs* No. 4 (July/August 2013) 32; Kurth Cronin, 'Why Drones Fail: When Tactics Drive Strategy', ibid. 44.

837 Zemanek, War Crimes in Modern Warfare', 24 *Schweizerische Zeitschrift für internationales und europäisches Recht* (2014) 206.

Index

Note: *'n'following the page numbers denotes footnotes*